BECOME LIKE JESUS

BY
JAMES
McKEEVER

BECOME LIKE JESUS

Printed in the United States of America
First printing June, 1984

Omega Publications
P. O. Box 4130
Medford, Oregon 97501 (U.S.A.)

ISBN 0-86694-100-2 (Softback)
ISBN 0-86694-101-0 (Hardback)

TABLE OF CONTENTS

This book is dedicated first and foremost to the glory of God and His Son, Jesus Christ.

This book is further dedicated to all Christians who make becoming like Jesus Christ the goal of their life and are earnestly pressing toward that goal.

FOREWORD

In beginning to think about becoming like Jesus, we must consider His love. The greatest expression of life is love. The greatest effect of love is an intimate relationship leading to sweet fellowship with God. We are to allow God to renew our minds and have His thoughts become our thoughts. We are to bring every thought captive to Jesus. We need to put on the mind of Christ.

We must be drawn by the Holy Spirit to Holy God to receive His holy work, but we can't come full of self-seeking and pride. We must be willing to forsake all. We must be willing to be mocked, abased and persecuted to receive the life of Jesus. He said we must lose our lives for His sake if we want to find them.

We are not fit in the body of Christ to receive the release of power that God would like to release. We would tend to merchandise it, market and parade it. We are not in a position to receive it because our focus is not on Jesus properly. We don't discern the body properly. We don't love one another, and we're not seeing the ministry of Jesus come.

When we abide in Him, when we walk in love and when we live in the light, the works that He did we will do. He will do them through us. We will see the very same release of power that came through Jesus. We are going to see more of the supernatural. In Christ, we can do all things.

Jesus would like to heal every kind of disease and sickness. If we preach Jesus, we must preach healing in Jesus, because it is there. Healing is important, because it is a visible manifestation of supernatural power, and no one can deny it.

I feel sorry for the Christians who do not overcome. God wants them to go out and let the world see Jesus living inside them. It breaks my heart to see Christians defeated. Every Christian could go out and change the world through the power of God.

The disciples of Jesus are described in Matthew 10 and if we don't look like that, we are not one of His disciples. When we do what He said to do in that chapter, what He said will happen will happen, including all the flak and all the persecution, but also will come the release of the power. The deep desire of a disciple is to be like his Master.

As we press toward becoming like Jesus, God will make us abound in spiritual fruit as an overcomer with victory, joy unspeakable and peace that passes understanding. We are all going to see the Holy Spirit bring forth fruit that looks like Jesus. What matters is the fruit of Jesus in our lives.

Every Christian should seek to become like Jesus, especially in his love and compassion. He had compassion for the multitudes, He loved the unlovely and touched the untouchable. God is going to bring forth a love and a unity in Christ and tear down the boundaries.

I believe that this book, BECOME LIKE JESUS, will be a significant help in your pursuit of your goal of becoming like Jesus, having His power flow through you and loving God and each other with the love of Christ. We need to see through the eyes of Jesus and to love like He loved. We need to become like Jesus. This book can help you do that.

I do not agree one hundred percent with every word in this book. There is no book that I know of, except the Bible, that I agree with one hundred percent. We've got to realize that we are all in error, none of us knows much, we've all got a long way to go and we all see through a glass darkly.

However, there's a light that comes through this book, and that light is Jesus. May God bless you as you read it and as you press on toward becoming like our Savior, Jesus Christ.

JAMES ROBISON

INTRODUCTION

Instead of the regular introduction that most books have, I would like to say a prayer for you as you read this book:

Almighty God, Creator of the universe, and our loving Heavenly Father, the reader and I both ask You to forgive our sins and to cleanse us of all unrighteousness by the blood of Christ. We ask You to fill us afresh with your Holy Spirit, so that He may teach us Your truth.

Father, you know that I yearn to become like Jesus Christ and I pray that You would place that same burning desire in the heart of this precious believer, who is about to read this book. I pray that You would help this person, for whom Christ died, to understand what it means to become like Christ and build a fire in his soul, that he or she might move in that direction.

Father, I pray that anything in this book that is not Your truth, You will eradicate from the memory of this beloved individual, and the things contained in this book that are Your truth, You will burn deep into his heart and let them transform his life and his daily behavior.

Oh Father, how we yearn to have a perfect heart toward You, to bring every thought into captivity into the obedience of Christ, and to be holy and pure in all of our ways. We want to seek first Your kingdom and Your righteousness. We want to answer, very positively, Your new call to holiness, righteousness and purity that is going out to the body of Christ.

Father, we want to become like Christ, not in an elitest way, not for pride, but humbly, as Your servants. I pray that we would use Jesus as our Example and, like Paul, press on toward becoming like Him. We want to do this for Your glory, Father, and for the glory of Jesus Christ in Whose name we pray.

Amen.

I wish that I could sit with you here in my study and that we could personally pray and fellowship together, but I trust that, as you read this book, we can have fellowship in the Spirit, around the Person of our Savior and Master, Jesus Christ. May the Lord bless you, may the Holy Spirit teach you, and may Jesus Christ become very real to you as you read this work.

James McKeever

ACKNOWLEDGEMENTS

In thinking of whom to acknowledge for this book, the persons Who instantly come to my mind are Jesus Christ and the Holy Spirit. I thank Jesus for dying for me and giving me new life, and I thank the Holy Spirit for teaching me, guiding me and bringing my heart to a position where I desire to be like Jesus Christ.

On the human level, I am indebted to so many who have helped me in my spiritual growth. I especially appreciate those men of God who read through the rough manuscript and gave me constructive feedback, much of which is included in this book:

Jon Allen	Finance and Investments
Jim Andrews	President, Omega Corporation
Dr. Carlton Booth	Treasurer, World Vision
Jamie Buckingham	Pastor and Author
Jim Burck	Pastor, Christ's Church
Giff Claiborne	Pastor, Faith Community Church
Ed Gruman	Management, World Vision
Jack Gustafson	Pastor, Foursquare
Roger Minor	Christian Attorney
Carl Nine	Pastor, Foursquare
Wade Parker	Physicist, Professor
Jimmy Smith	Evangelist
Mike Vessey	Finance and Real Estate
David Wilkerson	Evangelist

I also appreciate the outstanding work in typing the manuscript and typesetting the final book done by Lenore Lantzsch, Lillian Allen and Jim Andrews.

Most of all, my appreciation goes to my wonderful wife, Jeani. She edited the book and provided many helpful suggestions and insights. At the same time, she performed the critical functions of a writer's wife, giving me encouragement and inspiration. I praise the Lord for her, not only for her contribution to this book, but also for her encouragement to me to become like Christ and for pursuing that same goal herself. She has been the perfect wife and co-laborer and I continually thank the Lord for her.

I also want to thank all of those who are members of the Omega Team, the Omega Club and those who receive the newsletter, END-TIMES NEWS DIGEST, who have been praying diligently for me and for this book. Satan did not want this book written nor published and, without their faithful prayers, intercession and support of this ministry, this book may never have come into being. I praise the Lord for each one of them and I love them with the warm love of Jesus.

James McKeever
P.O. Box 1788
Medford, Oregon 97501

PREFACE

I have spent many hours working on all of James' books and I know each of them inside out. Without question, BECOME LIKE JESUS has impacted my life more profoundly and in more areas than any one of them. It is the natural stepping stone after one commits to be a bondslave of God. It is a pathway, a guide as to how to be an overcomer.

As James and I have worked on this book, we have found ourselves putty in the Master's hands again and again, as He worked us over and made changes in our lives. In four months, as we have worked hard and prayed much over this book, I have watched my husband grow more and more into the likeness of our Lord and Savior, Jesus Christ. It is really an amazing thing to watch such an extraordinary transformation occur in the life of one you love dearly. I pray that the changes God has been making in me might be as evident to a world so much in need of God's love.

I truly believe this book can revolutionize your life as a Christian, if you read it with an open heart, asking God to speak to you personally through it. God bless you as you embark on an exciting adventure!

Celebrating His love--

Jeani McKeever

1
CAN YOU REALLY BE LIKE JESUS

Just about everyone would say that we should be like Jesus. I have even heard ministers that did not know Christ as their Savior advocate becoming like Jesus. However, even though everyone agrees that we should do this, few people do much, if anything, about it.

When someone tells you that you can be like Jesus Christ, your reaction probably is that it may be possible theoretically, but there is no way that it is going to happen. This is the same kind of reaction that you would have if someone were to tell you that you could become the world's most beautiful woman or the world's strongest man. The hard, cold facts of reality tend to make you shrug off such statements and never even seriously consider them.

But before we shrug off "becoming like Jesus" too quickly, let's at least pause for a minute and take a second look at it. In order to examine it properly, we need first to go back in time and review how various churches have looked at Christ.

CHRIST OUR EXAMPLE--SALVATION BY WORKS

In the early 1900's, many of the more liberal churches and denominations began to preach Jesus as our Example, but they really did not preach Him as our Savior. The sermons began to take on a nature of doing good works, such as feeding the hungry, helping the poor, and caring for orphans. There is nothing wrong with these works; in fact, they have a very important place in a Christian's life, as we will see later in this book. However, in many of these liberal churches and denominations, whether by design or accident, the message began to be "salvation by works." The philosophy was that if you didn't beat your wife, kill anyone, or rape anyone, and if you went to church and led a moral life, you would in all likelihood get to heaven.

I know that this was the essence of many of the sermons in the liberal churches, because I sat through them for the first twenty-two years of my life. I did everything they said to do, and yet I did not know Jesus Christ as my personal Savior. As a young Methodist boy, I spent hundreds of hours reading the Bible, because I was planning to be a preacher. I was even a licensed local Methodist preacher at age 16. After that, I preached one Sunday night each month at our Methodist church. I preached the same kind of sermons that I had been hearing all of my life. My sermons were about doing good, reading your Bible and praying, and how these things would make you right with God. I had a hard time preaching for fifteen minutes because the Lord had not really placed a burning message within my heart.

To be fair, these liberal churches do give lip service to the fact that Jesus is the Son of God and our Savior; however, they never preach about people being lost and needing to receive Jesus as Lord and Savior in order to go to heaven. Their message is really one of good works. In fact, some of the preachers don't even believe in the divinity of Jesus.

CHRIST AS OUR SAVIOR

Many churches and denominations realized that there was no way that good works alone could save anyone and that salvation comes only through the blood of Jesus Christ and faith in Him and what He has done on the cross:

> **8 For by grace you have been saved through faith, and that not of yourselves, it is the gift of God;**

9 not as a result of works, that no one should boast.

--Ephesians 2

Based on these and similar verses, these churches recognized that salvation is indeed a gift of God and not a result of works, or even of doing things that are "Christlike." Perhaps they were so very proud of the fact that they knew the truth--that works could not save a man, but Christ alone--that they wanted in no way to be identified with the liberal churches which preached Jesus Christ just as our Example.

Thus, these fundamental, evangelical and pentecostal churches swung over to the other extreme and preached Christ as Savior, but they did not preach Him as our Example. They were so against the message of salvation by works that they became almost "anti-works." They became so disgusted with the liberal churches that were **only** preaching Christ as our Example that they themselves unfortunately neglected to preach that He was **also** our Example.

JESUS CHRIST IS BOTH OUR SAVIOR AND OUR EXAMPLE

I would like to humbly suggest that neither of those extremities is a valid position. The Scriptures that we will be examining show that Jesus Christ is **both** our Savior **and** our Example. If He came only to be our Savior, He could have been crucified at age 18 and the blood of that spotless young Lamb could have washed away our sins and paid the death penalty that we deserve.

Why then did He remain on earth until He was 33 years old? I believe He remained here to show us what a Christian could be, what a Christian should be, and what God **expects** a Christian to be.

That last sentence may have set your head reeling a little bit. How could God expect us to be like Jesus Christ, His very own Son? Christ was both human and divine. How could we possibly be like Him? You might be resisting in your heart and thinking that there is no way that you could ever become like Jesus Christ and live like He lived when He was here on the earth.

Before you reject that, let me ask you a question.

> **When He was here on the earth, do you think Jesus Christ utilized power not available to you and me?**

Think about that question very carefully, because the answer to it can indeed transform your life. When Christ walked here on the earth, did He utilize power not available to you and me? Pause and think about that, if you would. What is your answer?

(I would really like for you to pause and ponder that question and determine what your answer is.)

I believe the answer to that question is that Christ had divine, creative power, in heaven before He came to earth, but He laid this aside and restricted Himself while He was here on planet earth, to utilizing only the power that is also available to you and me. One way we can know this is that every miracle that Christ did was essentially duplicated by somebody else, somewhere else in the Bible.

Christ raised the dead, but so did Peter and Paul (Acts 9:36-41;20:8-10). Christ multiplied food, but so did Elijah with the oil and the meal in the situation with the widow (1 Kings 17:11-16). Christ walked on water, but in the Old Testament an axehead floated up from the bottom of a river, utilizing the same spiritual force (2 Kings 6:5-7). Christ healed the sick and cast out demons, but so did Peter, Paul and the other apostles.

Do you begin to see that the power that enabled Jesus to do all of these things was available to and was used by the early Christians, and it is available to you and me? In John 14, Jesus said this:

> **12 "Truly, truly, I say to you, he who believes in Me, the works that I do shall he do also; and greater works than these shall he do; because I go to the Father. . . .**

This says that those who believe in Jesus shall do even greater works than He did! In other words, all of the power that Jesus utilized while He was here on the earth is available to you and me as Christians. Think about that. Isn't it absolutely fantastic!

Let's consider another point to help us realize that Christ limited Himself to using only the power that is available to Christians today. The Bible says Christ was tempted in all points as we are:

> **18 For since He Himself was tempted in that which He has suffered, He is able to come to the aid of those who are tempted.**
>
> **--Hebrews 2**

> **14 Since then we have a great high priest who has passed through the heavens, Jesus the Son of God, let us hold fast our confession.**
>
> **15 For we do not have a high priest who cannot sympathize with our weaknesses, but one who has been tempted in all things as we are, yet without sin.**
>
> **--Hebrews 4**

These two passages point out that Christ was tempted in every way that we are tempted, so He could understand us. If He had power not available to you and me to withstand these temptations, that would mean that He had an unfair advantage and really could not understand us and our struggles.

As far as I am concerned, that is totally contradictory to the Scriptures. When Jesus was tempted, He resisted those temptations, utilizing only the same power that is available to you and me.

This means that when we are tempted, we have the same power available to us to resist temptations that Jesus Christ had. Praise the Lord for His gift of that incredible, wonderful power.

Do you begin to see that Jesus is not just our Savior, but He is also our Example? He is an example of what a Christian can be, what a Christian should be and what God expects a Christian to be. Jesus came down not only to save us but also to show us **how to live.**

To try to live like Christ without first receiving Him as your personal Savior--being born anew by the Holy Spirit and receiving the power of the Holy Spirit--is an impossible exercise. If you are not absolutely sure that you have received Jesus Christ as your personal Savior and have been born of the Holy Spirit, please stop now and read Appendix A, "How You Can Know You Have Been Born of the Spirit." For the Bible says:

> **5 Jesus answered, "Truly, truly, I say to you, unless one is born of water and the Spirit, he cannot enter into the kingdom of God. . . ."**
>
> --John 3

As you can see, it is super important for you to get it settled that you have been born of the Spirit--that is, have received Jesus as your personal Savior. We cannot even begin to live like Jesus without that.

However, after one receives Jesus as Savior and receives the power of the Holy Spirit, the goal of living like Jesus becomes not only feasible and desirable, but I believe it just might be attainable. But before we conclude that, let's look further.

WALKING DAILY IN HIS STEPS

As a young Methodist boy, I read a book entitled IN HIS STEPS by Charles M. Shelton. This was a novel about a group of people who tried to walk daily in the steps of Jesus and to follow Him as their Example. I tried to do this and it was a dismal failure. It was a failure because I did not know Christ personally at that time, nor did I have any supernatural power in my life. However, in recent years, I find that this concept, of walking in His steps, is very biblical:

> **21 For you have been called for this purpose, since Christ also suffered for you, leaving you an**

example for you to follow in His steps, . . .
--1 Peter 2

This verse clearly says that Christ left us an example to follow and that we should daily follow this example and walk in His steps. What kind of example did He leave for us? Jesus gave us an example of how we are to live!

The apostle Paul spent his life trying to imitate (become like) Jesus:

1 Be imitators of me, just as I also am of Christ.
--1 Corinthians 11

Have you ever seen a child striving to imitate an adult? Have you seen little girls playing "dress up?" The imitation isn't perfect, but they are trying with all their little hearts to imitate the people they are representing or the people they admire. You might ask yourself, are you trying with all of your heart to imitate Jesus? Why not? Paul was doing so. Shouldn't you and I also try with all our hearts to imitate Jesus?

If we use a cookie cutter on dough, the dough conforms to the image of the cookie cutter. If we pour plaster of Paris into a mold, out comes a casting that is perfectly conformed to the image of the mold. God desires that you and I be conformed to the image of His Son Jesus:

29 For whom He foreknew, He also predestined to become conformed to the image of His Son, that he might be the first-born of many brethren; . . .
--Romans 8

This verse says that we are to be poured into the mold of Jesus and come out "looking like" Him. You might be thinking, "If that were true, I would essentially be perfect." The answer is, "Yes, you would be, and that is exactly what God wants you to be."

JESUS COMMANDED US TO BE PERFECT

Would Jesus ever command you to do anything that was impossible? If so, He is an intolerant, unreasonable task master. However, I believe that He would never ask you or me to do anything that was impossible. Let's look at one of Christ's commands to you and me:

> **48 "Therefore you are to be perfect, as your heavenly Father is perfect. . . ."**
>
> **--Matthew 5**

This is not a suggestion from Jesus, nor something that He would like for you to do halfheartedly. It is a direct command from Jesus Christ, just as much as any of any of His other commands.

Satan will say to you: "You could never be perfect. Don't bother trying." Yet Jesus says to you: "You can become perfect; you can become like me. Go for it." Who are you going to believe? If you believe Jesus and really press on toward becoming an imitator of Him and becoming conformed to His image, yet only get 98 or 99 percent there, how much better off you will be than if you believe Satan's lie and don't even bother trying.

Many ministries and churches emphasize the five-fold ministries. Yet we need to examine why these ministries are given. Let's first look at what the Bible has to say:

> **11 And he gave some, apostles; and some, prophets; and some, evangelists; and some, pastors and teachers;**
>
> **12 For the perfecting of the saints, for the work of the ministry, for the edifying of the body of Christ:**
>
> **13 Till we all come in the unity of the faith, and of the knowledge of the Son of God, unto a perfect man, unto the measure of the stature of the fulness of Christ:**
>
> **--Ephesians 4, KJV**

As we can see, the fivefold ministries are given for "the perfecting of the saints." That means that these ministries are given so that they can help the saints become perfect, so they can help the believers become like Jesus Christ.

Did you notice how verse 13 ends? Another reason that these ministries are given is to help each Christian become **"a perfect man, unto the measure of the stature of the fulness of Christ."** These ministries are to help Christians become perfect in the full likeness of Jesus Christ.

In evaluating the ministry of an apostle, prophet, pastor, teacher or evangelist, you might ask yourself if that individual is really fulfilling the biblical purpose of that ministry. Is he or she helping Christians to become perfect, to become like Jesus Christ?

If you are a man or woman called into one of these ministries, you may want to reevaluate your ministry to see if the main thrust of it is really helping fulfill this purpose of helping Christians become perfect, (become like Jesus Christ).

THE GOAL OF MY LIFE

In the financial newsletters that I write, I have advised people at times to buy gold. Some people have asked me if I was a "gold bug." My response to them was a definite "no," but rather that I am a "goal bug."

Those of you who have read my book on the Christian and his financial affairs, FINANCIAL GUIDANCE FOR CHRISTIANS (formerly THE ALMIGHTY AND THE DOLLAR), know that I am a strong advocate of setting goals. Most people's financial affairs are in a less-than-desirable condition, because they have not established goals. "He who aims at nothing usually hits it."

Likewise, in our churches and our ministries we frequently set goals. If you were to ask many television ministers what their goal was, it might be to have their television programs broadcast in every country in the world, for example. If you were to ask the head of a campus ministry what his goal was, it might be to double his staff so that they could reach more campuses. If you were to ask some pastors what their goal was, it might be to conduct an evangelistic campaign in their neighborhood that would reach every home.

Similarly, before June, 1982, I had a goal for Omega Ministries to grow and expand in order to get the vital end-times message out to the body of Christ. I spent much of the month of June, 1982, in prayer and fasting. During that month, the Lord completely changed my goal. My goal from that time forward has simply been "to become like Jesus Christ." He told me that at the end of the trail, when I stand before the judgment seat of Christ, it will not matter how big or small my ministry became or how "successful" I became. The key question is going to be: How much like Jesus did I become?

From that time on, if anyone asked me what the goal of my life was, I would instantly say, "To become like Jesus." The burning desire of my life is to become like Him. Numerous times each day, I ask Father God to make me more like Jesus, to conform me to the image of His very own Son. How I yearn to be continually imitating Jesus Christ, my Lord and Savior.

Becoming like Jesus really must become the goal of our lives before we can help others make that the goal of their lives. Right? If I were to ask you right now what the burning goal of your life is, what would you answer?

PRESSING TOWARDS THE GOAL

It is not enough simply to have a goal. For a goal to have any meaning, we need to press toward it. To help you understand this, I would like to share with you something that happened when I was in high school.

I was on the track team and ran the sprints--the 100-yard dash and the 220 dash. We sprinters would take a few sprints and then lie around on the grass and make fun of the distance runners, who ran round and round the oval track to build up their wind and endurance.

One day we were in a significant track meet and our quarter miler was sick. The coach asked me to run the quarter-mile race and told me that we really needed to win it in order to win the track meet. I was in no shape to run a quarter mile. My wind and endurance were not up to it. I figured that the only way I could win that race was not to let anybody pass me.

The starting gun sounded and I shot out like a sprinter and got way ahead of the pack. Then I slacked off on my running pace. When I heard the sound of someone coming up behind me, I began to sprint again until I was able to put some distance between him and myself, and then I eased off again. When I heard someone come up behind me again, I would floor it and put some distance between me and whomever was behind me. This happened time after time. As we were rounding the final curve into the finish line, my legs were burning like fire and I was gasping for breath, but I was so determined to hit that tape before anyone else that it would have taken a Sherman tank to have stopped me. My eyes were probably white-hot with determination to hit that tape first, and I did.

That is the same sort of determination and concentration that we need to have in pressing toward the goal of becoming like Jesus Christ. We need to press toward it with every fiber of our being. I think this is what Paul must have had in mind when he was writing to the Philippians:

> 7 But whatever things were gain to me, those things I have counted as loss for the sake of Christ.
>
> 8 More than that, I count all things to be loss in view of the surpassing value of knowing Christ Jesus my Lord, for whom I have suffered the loss of all things, and count them but rubbish in order that I may gain Christ,
>
> 9 and may be found in Him, not having a righteousness of my own derived from the Law, but that which is through faith in Christ, the

righteousness which comes from God on the basis of faith,

10 that I may know Him, and the power of His resurrection and the fellowship of His sufferings, being conformed to His death;

11 in order that I may attain to the resurrection from the dead.

12 Not that I have already obtained it, or have already become perfect, but I press on in order that I may lay hold of that for which I also was laid hold of by Christ Jesus.

13 Brethren, I do not regard myself as having laid hold of it yet; but one thing I do: forgetting what lies behind and reaching forward to what lies ahead,

14 I press on toward the goal for the prize of the upward call of God in Christ Jesus.

--Philippians 3

Here Paul encourages us to forget what is behind us--what happened yesterday, last month or last year--and to press on towards the goal of becoming like Christ Jesus. I urge you with every fiber of your being to press toward the "finish line" of being conformed to His image, or of being perfect.

REALISTIC VIEW OF JESUS

In the book the Lord had me write about the third stage of the Christian life, YOU CAN OVERCOME, there was an important chapter entitled "Your Image of Jesus." In that chapter, I discussed differing views that Christians have of what Jesus was really like:

> About two years ago, right before I went to Hawaii to speak at a monetary conference, a brother in Medford and I had a real conflict. During my week in Hawaii I had a lot of time to do some thinking and I kept asking the Lord what the cause of it was. I knew that I was sincerely seeking to be like Jesus and I knew that this

> brother also sincerely desired to be like Jesus, so what could be causing the conflict?
>
> After praying about it a great deal during that week, finally the Lord showed me that the reason we were having problems was because my image of what Jesus was like was very different from this brother's image of what Jesus was like. We were both trying to become like our image of Jesus, but those images were very different.
>
> To help you understand how different two brothers' images of Jesus can be, let's take this one example.
>
> I have heard a well-known Christian author say that Christ did not create wine at the wedding feast of Cana; it was a "heavenly nectar," but definitely not fermented wine. He would probably say that Christ never created nor drank wine with any alcoholic content.
>
> Other Christian leaders have a very different view of the same facts and feel that Christ created and drank real wine. They would point out that the same word was used when the good Samaritan poured the "wine" into the stranger's wounds as when Christ turned water into "wine" and that the good Samaritan certainly would not pour grape juice into wounds; all grape juice would do would be to attract flies, whereas wine would at least have some medicinal and sterilizing value. If two such brothers were both trying to be like their images of Jesus, one might totally reject wine (and unfortunately usually also reject Christians who drink wine), while the other would feel at liberty to drink wine.
>
> --Omega Publications, p. 82

You can see that Christians can indeed have different ideas about what Jesus was like. In order to get a more realistic view of Jesus, what we need to do is to go back to the Scriptures, with an open heart and mind, and ask the Holy Spirit to show us how Jesus acted, lived and what He was like.

In the following chapters of this book, we will be examining, from the Bible, the prayer life of Jesus, His fasting life and how He healed and cast out demons. We will look at some of the things that the Scriptures say about Him; for example, they say He was holy and pure. All of these things are important for us to understand if we are going to press on to become like Him.

I am certainly not claiming that I have a perfect picture of what Jesus was like, but I believe God has shown me some exciting things about Him from the Scriptures that might be of help to you. I would encourage you to examine the Scriptures for yourself to get a fresh and realistic view of Jesus.

Praise the Lord! I believe it will be a real blessing as we discover more about what Jesus was like, and press on to become like Him.

YOU CAN'T DO IT, BUT HE CAN

Becoming like Jesus Christ may seem, at the outset, an impossible task. There is no way that you can legalistically do a set of things with the end result being that you become like Christ. We need to keep reminding ourselves that becoming like Jesus is not a legalistic set of things we go through. I hope this book will give you a direction and an indication of what becoming like Jesus Christ is really all about. Without Christ inside you doing the work, you could never achieve the goal of becoming like Him. The Scriptures point this out:

> **27 to whom God willed to make known what is the riches of the glory of this mystery among the Gentiles, which is Christ in you, the hope of glory.**
>
> --Colossians 1

If we are going to achieve this glorious goal of becoming like Jesus Christ, it will only be because Christ is in us and living out His life through us. Paul stated this over and over again in his writings:

21 For to me, to live is Christ, and to die is gain.

--Philippians 1

20 "I have been crucified with Christ; and it is no longer I who live, but Christ lives in me; and the life which I now live in the flesh I live by faith in the Son of God, who loved me, and delivered Himself up for me.

21 "I do not nullify the grace of God; for if righteousness comes through the Law, then Christ died needlessly."

--Galatians 2

In these verses we see that it was Jesus Christ who was really living out His life through Paul. Paul's responsibility was to die to himself (be crucified with Christ) and allow Christ to totally control him and to conform him to the image of Christ.

Verse 21 above points out that we can never achieve this by legalistically doing a set of things. Even though we can't do it ourselves in our own strength, we can and will do it in the strength and power of Jesus Christ, Who lives in us and will conform us to His image as we move forward toward that goal.

SUMMARY AND CONCLUSION

In this chapter, we have looked at the fact that some churches preach Jesus Christ as our Example and not as our Savior. Other churches have swung over to the opposite extreme and preach Him as our Savior, but do not really preach Him as our Example. I believe both are true and that Jesus is indeed our Savior and also our Example.

There are ample passages in the Bible that tell us we are to be imitators of Christ, that He was our Example, that we are to be conformed to His image and that we are to follow in His steps. This seems so far above us that we prefer to ignore it, rather than deal with it. However, I believe that the goal of becoming like Jesus Christ is realistic, is attainable, and God wants us to press toward it.

If I asked you afresh right now what the goal of your life was, what would you say? If it is anything other than "to become like Jesus Christ," I would encourage you to reevaluate your life's goals and consider changing them. You might want to pause and have a little talk with Father God and ask Him what the goal of your life should be. If He tells you that it should be "to become like Jesus Christ," then I would encourage you to ask God to cause that to become the goal of your life and to help you press toward that goal, forgetting what lies behind.

If becoming like Jesus is, or has just become, the overpowering goal of your life, then this book should be of a tremendous help to you. We need to see what Jesus was like in many areas and we are to become like Him in those same areas in our lives. Now let's start at the very beginning of this exciting new venture in your Christian life.

2
IT ALL STARTS WITH HUMILITY

If we really want to become like Jesus Christ, a good place to start is at the same position He started His earthly life--a position of humility. He existed from time without beginning, equal with God in every way. However, He was willing to put aside that divine power that He exercised in heaven and become a very humble bondslave:

> 5 Have this attitude in yourselves which was also in Christ Jesus,
> 6 who, although He existed in the form of God, did not regard equality with God a thing to be grasped,
> 7 but emptied Himself, taking the form of a bond-servant, and being made in the likeness of men.
> 8 And being found in appearance as a man, He humbled Himself by becoming obedient to the point of death, even death on a cross.
>
> --Philippians 2

We see in these verses from Philippians that Jesus humbled Himself and became an obedient bondslave. He was willing to be obedient, even when the Father told Him to die on a cross. To go from being ruler of the heavenly hosts down to being despised and rejected by men and tortured to death on the cross is an incredible humbling.

The next few verses in this passage continue this discussion and talk about Jesus being exalted.

However, we must remember that becoming humble--to the point of being an obedient bondslave, willing to do anything Father God asks--must of necessity precede the exaltation. Humbling comes first; exaltation comes later:

> **9 Therefore also God highly exalted Him, and bestowed on Him the name which is above every name,**
> **10 that at the name of Jesus EVERY KNEE SHOULD BOW, of those who are in heaven, and on earth, and under the earth,**
> **11 and that every tongue should confess that Jesus Christ is Lord, to the glory of God the Father.**
>
> **--Philippians 2**

JESUS WAS A BONDSLAVE OF GOD

Verse 7 of the passage we quoted from Philippians 2 said that Christ was a bond-servant. A better term for that is a "bondslave." When we think of the word "slave," we think of those people of Africa who were captured by force, taken to America and forced into slavery. We also might think of slaves in the ancient times, such as under the Roman Empire, when a country was captured and some or most of the people in the captured country were forced into slavery at the hands of the victors. Of course, children born to slave parents were born into slavery. Thus, our basic concept of slavery is that people are either forced into it or born into it.

It would be almost impossible for most people to conceive of a free person walking up to a slave master and volunteering to become a permanent slave. To us this would almost seem like an act of a psychotic, a sadist, or a lunatic. Yet, that is precisely what God asks us to do. To those who don't know God and Christ in an intimate way, to do so may indeed seem like lunacy or psychotic behavior, but those who know God well realize that it is the only path to victory and an overcoming life.

Unfortunately, some of the newer translations of the Bible use the words **slave** and **servant** almost interchangeably. In many instances where the word would more accurately be translated "bondslave," it is unfortunately translated "bond-servant." The terms **slave** and **servant** are far from interchangeable.

A servant gets paid a wage, however small it may be. That servant then can go out and buy with that wage anything he or she wants to buy. The servant also has days off, during which he can do anything that he desires. Thus, he has control over a good portion of his life. Servants may live in virtual poverty, or have a low standard of living, but they are still in control of their spending and a portion of their time.

On the other hand, a slave never receives any money of his own whatsoever. Anything that he wants he must ask of his master. If he wants some new clothes, he must ask his master for them. His master may say "yes" or "no" and, if the answer is "yes," he might also specify what kind and what color. If the slave wants to take a wife, he goes and asks his master if he may have one. His master answers "yes" or "no." If the answer is "yes," the master can also decide who the slave must marry. The slave has no "rights" to marry whomever he pleases. He does his master's bidding. If the slave wants to live in a different house, have a piece of furniture or anything else, he cannot make the decision himself for he has no money to purchase these items; he must go to the master and ask him and then do whatever the master says or receive whatever the master gives.

Similarly, there is never any time at all when the slave is not a slave. He doesn't have any "days off." His time is 100 percent under the control of his master. He may be dead tired and need a vacation, but if his master says, "Work," he works. He may be sick, but if his master tells him to do something, the slave must do it, in spite of his sickness. His time is not his own.

In the time of the fuedal lords where there were feudal slaves, the slaves were used as part of the army of the feudal lord in the event of any attack. Thus, if a master told a slave to go out into battle and charge up a particular hill, the slave had to do it, even if it meant his death. For a person to voluntarily become a slave, he was voluntarily making a commitment to die for his master, if his master wanted him to die, to have no possessions except what the master gave him, to have no discretionary spending money of his own, to have no time of his own and no rights at all. As you can see, being a slave is far, far different from being a servant. If one is a servant, one can quit whenever one wants to. If one is a slave, one can never quit.

Now let's take a look at bondslaves in the Old Testament, followed by bondslaves in the New Testament, and what implications it has for you and me.

The concept of a bondslave (a voluntary slave) in the Old Testament is found in many places. One of the best descriptions of it is in Exodus:

> 2 "If you buy a Hebrew slave, he shall serve for six years; but on the seventh he shall go out as a free man without payment.
>
> 3 "If he comes alone, he shall go out alone; if he is the husband of a wife, then his wife shall go out with him.
>
> 4 "If his master gives him a wife, and she bears him sons or daughters, the wife and her children shall belong to her master, and he shall go out alone.
>
> 5 "But if the slave plainly says, 'I love my master, my wife and my children; I will not go out as a free man,'
>
> 6 then his master shall bring him to God, then he shall bring him to the door or the doorpost. And his master shall pierce his ear with an awl; and he shall serve him permanently. . . ."
>
> --Exodus 21

As you can see in this passage, if a person has come to be your temporary slave, for whatever reason (whether because he owed you money or because he sold himself to you to raise money) at the end of the seventh year, you were to set him free.

On the other hand, he could say to you that he did not want to go away and be free again, but instead he wanted to voluntarily become your permanent slave (bondslave). If he told you that, you would stand him against the doorpost and pierce his ear with an awl, a nail or something of that nature. The pierced ear was the mark of a permanent slave. Since he was not born into slavery, but he voluntarily became a permanent slave, he was called a bondslave.

I used to think of this passage only from the master's viewpoint. He had gotten a slave for life who would have to do his bidding, work for him, fight for him and even die for him. But as I reread it considering the slave's side, I realized that the master was also taking on the obligation and responsibility to care for that slave for the rest of his life, to protect him and to provide for him. It required a two-sided commitment, the master and the slave each committing themselves to the other and each assuming a certain responsibility.

What would cause an individual to voluntarily become a permanent slave? One certainly would not want to do so if the master were cruel, harsh or unjust. However, if the master were loving, kind, considerate and just, and if serving him were a joy, one might well consider being a voluntary permanent slave. Even though a slave might live in material luxury, he still had no freedoms of his own.

I think this passage from Exodus 21 beautifully portrays the reason for voluntarily becoming a permanent slave--that of love for the master. If the slave plainly says that he wants to stay because he loves his master, he can become a permanent bondslave.

This passage also clearly affirms that even a temporary slave had no rights at all. If the master had given the slave a wife and they had children, the wife and the children still belonged to the master. If the slave decided to leave, he had to leave his wife and children with the master. As you can see, when one is a slave, everything that person has, including his wife (or her husband) and children, belong to the master and not to the slave. Yet that is a temporary condition of one who is a temporary slave, but if one volunteers to become a permanent slave, that becomes a permanent condition.

SLAVES VERSUS SERVANTS

In the Hebrew of the Old Testament, there are two distinct words for servant and slave, a servant being one who is hired and a slave being one who doesn't receive wages, and who is more of a possession of his master.

The Hebrew word for "servant" really means a "hired man." Yet whenever the Old Testament talks about being a "bond-servant," the Hebrew word that is used really means a servant who is not hired, but one who is indeed a slave, in permanent or semipermanent bondage to his master.

In the New Testament, again we find that there are distinct words for slave and for servant (hired servant). There are actually two Greek words translated "servant," both of which have the concept of a hired servant. The Greek word for slave or bondslave, on the other hand, definitely denotes subjection or subserviency. This is the word used whenever the New Testament talks of Paul being a "bondslave" of Christ or any other time slavery is mentioned. (This is covered in more detail in my book, YOU CAN OVERCOME.)

BONDSLAVES IN THE NEW TESTAMENT

We find many examples of people who were called bondslaves of God in the New Testament. One of the first and most beautiful is found in Luke:

> **25 And behold, there was a man in Jerusalem whose name was Simeon; and this man was righteous and devout, looking for the consolation**

of Israel; and the Holy Spirit was upon him.
26 And it had been revealed to him by the Holy Spirit that he would not see death before he had seen the Lord's Christ.
27 And he came in the Spirit into the temple; and when the parents brought in the child Jesus, to carry out for Him the custom of the Law,
28 then he took Him into his arms, and blessed God, and said,
29 "Now Lord, Thou dost let Thy bond-servant depart
In peace, according to Thy word;
30 For my eyes have seen Thy salvation,
31 Which Thou has prepared in the presence of all peoples,
32 A LIGHT OF REVELATION TO THE GENTILES,
And the glory of Thy people Israel."
33 And His father and mother were amazed at the things which were being said about Him.
34 And Simeon blessed them, and said to Mary His mother, "Behold, this Child is appointed for the fall and rise of many in Israel, and for a sign to be opposed--
35 and a sword will pierce even your own soul--to the end that thoughts from many hearts may be revealed."

--Luke 2

As we discussed earlier, where Simeon refers to himself as a "bond-servant" in this translation, it really should be translated "bondslave." What are some of the things that we can discern about being a bondslave by looking at Simeon's life?

1. He was righteous.
2. He was devout.
3. The Holy Spirit was upon him.
4. The Holy Spirit revealed things to him.
5. He could give blessings in the name of God.
6. He could prophesy in the name of God.

Here is a picture of a pure, holy, righteous, devoted man of God, who has the gifts of the Spirit functioning through him.

Another New Testament example, in this case said to be a bondslave of Christ rather than a bondslave of God, is the apostle Paul. We find this mentioned several places in the New Testament:

> **1 Paul, a bond-servant of Christ Jesus, called as an apostle, set apart for the gospel of God, . . .**
>
> --Romans 1

> **10 For am I now seeking the favor of man, or of God? Or am I striving to please men? If I were still trying to please men, I would not be a bond-servant of Christ.**
>
> --Galatians 1

> **1 Paul and Timothy, bond-servants of Christ Jesus, to all the saints in Christ Jesus who are in Philippi, including the overseers and deacons: ...**
>
> --Philippians 1

These verses shed some additional light on what a bondslave of Christ is. In Romans 1:1, we see that a bondslave of Christ is set apart for the gospel of God, or we could say "sanctified" for the gospel of God.

In Galatians 1:10 we learn that a bondslave of Christ strives only to please Christ and not to please men. His aim is to do that which will glorify Christ, even if it makes him unpopular with men.

As Christians, we want to be like Jesus. If Christ was a bondslave of God, we too should yearn to be bondslaves of our heavenly Father. If we do, and if we are faithful to obey, in God's good time He will exalt us with Christ and we will rule and reign with Him, not because we deserve it, but simply because of His love and grace.

Incidentally, when I first became a Christian I thought that the better and finer things of God were on higher and higher shelves. Thus, I wanted to grow so that I could reach them. Now I know that the best things of God are on lower and lower shelves. Only lowly slaves of God can partake of them, both in this age and in the age to come. As we become less and less, the power of God can flow through us more and more.

Just as Christ, a bondslave of God, fought against Satan and evil and overcame them victoriously, God wants you and me, His bondslaves, to also become soldiers and overcomers in this spiritual warfare.

If God is speaking to your heart that you should be His bondslave, you may wish to use the "Bondslave Commitment" on the next to last page of this book to seal that decision right now. This is such an important step that I would encourage you to take it now while the Holy Spirit is speaking to you.

JESUS WAS A SERVANT OF MAN

Jesus was not only a bondslave of God; He was also a servant of man. He came to serve:

> 26 "It is not so among you, but whoever wishes to become great among you shall be your servant,
> 27 and whoever wishes to be first among you shall be your slave;
> 28 just as the Son of Man did not come to be served, but to serve, and to give His life a ransom for many."
>
> --Matthew 20

> 24 And there arose also a dispute among them as to which one of them was regarded to be greatest.
> 25 And He said to them, "The kings of the Gentiles lord it over them; and those who have authority over them are called 'Benefactors.'
> 26 "But not so with you, but let him who is the greatest among you become as the youngest, and the leader as the servant.
> 27 "For who is greater, the one who reclines

at the table, or the one who serves? Is it not the one who reclines at the table? But I am among you as the one who serves."

--Luke 22

Jesus was among the disciples as a servant. Perhaps the best-known example of this is when He washed the disciples' feet:

3 Jesus, knowing that the Father had given all things into His hands, and that He had come forth from God, and was going back to God,
4 rose from supper, and laid aside His garments; and taking a towel, He girded Himself about.
5 Then He poured water into the basin, and began to wash the disciples' feet, and to wipe them with the towel with which He was girded.
6 And so He came to Simon Peter. He said to Him, "Lord, do You wash my feet?"
7 Jesus answered and said to him, "What I do you do not realize now, but you shall understand hereafter."
8 Peter said to Him, "Never shall You wash my feet!" Jesus answered him, "If I do not wash you, you have no part with Me."
9 Simon Peter said to Him, "Lord, not my feet only, but also my hands and my head."
10 Jesus said to him, "He who has bathed needs only to wash his feet, but is completely clean; and you are clean, but not all of you."
11 For He knew the one who was betraying Him; for this reason He said, "Not all of you are clean."
12 And so when He had washed their feet, and taken His garments, and reclined at the table again, He said to them, 'Do you know what I have done to you?
13 "You call Me Teacher and Lord; and you are right, for so I am.
14 "If I then, the Lord and the Teacher, washed your feet, you also ought to wash one

> another's feet.
> 15 "For I gave you an example that you also should do as I did to you.
> 16 "Truly, truly, I say to you, a slave is not greater than his master; neither is one who is sent greater than the one who sent him.
> 17 "If you know these things, you are blessed if you do them. . . ."
>
> --John 13

What an example Jesus gave us! As we become like Him, we will be eager to serve each other.

PRIDE AND HUMILITY ARE OPPOSITES

I believe we would all agree that Jesus Christ, a bondslave of God and a servant of man, had not an ounce of pride in Him but was totally humble before His Father. We, too, certainly need to be devoid of pride, but we are not. Probably the worst sin among Christians today is that of pride. At a recent Christian meeting, I spoke on the subject and read these verses:

> 5 You younger men, likewise, be subject to your elders; and all of you, clothe yourselves with humility toward one another, for GOD IS OPPOSED TO THE PROUD, BUT GIVES GRACE TO THE HUMBLE.
>
> --1 Peter 5

> 6 But He gives a greater grace. Therefore it says, "GOD IS OPPOSED TO THE PROUD, BUT GIVES GRACE TO THE HUMBLE."
>
> --James 4

I pointed out to that group that these verses were written to Christians and what they are saying is that God is directly opposed to any Christian who is proud or has a pride problem. Literally, that means that God and that Christian are going to have a head-on collision. When that proud Christian and God have a head-on collision, what do you think will happen? I then read a few verses to that group which showed the end result of pride:

> **25 The Lord will tear down the house of the proud,**
> **But He will establish the boundary of the widow.**
>
> **--Proverbs 15**

> **11 The proud look of man will be abased,**
> **And the loftiness of man will be humbled,**
> **And the Lord alone will be exalted in that day.**
> **12 For the Lord of hosts will have a day of reckoning**
> **Against everyone who is proud and lofty,**
> **And against everyone who is lifted up,**
> **That he may be abased.**
>
> **--Isaiah 2**

> **51 "He has done mighty deeds with His arm;**
> **He has scattered those who were proud in the thoughts of their heart.**
> **52 "He has brought down rulers from their thrones,**
> **And has exalted those who were humble."**
>
> **--Luke 1**

Did you notice in these last two verses from Luke that not only does God scatter and bring down the proud, but He exalts the humble. The humbling comes first, then the exaltation. But the main thing that we should notice in these verses is that God is definitely directly opposed to the proud, and that includes proud Christians.

At that particular meeting, shortly after my message on pride had begun and I had read these verses, I felt the Lord wanted me to do something that He had never asked me to do before. He had me ask all of those who had a problem with pride to stand up and, by standing, to humble themselves before God and before the people there. A goodly number stood up, and as we took authority over the spirit of pride and led those people in a prayer of repentance and confession, the Holy Spirit did a mighty deliverance and work in their hearts. There was one man who repented with loud moanings for about ten minutes.

Before we proceed to see how to humble ourselves, we need first to look at what pride really is.

PRIDE IS THE LUST FOR GLORY

To help you understand pride, we need to look at the three major sins about which we are warned:

> **15 Do not love the world, nor the things in the world. If anyone loves the world, the love of the Father is not in him.**
> **16 For all that is in the world, the lust of the flesh and the lust of the eyes and the boastful pride of life, is not from the Father, but is from the world.**
>
> --1 John 2

This says that if anyone loves any part of the world, the love of the Father is not in him. It then lists three things that are specifically of the world:

1. Lust of the flesh
2. Lust of the eyes
3. Pride (Lust for glory)

To help you understand why I believe that pride is a "lust for glory," we need to first look at why man was created. The only verse I can find in the Bible that tells why you and I were created is this:

> **7 Even every one that is called by my name: for I have created him for my glory, I have formed him; yea, I have made him.**
>
> --Isaiah 43, KJV

According to this verse, the reason we were created was to glorify God in everything we say and do and think all of our lives. If this is true, the verse in Romans begins to make some sense:

> **23 for all have sinned and fall short of the glory of God, . .**
>
> **--Romans 3**

Here we see the basic definition of sin, which is not glorifying God, or not doing what you were created to do. If you accept that, which I believe to be true, it can significantly affect how you live. If you strive to glorify God in all that you do, you are going to live a much purer, more holy life. These verses indicate that anything that you do that does not glorify God is sin.

Let's take an example. Let's say there is a widow lady down the street who needs her garden spaded up and you go down and spade it up for her. Afterwards she says: "Oh, that was so sweet and wonderful of you. I really appreciate it." If your response is, "Oh, it was nothing," who gets the glory? You do.

On the other hand, your response to her could be: "Well, I'm a bondslave of God and He told me to come spade up your garden. He wanted to show you that He loves you, and He just used me as a tool." In that case, who gets the glory? God does.

Now, think with me carefully. If you go down and spade up a neighbor's garden or haul her trash to help her out, and you get the glory, it is sin. Most observers would think that spading up her garden was a wonderful thing to do; but looking through God's eyes, if you steal the glory that belongs to Him, it is sin. God looks at our hearts, but the words that we speak are an important reflection of what is in our hearts.

We are talking about a higher and a more pure definition of sin than you may be used to. In the beginning of our Christian life, we die to that which is overtly wrong and against God's commandments. As we move on in the Christian life, particularly as we move into the bondslave and overcomer realm, then we also die to those things which are perfectly legal and even "good" in most people's eyes, if they do not glorify God.

For example, a family in the neighborhood could have a sickness or a death and a sweet Christian lady could bake a casserole or some other dish and take it over to them. They could say: "We really appreciate it. You are so thoughtful." If she responds, "Oh, it was nothing. I was glad to do it," who gets the glory? She does, and I believe that is sin. Do you see what the Scriptures tell us? Anything in which you get the glory, and God does not, is sin.

The basic problem with Satan all along has been pride. He wants the glory that is given to God. If pride is carried to its final extremity, the end result is a lust for power and, ultimately, the desire to be worshiped. Satan is despicable in God's eyes because he is proud and arrogant.

When we receive glory that should go to God, we have a pride problem. At that moment, we are taking on Satan's worst characteristic, which God hates and to which He is opposed.

JESUS WAS HUMBLE

In our desire to put away pride and to be humble, the first place to start is by looking at Jesus. Jesus was humble and we should learn to be like Him:

> 29 "Take My yoke upon you, and learn from Me, for I am gentle and humble in heart; and YOU SHALL FIND REST FOR YOUR SOULS."
>
> --Matthew 11

In this verse in Matthew, Jesus points out that He was humble and gentle. If we learn to be like Christ, then we will learn to be humble and gentle. As you let God work this in your heart, it may change many things in your life. It may change your ministry, your public prayers, your business and family relationships, and the list could go on and on.

A minister can be enthusiastic and speak loudly with vigorous gestures and still be humble and gentle. Jesus gave us an example of how to preach and how to minister. He spoke to thousands, but evidently He did so in a gentle, humble way.

Many Christians, including many ministers, and leaders have a hard time laughing at themselves when they make a public mistake. That is probably a form of pride and God wants to purge that out of their lives so they will be able to relax and laugh at themselves.

Some Christians are afraid to go knock on someone's door and tell them about Jesus. They are afraid that they might get laughed at, might stumble for words, or might not have the answer to a question. Why are they afraid? I believe it is pride. If they were truly humble, those things would not matter. As they go forth at Christ's command, it doesn't matter if they are laughed at, spat at or even shot at. We are to please Him, not men.

Oh, that God's people would do what 2 Chronicles admonishes:

> **14 and My people who are called by My name humble themselves and pray, and seek My face and turn from their wicked ways, then I will hear from heaven, will forgive their sin, and will heal their land.**
>
> **--2 Chronicles 7**

This does not say anything about non-Christians humbling themselves, praying, seeking God's face and turning from their wicked ways. This verse is talking about **God's** people--Christians. Oh, that God's people would first confess their sin of pride and then humble themselves before Almighty God!

TWO WAYS TO BECOME HUMBLE

I trust that you would like to get rid of any pride left in you and humble yourself before God. Let's read what Jesus had to say about this:

> **13 "But the tax-gatherer, standing some distance away, was even unwilling to lift up his eyes to heaven, but was beating his breast,**

saying, 'God, be merciful to me, the sinner!'
14 "I tell you, this man went down to his house justified rather than the other; for everyone who exalts himself shall be humbled, but he who humbles himself shall be exalted."

--Luke 18

11 "For everyone who exalts himself shall be humbled, and he who humbles himself shall be exalted."

--Luke 14

What these verses say is that whoever exalts himself, God will humble, and whoever voluntarily humbles himself before God, God will exalt, in His time and in His way. The exalting may come during this life, during the millennium, or during eternity, but eventually God will exalt him. If you study these passages very carefully, you will realize that either way you are going to become humble.

If you exalt yourself, God will humble you under His mighty hand, but if you voluntarily humble yourself, God will exalt you in due time. Thus, you are indeed going to become humble in one of two ways:

1. By being crushed humble by God.
2. By voluntarily humbling yourself.

I have tried it both ways and I highly recommend the voluntary method. It is a terrible thing to be crushed humble under the hand of Almighty God.

Peter says a similar thing and adds some additional thoughts to it:

6 Humble yourselves, therefore, under the mighty hand of God, that He may exalt you at the proper time,
7 casting all your anxiety upon Him, because He cares for you.

--1 Peter 5

Here we see that we are to voluntarily humble ourselves and that, if we do this, God will exalt us at the proper time. But humbling ourselves can create anxiety within, because our wills and our egos rebel. Peter then goes on to tell us that we are to cast all of this internal struggle upon God, because He loves and cares for us.

What we need to do then is to confess any pride that is within us, voluntarily humble ourselves before God and pledge to Him to give Him all the glory for anything that we do. This is an essential first step if you really want to become like Jesus Christ. If this is the desire of your heart, you might pray a simple prayer something like this:

> **Father God, I confess to you that I have pride in my heart and soul. I confess to you that I have taken credit and glory when it should have been given to You. I confess that this pride is evil and satanic. Now Father, I claim the promise that if I confess, You are faithful and just to forgive me my sins and to cleanse me from all unrighteousness. I thank you that I am now cleansed of that sin.**
>
> **Father, I voluntarily humble myself before you. I dedicate myself to living for your glory and to giving You the glory and the credit for everything good that I do. Help me, Father, to be humble and gentle in my dealings with people, in my ministry and in my personal relationships, for I yearn to be like Jesus Christ, Your precious Son and my Savior. In His name I pray. Amen.**

I believe that if you have had a long talk with God and prayed a prayer similar to that, God has now cleansed you from that pride and you have begun your journey toward becoming like Jesus Christ. It is possible to be like Jesus. God wants you to be like Jesus. The Holy Spirit will give you the power. So, let's press on toward that goal of being like our precious Savior. As we are conformed to His image, transformed into His likeness, what a peace and a joy we will have! Praise the Lord!

SUMMARY AND CONCLUSION

As we desire strongly to become like Jesus Christ, we need to begin where He began. He began His earthly ministry by putting aside His divine creative power, humbling Himself and being born in a barn and laid down in a dirty feeding trough for the animals. He was raised as a working man, a carpenter, and when He began His ministry, He was not accepted by the religious leaders and was openly turned upon by the people.

Through all of the persecution, He remained humble and gentle, not striking back, not calling down hosts of angels to protect Him. He humbly laid aside His own will to only do the will of the Father. The ultimate humility was that He was willing to be tortured to death so that you and I can have eternal life as we believe on Him as our personal Savior.

We, too, need to lay aside our pride and our own egos and to voluntarily humble ourselves before God. As we do this, we are getting rid of some the major weights that would prevent us from becoming like Jesus Christ.

One thing that the Scriptures say is a very humbling experience is fasting. Let's turn now and look at how fasting and humility go together.

3
FASTING BRINGS POWER IN PRAYER

In our desire to become like Jesus Christ, to let Him be our Example, I believe fasting is an important thing. Before you react to the idea of fasting, and before we get into the details of fasting, we need to observe the fact that Jesus fasted:

> 1 Then Jesus was led up by the Spirit into the wilderness to be tempted by the devil.
> 2 And after He had fasted forty days and forty nights, He then became hungry.
>
> --Matthew 4

Jesus evidently fasted many more times than just that initial fast. When the disciples tried to cast out the demon and could not, we have this recorded:

> 19 Then came the disciples to Jesus apart, and said, Why could not we cast him out?
> 20 And Jesus said unto them, Because of your unbelief: for verily I say unto you, If ye have faith as a grain of mustard seed, ye shall say unto this mountain, Remove hence to yonder place; and it shall remove: and nothing shall be impossible unto you.
> 21 Howbeit this kind goeth not out but by prayer and fasting.
>
> --Matthew 17, KJV

Even though the disciples had previously been given authority over demons, Jesus tells them here that, in addition to authority, they needed faith and to pray and fast in order to cast out the stronger demons. Since Jesus cast out the demon, evidently He had been praying and fasting.

We know that, referring to Christ, it says in the New Testament: "For zeal for Thy house will consume me" (John 2:17). This was quoted from Psalms, but let's look at the companion verse with that:

> 9 For zeal for Thy house has consumed me,
> And the reproaches of those who reproach
> Thee have fallen on me.
> 10 When I wept in my soul with fasting,
> It became my reproach.
>
> --Psalm 69

These two verses out of Psalm 69 tell us that Jesus was reproached, and part of the reproach was because of zeal for God's house, but part was because He was weeping and fasting.

FASTING AND HUMBLING

To tie fasting back to the previous chapter, it is helpful to realize that one of the chief ways to show God that you are indeed humble is through fasting. The connection between humbling oneself and fasting is found repeatedly in the Scriptures. For example:

> 21 Then I proclaimed a fast there at the river of Ahava that we might humble ourselves before our God to seek from Him a safe journey for us, our little ones, and all our possessions.
> 22 For I was ashamed to request from the king troops and horsemen to protect us from the enemy on the way, because we had said to the king, "The hand of our God is favorably disposed to all those who seek Him, but His power and His anger are against all those who forsake Him."
> 23 So we fasted and sought our God concerning this matter, and He listened to our entreaty.
>
> --Ezra 8

In this passage from Ezra, we see that they humbled themselves with a fast, they prayed to God, and because of this, verse 23 tells us that He listened to their prayer and answered it. If you feel that your prayers are not being answered, fasting might help. However, we should not use fasting like a "hunger strike" to try to force God to answer our prayers or to try to manipulate Him into action.

In addition to humbling ourselves, in the following passage from Isaiah, we find that fasting has other benefits:

> 4 "Behold, you fast for contention and strife
> and to strike with a wicked fist.
> You do not fast like you do today to make
> your voice heard on high.
> 5 "Is it a fast like this which I choose, a
> day for a man to humble himself?
> Is it for bowing one's head like a reed,
> And for spreading out sackcloth and ashes
> as a bed?
> Will you call this a fast, even an
> acceptable day to the Lord?
> 6 "Is this not the fast which I choose,
> To loosen the bonds of wickedness,
> To undo the bands of the yoke,
> And to let the oppressed go free,
> And break every yoke? . . ."
>
> --Isaiah 58

Here we see that fasting not only is a humbling thing, but it can loosen the bonds of wickedness, break the yoke and let the oppressed go free. Many Christians have bonds of wickedness tightened upon them and have the yoke of immorality or bad habits weighing them down. By prayer and fasting, those bonds can be loosened and those yokes broken. God will hear and answer us as we humble ourselves.

If one really has his heart set on becoming like Jesus Christ, he will fast.

There are many spiritual reasons to fast and other things about fasting that we will cover in this chapter;

but, perhaps we should first breathe a prayer and ask God's Holy Spirit to show us His truth about fasting and whether or not He wants us to fast.

LET'S EXAMINE FASTING

Let's come to the subject of fasting with an open heart and a teachable mind. First we must realize that God designed our bodies to fast. Fasting was God's idea, not man's.

By and large, our human bodies eliminate any excess water that we drink. However, God designed a camel so that any excess water that it drinks is stored. God could have designed us so that any excess food that we eat is also eliminated, but He did not. He designed us so that any excess food that we eat is stored in our bodies for future energy needs.

Initially, this energy is stored in such places as our bloodstream and the marrow of our bones. As all of these hidden storage places are filled up, the energy reserves begin to be stored externally as visible fat.

God has also designed our bodies so that 48 hours after we eat our last bite of food, a biological "switch" is thrown (our pituitary gland emits a hormone), which tells the body no longer to rely on incoming food for energy, but to start utilizing the stored energy. About that time, or within 24 hours after that, all hunger disappears. Real hunger does not return for about 40-60 days, for the average, healthy individual. During this time, the body is consuming the stored energy.

Once all of the stored energy is gone, then an intense hunger comes back that cannot be shaken. If you did not resume eating at this point, this is when starvation would begin. The Bible tells us when hunger returned in the first major fast of Christ:

> **1 And Jesus, full of the Holy Spirit, returned from the Jordan and was led about by the Spirit in the wilderness**
>
> **2 for forty days, being tempted by the devil. And He ate nothing during those days; and when**

> **they had ended, He became hungry.**
>
> **--Luke 4**

As you can see in verse 2, it was **after** the 40 days had ended that Jesus became hungry.

We will talk later in this chapter about some of the physical benefits of fasting and some mechanics that might be helpful to you as you fast, but first let's look further at the spiritual side of fasting, which is by far the most important aspect.

JESUS EXPECTS US TO FAST

We have already seen that Jesus fasted. Now let's look at some of His teaching on this vital subject:

> **14 Then the disciples of John came to Him saying, "Why do we and the Pharisees fast, but Your disciples do not fast?"**
>
> **15 And Jesus said to them, "The attendants of the bridegroom cannot mourn as long as the bridegroom is with them, can they? But the days will come when the bridegroom is taken away from them, and then they will fast. . . ."**
>
> **--Matthew 9**

Here Jesus plainly said that after He went back to heaven and left the disciples here on the earth, then they would indeed fast.

From His teaching in the Sermon on the Mount, we also know that Christ expects us to pray.

> **2 "When therefore you give alms, do not sound a trumpet before you, as the hypocrites do in the synagogues and in the streets, that they may be honored by men. Truly I say to you, they have their reward in full. . . ."**
>
> **--Matthew 6**

In the verse above, Jesus did not say **"if** you give," but **"when** you give," which means that He expected them to give. Let's look at the next thing that He expects:

> 5 "And when you pray, you are not to be as the hypocrites; for they love to stand and pray in the synagogues and on the street corners, in order to be seen by men. Truly I say to you, they have their reward in full. . . ."
>
> --Matthew 6

Here again, Jesus did not say "if you pray"; He said "when you pray." He obviously expected them to pray. Let's look at a third thing He expected them to do:

> 16 "And whenever you fast, do not put on a gloomy face as the hypocrites do, for they neglect their appearance in order to be seen fasting by men. Truly I say to you, they have their reward in full.
> 17 "But you, when you fast, anoint your head, and wash your face
> 18 so that you may not be seen fasting by men, but by your Father who is in secret; and your Father who sees in secret will repay you."
>
> --Matthew 6

Here Jesus did not say, "if you fast," but He says, "whenever you fast." He expected them to fast and told them a little bit about how they were to behave when they were fasting.

There is no doubt that Jesus expected the disciples to fast and that they followed His commands and expectations, because all the way through the book of Acts, fasting was involved with the early church:

> 23 And when they had appointed elders for them in every church, having prayed with fasting, they commended them to the Lord in whom they had believed.
>
> --Acts 14

Incidentally, this idea of "prayer and fasting" going together is mentioned over and over again in the Bible. Remember, we have already pointed out that

Christ said certain kinds of demons do not come out but by prayer and fasting.

SPIRITUAL REASONS TO FAST

We have already seen four good reasons for fasting:

1. To humble ourselves before God
2. To have our prayers answered
3. To break the yoke and bonds of wickedness
4. To have power to cast out demons

Now let's look at some other excellent spiritual reasons for fasting. One reason is for guidance:

> 24 Then the sons of Israel came against the sons of Benjamin the second day.
> 25 And Benjamin went out against them from Gibeah the second day and felled to the ground again 18,000 men of the sons of Israel; all these drew the sword.
> 26 Then all the sons of Israel and all the people went up and came to Bethel and wept; thus they remained there before the LORD and fasted that day until evening. And they offered burnt offerings and peace offerings before the LORD.
> 27 And the sons of Israel inquired of the LORD (for the ark of the covenant of God was there in those days,
> 28 and Phinehas the son of Eleazar, Aaron's son, stood before it to minister in those days), saying, "Shall I yet again go out to battle against the sons of my brother Benjamin, or shall I cease?" And the LORD said, "Go up, for tomorrow I will deliver them into your hand."
> --Judges 20

Here we see that as the sons of Israel fasted and sought God's guidance, God gave it to them. That appears to be another very valid reason to fast.

Another reason is so that we can really prove to God that we are repentant. One example of this is found in the story of Ahab:

> 19 "And you shall speak to him, saying, 'Thus says the LORD, "Have you murdered, and also taken possession?"' And you shall speak to him, saying, 'Thus says the LORD, "In the place where the dogs licked up the blood of Naboth the dogs shall lick up your blood, even yours. . . ." ' "
>
> 27 And it came about when Ahab heard these words, that he tore his clothes and put on sackcloth and fasted, and he lay in sackcloth and went about despondently.
> 28 Then the word of the LORD came to Elijah the Tishbite, saying,
> 29 "Do you see how Ahab has humbled himself before Me? Because he has humbled himself before Me, I will not bring the evil in his days, but I will bring the evil upon his house in his son's days."
>
> --1 Kings 21

We find in Daniel that fasting, along with repentance, also brought insight and understanding:

> 3 So I gave my attention to the Lord God to seek Him by prayer and supplications, with fasting, sackcloth, and ashes.
> 4 And I prayed to the LORD my God and confessed and said, "Alas, O Lord, the great and awesome God, who keeps His covenant and lovingkindness for those who love Him and keep His commandments,
> 5 we have sinned, committed iniquity, acted wickedly, and rebelled, even turning aside from Thy commandments and ordinances.
> 6 "Moreover, we have not listened to Thy servants the prophets, who spoke in Thy name to our kings, our princes, our fathers, and all the people of the land. . . .
>
> 20 Now while I was speaking and praying, and

confessing my sin and the sin of my people Israel, and presenting my supplication before the LORD my God in behalf of the holy mountain of my God,

21 while I was still speaking in prayer, then the man Gabriel, whom I had seen in the vision previously, came to me in my extreme weariness about the time of the evening offering.

22 And he gave me instruction and talked with me, and said, "O Daniel, I have now come forth to give you insight with understanding. . . ."

--Daniel 9

We have now seen at least seven very good reasons to fast:

1. To humble ourselves before God
2. To have our prayers answered
3. To break the yoke and bonds of wickedness
4. To have power to cast out demons
5. To seek guidance
6. To prove repentance
7. To obtain understanding and insight

Would you like to have your prayers answered? Would you like guidance? Would you like to have the bonds of unrighteousness broken in your life? Would you like to be able to cast out demons and to have understanding and insight? If your answer to any of these is "yes," then fasting is for you.

TYPES OF FASTS

There is some confusion as to what fasting is. We would like to look at the two types of fasts mentioned in the Bible:

1. Normal fast (water only)
2. Absolute fast (no water)

NORMAL FAST: In a normal fast you eat no food (this would include fruit and vegetable juices), but you may drink all of the water you want. This is the type of fast that Jesus went on after He was baptized:

> 1 And Jesus, full of the Holy Spirit, returned from the Jordan and was led about by the Spirit in the wilderness
> 2 for forty days, being tempted by the devil. And He ate nothing during those days; and when they had ended, He became hungry.
>
> --Luke 4

Verse 2 says, "He ate nothing," but there is no implication that He did not drink water. We can go forty or maybe sixty days without food, but we can only go three or four days without water before dying, unless God does a miracle.

ABSOLUTE FAST: In an absolute fast, no food nor any water is taken into the body. With one exception in the Scriptures, an absolute fast has never exceeded three days:

> 8 And Saul got up from the ground, and though his eyes were open, he could see nothing; and leading him by the hand, they brought him into Damascus.
> 9 And he was three days without sight, and neither ate nor drank.
>
> --Acts 9

Another example of the absolute fast is found in the story of Esther:

> 16 "Go, assemble all the Jews who are found in Susa, and fast for me; do not eat or drink for three days, night or day. I and my maidens also will fast in the same way. And thus I will go in to the king, which is not according to the law; and if I perish, I perish."
> 17 So Mordecai went away and did just as Esther had commanded him.

1 Now it came about on the third day that Esther put on her royal robes and stood in the inner court of the king's palace in front of the king's rooms, and the king was sitting on his royal throne in the throne room, opposite the entrance to the palace.

2 And it happened when the king saw Esther the queen standing in the court, she obtained favor in his sight; and the king extended to Esther the golden scepter which was in his hand. So Esther came near and touched the top of the scepter.

--Esther 4,5

When no water was taken in, the fasts described above lasted only three days.

RESTRICTED DIET: There are cases in which one's diet is restricted in one form or another. However, in the Bible these situations are never called fasts. One could drink only fruit and vegetable juices and that would be a restricted diet but not a fast, according to biblical definitions. One could eat no meat for a period of time and that would be a restricted diet but not a fast. Probably the most well-known example of a restricted diet was that of Ezekiel:

9 "But as for you, take wheat, barley, beans, lentils, millet and spelt, put them in one vessel and make them into bread for yourself; you shall eat it according to the number of the days that you lie on your side, three hundred and ninety days.

10 "And your food which you eat shall be twenty shekels a day by weight; you shall eat it from time to time.

11 "And the water you drink will be the sixth part of a hin by measure; you shall drink it from time to time.

12 "And you shall eat it as a barley cake, having baked it in their sight over human dung."

--Ezekiel 4

GROUP FAST: In addition to individual fasting, sometimes the Lord has led a group of people to fast. We will give three examples of this:

14 Consecrate a fast,
Proclaim a solemn assembly;
Gather the elders
And all the inhabitants of the land
To the house of the LORD your God,
And cry out to the LORD.

--Joel 1

15 Blow a trumpet in Zion,
Consecrate a fast, proclaim a solemn
assembly,
16 Gather the people, sanctify the
congregation,
Assemble the elders,
Gather the children and the nursing
infants.
Let the bridegroom come out of his
room
And the bride out of her bridal
chamber.

--Joel 2

5 Then the people of Nineveh believed in God; and they called a fast and put on sackcloth from the greatest to the least of them.

--Jonah 3

The reason we have gone through these various types of fasts is that usually when fasting is mentioned in the Bible, it is talking about the "normal fast." That is a fast wherein you drink all the water you want, but you eat no food or nutrients of any kind, including vitamin supplements. So when we use the word "fasting" in this book, we will be referring to the "normal fast."

OUR BODIES SHOULD GLORIFY GOD

We certainly want our spiritual lives to glorify God, but God also wants our bodies to glorify Him. Sometime you might want to take five minutes and stand before a full-length mirror and really examine your body from various angles, asking yourself if your body brings glory to God. If not, you may have to do what Paul did:

> 24 Do you not know that those who run in a race all run, but only one receives the prize? Run in such a way that you may win.
> 25 And everyone who competes in the games exercises self-control in all things. They then do it to receive a perishable wreath, but we an imperishable.
> 26 Therefore I run in such a way, as not without aim; I box in such a way, as not beating the air;
> 27 but I buffet my body and make it my slave, lest possibly, after I have preached to others, I myself should be disqualified.
>
> --1 Corinthians 9

In this passage, Paul says that he buffets his body in order to make it glorify God. In writing to the Romans, Paul encouraged them to present their bodies as a living sacrifice to God:

> 1 I urge you therefore, brethren, by the mercies of God, to present your bodies a living and holy sacrifice, acceptable to God, which is your spiritual service of worship.
> 2 And do not be conformed to this world, but be transformed by the renewing of your mind, that you may prove what the will of God is, that which is good and acceptable and perfect.
>
> --Romans 12

For most of us, our bodies really are not a living sacrifice and really do not glorify God. One recent survey showed that 80 percent of Americans are overweight by an average of 20 pounds. As I travel and minister, it is my observation that Christian groups tend to reflect those same statistics.

As the end of this age rapidly approaches, I believe Christians are going to need to have their bodies in shape. We are going to need to be toned up, with the "excess baggage" eliminated. There are probably changes in dietary habits that are necessary for us to indeed be good soldiers of Jesus Christ.

I believe that one of the very first steps in helping to make your body glorify God is to go on a fast. I recommend a ten-day fast, unless there are medical reasons why you should do otherwise. However, for any normal, healthy individual, a ten-day fast should be no problem. Don't ask your doctor if you **should** fast; he will likely say "no," since the benefits of fasting were probably not a part of his traditional medical training. Instead ask him if there is any biological reason why you could not go on a ten-day fast. In most cases, he will tell you that there is no reason why you could not fast.

Many Christians are addicted to coffee, whether they realize it or not. Coming off of coffee can give tremendous headaches and other physical withdrawal problems. I encourage a person who drinks coffee to stop drinking it one week before he starts a fast. This way he goes through the physical discomfort of coffee withdrawal without confusing it with fasting. Since it is the caffeine that is addictive, this would also apply to heavy drinkers of tea and colas, which also contain significant amounts of caffeine.

Now let's look at the mechanics of fasting. There are five distinct phases of fasting that you need to understand.

PHASE ONE: This is the "gearshift" phase. Forty-eight hours after you eat your last meal, the pituitary gland will begin to emit a hormone to tell your body to take its energy from the stored energy rather than from incoming food. During these first two days, you may have a bit of nausea, dizziness, headaches or weakness. Don't worry; this is normal.

One of the reasons that Jeani and I usually start a fast on Friday night or Saturday morning is so that we can get this out of the way and be ready to return to work on Monday.

All of the toxins that you have taken in, such as the insecticide residues on the skin of an apple, are stored in the fat cells of your body. Your body has only four ways to eliminate toxins: through bowel movements, urine, perspiration and your breath. Within about twenty-four hours after you start fasting, your bowel movements will stop. At that point, the primary ways that you will be eliminating toxins--some of which may have been stored in your body for many years--will be through your urine and your breath. Thus, you may experience very bad breath during the first part or even all of your fast. Jeani and I carry a little spray bottle of breath freshener with us during a fast and use it occassionally, both for our sake and for the sake of others.

PHASE TWO: This phase is short and you will tend to experience a bit of weakness that only lasts about a day. The energy that is stored is not quite the caliber of the energy from food you take in and, thus, for the remainder of your fast, you will likely be operating on about 80 percent of your normal energy level. After phase two is over, all hunger will disappear. Many Christians who fast for just one or two days at a time have never made it over this "hump" where hunger disappears. If you and God agree beforehand on how many days He wants you to fast, then you will have no trouble making it over this hunger hump.

PHASE THREE: The remainder of the fast, days four through ten (or even up to day forty, if God is so directing you) is a time of physical cleansing, as you give your digestive system a rest in order to repair itself and let your body rejuvenate itself. Also, after about the seventh day of the fast, you will find a heightened spiritual awareness. Your times of Bible reading and prayer will become more anointed than you have ever found them to be and very likely God will begin to speak to you in a more direct and clear way.

You can have real joy as you worship, praise and adore Him during the times that you would normally spend preparing and eating meals. What a wonderful experience this is!

PHASE FOUR: You will probably not get to this phase. It is the return-of-hunger phase. This would normally happen forty to sixty days after the fast begins. Some very obese patients have gone even more than one hundred days without hunger returning. Once that gnawing hunger returns, it is God's signal to you that starvation is beginning and you should definitely end your fast.

PHASE FIVE: This is the phase of breaking the fast. You want to come off your fast gently and gradually. Your first meal may be a glass of fruit or vegetable juice, diluted 50 percent with water. You can then gradually begin to add a little bit of solid food. Fresh fruit is a good thing to start with when you reintroduce solid foods; dairy products, such as cheese, are not good. Treat your body gently as it is coming off this fast and add quantity to your meals gradually, until you are back up to the meal size that God wants you to eat. (You may find that you don't need to eat meals as large as previously, once your system is cleansed and you are better able to digest your food.) Don't go from fasting to gluttony. Coming off of your fast properly is very important; be careful to do it in a way that will glorify God.

For most of us, our body is really a spoiled brat. We give it about anything it wants, when it comes to eating. Most Christians don't commit adultery, don't drink, and don't take dope, but boy can they eat! They walk around with a big girth advertising to the world: "Look, I'm yielding to lust of the flesh. I overeat routinely." Like any other spoiled brat, you cannot begin to discipline gradually; the iron curtain must fall. Fasting is the "rod" that will tame the spoiled brat called your body.

For some, the first extended fast (four days or more) is a little more difficult than subsequent ones. For others, subsequent fasts do not even have the hunger pangs during the first two or three days. If you find more physical discomfort than you expected during your first extended fast, do not be alarmed; many people do. If you do experience dizziness, weakness, nausea, headaches and so forth during the first few days of your fast, it is probably a combination of your body getting rid of a high level of toxins and Satan trying to discourage you. But hang in there--those symptoms will pass and the victory will be yours in Christ!

SUMMARY AND CONCLUSION

We have seen that Jesus fasted. If we really want to become like Jesus Christ, then we too will fast. Jesus said His disciples would fast and He expected it of them.

Fasting has tremendous spiritual benefits. It allows us to humble ourselves before God, and to have Him answer our prayers; it breaks the yoke of bondage; it can be proof of repentance and can bring understanding, guidance, and insight. Fasting can even cause us to have more faith and to be able to take authority over the strongest demons.

In addition, fasting can also free you from the fear of going without food. That freedom could be a source of tremendous peace and an opportunity to minister to others in the tough days that lie ahead when food may be scarce. An initial fast of more than three days (long enough to get over the "hunger hump") can help you get more comfortable with the idea of going without food and you will actually look forward to future fasts. Satan would love to keep Western Christians blinded to the benefits of fasting and the closer walk with God that it can bring.

In addition to spiritual benefits, fasting has considerable physical benefits. It detoxifies the body, cleanses and purifies it and helps us to bring our bodies under the control of the Holy Spirit. For many people, fasting can break Satan's stronghold over what has been an area of lust of the flesh--that of overeating or eating the wrong foods.

If you really want to be like Jesus and you prayed the prayer at the end of Chapter 2 about humbling yourself before God, God may well be speaking to you saying, "Prove it." One way indeed to prove your humility before Him is through fasting. I like to think of fasting as the dynamite that puts power behind our prayers.

While He was here on the earth, Jesus set an example for us of how Christians should live. Fasting was a part of the example He set for us. God, help us to walk in it.

4
PRAYER—JESUS STYLE

We have already seen that fasting is the dynamite that gives extra power to your prayers. As we now begin to think specifically about prayer, we need to examine Christ's prayer life and also what He taught about prayer. If we indeed have a burning desire to become like Jesus Christ, our prayer life will become like His prayer life. Our prayers will conform to His teachings on prayer and we know that He practiced what He taught.

One simple characteristic of Christ's prayer life is that He was usually **alone** with the Father when He was praying. It is fine to have little casual prayers as we drive down the highway, wash the dishes and go about our daily activities. These are necessary for moment by moment guidance, but the prayer time we are talking about in this chapter is the time when we are alone with God, concentrating on Him totally, with no distractions. One of the Scriptures that points this out is this:

> **23 And after He had sent the multitudes away, He went up to the mountain by Himself to pray; and when it was evening, He was there alone.**
>
> --Matthew 14

Here Jesus sent everyone away and He got alone with the Father in the evening to pray. This matches exactly with His teaching about prayer:

> **6 "But you, when you pray, go into your inner room, and when you have shut your door, pray to your Father who is in secret, and your Father who sees in secret will repay you. . . ."**
>
> **--Matthew 6**

If many Christians were honest with themselves and really evaluated how much time they spend in quality prayer alone with God, it would be not nearly as much as they assume. We need to exclude from this calculation any time when we are doing something else. We are talking about time alone with Him, wherein there are no distractions and we would be able to shut our eyes if we wanted to. There is nothing else that we are thinking about, listening to, or watching. This also would exclude prayer in church, in prayer meetings, or even with your spouse. What we are discussing in this chapter is prayer when you are alone concentrating solely on God.

How much time do you think the average Christian spends in this kind of prayer? . . . Right--not much! However, if we yearn to be like Christ, I believe we will have this kind of prayer time on a daily basis. If you desire to have this kind of time, alone with God, there will be some things that I will share later in this chapter that I believe will be a help to you.

We do not know if Jesus had a time of this type of prayer daily, but if not, it was certainly very frequently:

> **16 But He Himself would often slip away to the wilderness and pray.**
>
> **--Luke 5**

FERVENT PRAYER

What is the difference between regular prayer and fervent prayer? If you have heard a person pray that his Sunday School class might grow, for example, you have probably heard a regular, relaxed or maybe even casual prayer. However, if you have heard a father or mother praying for a child that was sick to the point of death, you have heard a fervent prayer. That fervent prayer not only involves every fiber of that individual's being, but it also tends to go on and on. It is not usually a short prayer.

From every indication, Christ's prayer life usually involved fervent prayer. We are all familiar with an extreme case of His fervent prayer in the garden of Gethsemane:

> 44 And being in agony He was praying very fervently; and His sweat became like drops of blood, falling down upon the ground.
>
> --Luke 22

Not only did He pray fervently in the garden of Gethsemane; let's see what the writer of Hebrews has to say about the prayer life of Jesus:

> 5 So also Christ did not glorify Himself so as to become a high priest, . . .
>
> 7 In the days of His flesh, He offered up both prayers and supplications with loud crying and tears to the One able to save Him from death, and He was heard because of His piety.
>
> --Hebrews 5

This says that Christ offered up prayers with loud crying and tears. That is fervent prayer. It also says that Christ was heard because of His piety. Would you like your prayers to avail much? The Bible tells us how they can:

> 16 Confess your faults one to another, and pray one for another, that ye may be healed. The effectual fervent prayer of a righteous man availeth much.
>
> --James 5, KJV

This verse tells us clearly that the fervent prayer of a righteous man will accomplish much. If your prayers are not accomplishing much, you might ask yourself if you meet the criteria of living a righteous life and praying fervently. If you are not living a righteous life, then you need to confess your sins and let God clean up your life. If your prayers are not fervent, ask God to lay a burden on your heart. When He does, your prayers will become fervent, like those of Jesus.

Fervent prayer can be full of joy or praise, as our heart is overwhelmed by the love, beauty and majesty of God. Fervent prayer of thanksgiving can cause one to dance, like it did David when he was finally able to bring the ark to its resting place. Whether it is prayer for healing, for a spiritual need (such as a yearning to be holy) or for something else, fervent prayer has an intensity. We need more of that in our prayers today.

REQUIREMENTS FOR PRAYERS TO BE ANSWERED

Many people have the idea that they can pray and ask for something, and then start claiming it and it will happen. Unfortunately, I do not believe that matches with what Christ taught and practiced about prayer. We have already seen that we need to spend some time alone in fervent prayer and at times we need to pray with fasting. Also, there are many other requirements in the Bible for our prayers to be answered. Our prayers need to meet all of these requirements, not just some of them. Following are some of the requirements that Jesus laid down for our prayers to be answered.

1. Pray In Jesus' Name

Praying in Jesus' name means more than just tacking His name on the end of your prayer. It means coming to God with a heart attitude of submission, recognizing that you could not come to God at all except through the sacrifice of Jesus Christ on the cross. Also, if you have not received Him as your Savior, you do not have His name. Thus, this is for those who have Jesus Christ as their personal Savior:

> 23 "And in that day you will ask Me no question. Truly, truly, I say to you, if you shall ask the Father for anything, He will give it to you in My name.
> 24 "Until now you have asked for nothing in My name; ask, and you will receive, that your joy may be made full. . . ."
>
> --John 16

2. We Must Pray Believing

Over and over again faith is stated as a requirement for answered prayer:

> 21 And Jesus answered and said to them, "Truly I say to you, if you have faith, and do not doubt, you shall not only do what was done to the fig tree, but even if you say to this mountain, 'Be taken up and cast into the sea,' it shall happen.
> 22 "And all things you ask in prayer, believing, you shall receive."
>
> --Matthew 21

> 24 "Therefore I say to you, all things for which you pray and ask, believe that you have received them, and they shall be granted you. . . ."
>
> --Mark 11

Faith is not generated by positive confession or repeating over and over again that your prayer has already been answered. Without a doubt, positive thinking has power, but it has nothing to do with faith and believing. The Bible tells us where faith comes from:

> 17 So then faith cometh by hearing, and hearing by the word of God.
>
> --Romans 10, KJV

This says that faith comes by hearing "the word of God." However, if you take the time to check the

Greek New Testament, this does not say that faith comes by hearing the "logos" of God; that is, faith does not come by hearing the Scriptures. The Greek word used here is "rhema." Correctly translated, faith comes by hearing the "rhema" of God.

The rhema of God is when the Holy Spirit speaks to your heart. The Holy Spirit can take a verse of Scripture and make it a rhema of God to you. However, you cannot randomly take a Scripture and start trying to make it the rhema of God for you, trying to have faith that God means that Scripture for you at that time.

Once the Holy Spirit speaks to your heart concerning something, you can know that it will happen. He may or may not use the Scriptures to speak to you. You may have had the same experience that I have had on many occasions, after seeking God about a particular request. In one instance, I had been praying for something for several weeks, then during a time of prayer God said, "It is yours." After that I could no longer ask God for it; I could only thank Him for it. I had received the rhema of God in that situation and it gave me total faith.

3. We Must Pray In His Will

In order for our prayers to be answered, we have to pray in His will. It may not be His will for us to be wealthy, for example. Jesus certainly wasn't wealthy, nor were His disciples. It may not always be God's will for someone to be healed. I believe this could be the case with Joni Eareckson Tada. Certainly Paul was not healed of his physical infirmity. Prayer should begin with the Holy Spirit. If He lays it on your heart to pray for a certain thing, then it is the rhema of God to you and you can know that it is the will of God.

> **14 And this is the confidence which we have before Him, that, if we ask anything according to His will, He hears us.**
> **15 And if we know that He hears us in what**

ever we ask, we know that we have the requests which we have asked from Him.

--1 John 5

If we are to pray in His will, prayer must begin with the Holy Spirit and not our own selfish desires.

4. Pray Without Any Iniquity In Your Heart

The Bible tells us that God will not hear sinners, and I believe that includes Christians who are sinning.

31 "We know that God does not hear sinners; but if anyone is God-fearing, and does His will, He hears him. . . ."

--John 9

18 If I regard wickedness in my heart,
The Lord will not hear; . . .

--Psalm 66

If we are harboring wickedness and known sin in our hearts, the Bible says that God will not even hear us, much less answer our prayers. Of course, He "hears us," in the sense that He hears every word spoken on the earth. What this means is that He does not receive our words as a prayer, if we are living in a way that is displeasing to Him. (There are exceptions to this, in that out of His mercy God may sometimes choose to answer our prayers in spite of our sin, but we have no guarantee that He will hear our prayers if we are harboring sin in our lives.)

5. Pray Having Forgiven All

Many of us have old, old hurts and we have never forgiven the people who have hurt us. This may have been a hurt inflicted by a parent or a close relative. It could have happened in our childhood or any other time in our past. If there is anyone that we have not forgiven, Jesus tells us that God cannot forgive us. If He has not been able to forgive us because of our unforgiveness, then we still have iniquity in our heart. Here is what Jesus had to say:

> 14 "For if you forgive men for their transgressions, your heavenly Father will also forgive you.
> 15 "But if you do not forgive men, then your Father will not forgive your transgressions. . ."
> --Matthew 6

> 25 "And whenever you stand praying, forgive, if you have anything against anyone; so that your Father also who is in heaven may forgive you your transgressions.
> 26 ("But if you do not forgive, neither will your Father who is in heaven forgive your transgressions.")
> --Mark 11

You might want to pause and consider whether there is anyone in your past, who has done you wrong, harmed you or hurt you, whom you have not forgiven. It does not matter whether or not that individual has repented or asked for forgiveness; God says you are to forgive him anyhow. If there is any unforgiveness in your heart, you might want to cry out to God right now and forgive that person. There is no need to live a moment longer with that unforgiveness blocking your clear communication with the Father.

6. Pray With Right Motives

If we pray with wrong motives, selfishly or for our own pleasure, the Bible says that God will not answer that prayer:

> 2 You lust and do not have; so you commit murder. And you are envious and cannot obtain; so you fight and quarrel. You do not have because you do not ask.
> 3 You ask and do not receive, because you ask with wrong motives, so that you may spend

it on your pleasures.

--James 4

If you stop to think about it, much of the praying done by Christians is somewhat selfish (for their pleasure or comfort).

7. Pray Not As A Friend Of The World

The world has a lot to offer, but if we are friends of the world, we make ourselves enemies of God. I do not believe that God will answer the prayers of His enemies:

> 15 Do not love the world, nor the things in the world. If anyone loves the world, the love of the Father is not in him.
> 16 For all that is in the world, the lust of the flesh and the lust of the eyes and the boastful pride of life, is not from the Father, but is from the world.
>
> --1 John 2

> 4 You adulteresses, do you not know that friendship with the world is hostility toward God? Therefore whoever wishes to be a friend of the world makes himself an enemy of God.
>
> --James 4

8. Keep On Praying

When Christ said to "ask and you will receive," the Greek is actually "keep on asking and you will receive." Williams, who translated a version of the New Testament (which was published by Moody Press), pointed out that the verbs in connection with prayer are in the continuous tense. For example, Matthew 7:7,8 is best translated:

> 7 Keep on asking, and it will be given to you; Keep on seeking, and you will find; keep on knocking (reverently) and the door will be

opened to you.

8 For every one who keeps on asking receives, and he who keeps on seeking finds, and to him who keeps on knocking it will be opened.

--Matthew 7, Amplified

All of the teaching of Christ on prayer portrayed this "continuous asking" form of prayer. The AMPLIFIED BIBLE again reflects this well in the following passage:

1 Then He was praying in a certain place, and when He stopped, one of His disciples said to Him, Lord, teach us to pray, as John taught his disciples.

2 And He said to them, When you pray, say, (Our) Father, (Who is in heaven,) hallowed be Your name. Your kingdom come. Your will be done--held holy and revered--on earth as it is in heaven.

3 Give us daily our bread (food for the morrow),

4 And forgive us our sins, for we ourselves also forgive every one who is indebted to us--who has offended us or done us wrong; and bring us not into temptation, but rescue us from evil.

5 And He said to them, Which of you who has a friend will go to him at midnight and will say to him, Friend, lend me three loaves (of bread),

6 For a friend of mine who is on a journey has just come, and I have nothing to put before him;

7 And he from within will answer, Do not disturb me; the door is now closed, and my children are with me in bed; I cannot get up and supply you (with anything)?

8 I tell you, although he will not get up and supply him anything because he is his friend, yet because of his shameless persistence and insistence, he will get up and give him as much

> as he needs.
> 9 So I say to you, Ask and keep on asking, and it shall be given you; seek and keep on seeking, and you shall find; knock and keep on knocking and the door shall be opened to you.
> 10 For every one who asks and keeps on asking receives, and he who seeks and keeps on seeking finds, and to him who knocks and keeps on knocking the door shall be opened.
> --Luke 11, Amplified

The NEW AMERICAN STANDARD BIBLE, gives the continuous tense in the marginal notes for the last two verses: "keep asking, keep seeking, keep knocking." This fits in perfectly with the example that Christ just gave--that of going to a friend at midnight and persistently asking. The main thing to note here is that the Greek tells us not to ask just once and then start "claiming" or "confessing" it. The Bible actually tells us to keep on asking.

Another example of prayer that Christ gave along this same line involved a woman going to a judge:

> 1 Now He was telling them a parable to show that at all times they ought to pray and not to lose heart,
> 2 saying, "There was in a certain city a judge who did not fear God, and did not respect man.
> 3 "And there was a widow in that city, and she kept coming to him, saying, 'Give me legal protection from my opponent.'
> 4 "And for a while he was unwilling; but afterward he said to himself, 'Even though I do not fear God nor respect man,
> 5 yet because this widow bothers me, I will give her legal protection, lest by continually coming she wear me out.'"
> 6 And the Lord said, "Hear what the unrighteous judge said;
> 7 now shall not God bring about justice for His elect, who cry to Him day and night, and

will He delay long over them? . . ."

--Luke 18

Jesus wanted His disciples to keep on praying and not to lose heart, so He told them about this woman who kept coming to the judge day after day. Thus, we see that, according to the teachings of Jesus, we do not just pray once and then start claiming that we have the answer. We "keep on praying" day after day. We should pray continually. The AMPLIFIED BIBLE gives an even better feeling for verse 1:

1 Now He was telling them a parable to show that at all times they ought to pray and not to lose heart, . . .

--Luke 18, Amplified

This persistence in prayer is found many places in the Scriptures:

17 pray without ceasing; . . .

--1 Thessalonians 5

18 With all prayer and petition pray at all times in the Spirit, and with this in view, be on the alert with all perseverance and petition for all the saints, . . .

--Ephesians 5

Jesus prayed multiple times for things:

44 And He left them again, and went away and prayed a third time, saying the same thing once more.

--Matthew 26

9. Obey God and Please Him

Another requirement to have our prayers answered is that we obey God's commandments and do the things that are pleasing to Him:

> 22 and whatever we ask we receive from Him, because we keep His commandments and do the things are are pleasing in His sight.
>
> --1 John 3

You could think of this another way. To have our prayers answered we need to avoid doing things that displease God.

JESUS PRAYED FOR LONG PERIODS OF TIME

We know that Christ frequently got up a great while before dawn to pray and on one occassion, of which we are aware, He prayed all night long:

> 35 And in the early morning, while it was still dark, He arose and went out and departed to a lonely place, and was praying there.
>
> --Mark 1

> 12 And it was at this time that He went off to the mountain to pray, and He spent the whole night in prayer to God.
>
> --Luke 6

If we want to become like Jesus Christ and have our prayer life become like His, then we are going to want to have a period of time set aside daily to spend in prayer alone with God. The question that arises is, "How much time should we daily spend in prayer?"

A good suggested standard is to regularly spend one hour in prayer. One of the passages of Scripture on which one could base this suggestion is the following:

> 40 And He came to the disciples and found them sleeping, and said to Peter, "So, you men could not keep watch with Me for one hour?
>
> 41 "Keep watching and praying, that you may not enter into temptation; the spirit is willing, but the flesh is weak."
>
> --Matthew 26

The alternative with the disciples, like with most of us, was to **sleep or pray.** If most Christians would spend one good, solid hour in prayer, alone with God, (not while doing something else), I believe that would satisfy that feeling of needing to spend more time in concentrated prayer. (Even if God leads you to begin spending an hour a day in prayer, be open to the possibility that sometime He may want you to spend all day or all night in prayer.)

One of the problems many Christians have is that after five or ten minutes of concentrated prayer, they run out of things for which to pray. If you would have difficulty in filling up an entire hour with prayer, I would like to give you some suggestions.

"PAC TALL POWER"

Rather than thinking of the hour as one big block of time, what the Lord has led me to do is to have twelve different areas of prayer and to aim to pray for each of those twelve areas for five minutes each. If the five minutes is not quite up, then I finish off by praying in tongues.

To make it easy to remember, the Lord gave me an acronym for these twelve areas. It is "PAC TALL POWER." We don't want to pack a little short power generator; we want to have a huge, tall power generator and, thus, we want to "PAC TALL POWER." Of course, the power is the power of prayer. Let me first list these twelve areas of PAC TALL POWER:

P - Praise
A - Adoration
C - Confession

T - Thanksgiving
A - Authorities
L - Leaders
L - Lost

P - Personal (including family)
O - Other Christians (including church members)

W - World
E - End Times
R - Rest

Do you think you could spend five minutes praising the Lord? You could use songs and choruses. That shouldn't be too difficult, should it?

Do you think you could spend five minutes adoring and worshiping the Lord? You could read some of the Psalms in connection with this.

What about confessing your sins and, like Daniel, confessing the sins of the nation? Do you think you could spend five minutes doing that? Of course.

What about the things for which we thank the Lord, usually on Thanksgiving day; could you spend five minutes thanking Him for the multitude of blessings in your life? Do you see how easy it is going to be to spend a fruitful hour in prayer? Now let's take these areas one at a time.

1. P = Praise

The first five minutes of this hour that we are going to spend in prayer is a joyful, wonderful time. In many of the verses in the Psalms, David is praising God. I always like to pray with my Bible open and frequently begin by reading Psalm 100:

> 1 Shout joyfully to the Lord, all the earth.
> 2 Serve the Lord with gladness;
> Come before Him with joyful singing.
> 3 Know that the Lord Himself is God;
> It is He who has made us, and not we ourselves;
> We are His people and the sheep of His pasture.
> 4 Enter His gates with thanksgiving,
> And His courts with praise.
> Give thanks to Him; bless His name.
> 5 For the Lord is good;
> His lovingkindness is everlasting,
> And His faithfulness to all generations.

This Psalm says that when we come to Him we should have joyful singing, thanksgiving and praise. This is evidently to be done aloud, because we are to use our mouth and our lips:

> **3 Because Thy lovingkindness is better than life,**
> **My lips will praise Thee.**
> **4 So I will bless Thee as long as I live;**
> **I will lift up my hands in Thy name.**
> **5 My soul is satisfied as with marrow and fatness,**
> **And my mouth offers praises with joyful lips.**
>
> **--Psalm 63**

I believe this hour of prayer should be aloud. If you are where you can speak and sing in a loud voice, that's wonderful. On the other hand, if you are in a confined living space, you can do it in a very quiet whisper, but let your lips actually be involved in it.

One morning the Lord may have you just read a number of Psalms. On another morning He may lead you to sing many of the songs that are sung in your fellowship. However He leads you, you should have no problem at all spending five minutes praising Him.

In addition to my open Bible, I like to have two other things with me when I start an hour of prayer. One of them is a notebook. You might want to copy over the "PAC TALL POWER" list into your notebook for reference and a quick reminder. You might also want to have a page for each of these twelve five-minute segments. On the praise page, you could list some of the Psalms that you especially like to praise the Lord with, and you could list the titles of some of the songs and choruses that you like to sing in praise to Him. Yes, you can have your eyes open during this hour. You can look at your watch or the Bible or the notebook.

The other thing I like to have handy is a stack of 3x5 cards. Don Moomaw, pastor of Bellaire Presbyterian Church, spends time each morning in prayer. In times past, as he was praying, the thought would come into his mind, "I need to call Mrs. Jones today." He would tell Satan to go away and quit distracting him from his time of prayer. Later during that same time of prayer, a thought would come into his mind, such as, "I must go by and pick up the new hymnals today." Again, he would rebuke Satan from distracting him from his prayer time.

Later, he shared with us that the Lord showed him how ignorant he was. He had asked the Lord at the beginning of the prayer to show him what he should do during that day. He realized that these things he thought were distractions were actually guidance from the Lord in setting up his schedule for the day. From then on, he kept a stack of 3x5 cards beside him when he prayed. When one of these thoughts would come into his mind (of something he needed to do that day), he would write it down on a 3x5 card, say, "Thank you Lord for your guidance," and go right back to praying.

We praise God as the Almighty Creator, the all powerful One who could bring galaxies into being at a single word.

2. A = Adoration

Praise deals with what God has done, whereas we adore Him as our loving heavenly Father. Adoration deals with our personal relationship with God. It is during this five minutes that we can tell Him how much we love Him, ask Him to cause us to love Him more and worship Him for who He is. We all remember the greatest commandment, which is the greatest thing for us to do:

> **36 "Teacher, which is the great commandment in the Law?"**
> **37 And He said to him, "'YOU SHALL LOVE THE LORD YOUR GOD WITH ALL YOUR HEART, AND WITH ALL YOUR SOUL, AND WITH ALL YOUR MIND.' . . ."**
>
> **--Matthew 22**

Loving God with all of your heart, soul and mind is by far the most important thing you can do. We should daily yearn to have a deeper love for God in all three of those areas. We also need to remember that the reason we were created was to glorify God:

> 7 Everyone who is called by My name,
> And whom I have created for My glory,
> Whom I have formed, even whom I have made." . . .
>
> --Isaiah 43

If we love Him with all of our heart, we will yearn to please Him and, certainly, glorifying Him in all that we do would please Him. Ask Him to show you this day what would glorify Him the most.

It is in adoring the Lord that I find the Psalms most helpful, because David loved and adored the Lord so much. A couple of Psalms that are good to use in this five-minute segment are Psalms 103 and 104:

> 1 Bless the Lord, O my soul;
> And all that is within me, bless His holy name.
> 2 Bless the Lord, O my soul,
> And forget none of His benefits;
> 3 Who pardons all your iniquities;
> Who heals all your diseases;
> 4 Who redeems your life from the pit;
> Who crowns you with lovingkindness and compassion;
> 5 Who satisfies your years with good things,
> So that your youth is renewed like the eagle.
> 6 The Lord performs righteous deeds,
> And judgments for all who are oppressed.
> 7 He made known His ways to Moses,
> His acts to the sons of Israel.
> 8 The Lord is compassionate and gracious,
> Slow to anger and abounding in lovingkindness.
>
> --Psalm 103

1 Bless the Lord, O my soul!
O Lord my God, Thou art very great;
Thou art clothed with spendor and
majesty,
2 Covering Thyself with light as with a
cloak,
Stretching out heaven like a tent
curtain.
3 He lays the beams of His upper chambers
in the waters;
He makes the clouds His chariot;
He walks upon the wings of the wind;
4 He makes the winds His messengers,
Flaming fire His ministers.

--Psalm 104

3. C = Confession

Many people think that confession should be the first thing that we do in a time of prayer. There are valid reasons for thinking this. However, in the model prayer that Jesus gave to the disciples, where did confession and asking for forgiveness come? It was about halfway through the prayer:

9 "Pray, then, in this way:
'Our Father who art in heaven,
Hallowed be Thy name.
10 'Thy kindgom come.
Thy will be done,
On earth as it is in heaven.
11 'Give us this day our daily bread.
12 'And forgive us our debts, as we also
have forgiven our debtors.
13 'And do not lead us into temptation,
but deliver us from evil. For
Thine is the kingdom, and the
power, and the glory, forever.
Amen.'. . ."

--Matthew 6

Once we have glimpsed afresh who God is, what He has done and how pure, holy and righteous He is, then we are ready to look at ourselves. We are so dirty in comparison that we are then eager to confess our sins. This is perhaps why confession comes later in the model prayer that Christ gave to the disciples.

One thing we can do in our time of confession for our personal sins is to ask God to shine His brilliant, pure searchlight into our hearts:

> 23 Search me, O God, and know my heart:
> Try me and know my anxious thoughts;
> 24 And see if there be any hurtful way in me,
> And lead me in the everlasting way.
> --Psalm 139

Once God shows us those sins, we are then to repent (turn 180 degrees away from those sins) and confess them to God:

> 9 If we confess our sins, He is faithful and righteous to forgive us our sins and to cleanse us from all unrighteousness. --1 John 1

Praise God! Once we confess our sins, He is faithful and has promised that He will forgive us our sins that we have confessed and He will cleanse us from all the unrighteousness that we don't even know about! Isn't that fantastic? Not only does He forgive us, but He also forgets about our sins:

> 12 "FOR I WILL BE MERCIFUL TO THEIR INIQUITIES
> AND I WILL REMEMBER THEIR SINS NO MORE."
> --Hebrews 8

This deals with our personal sins. However, I believe we should also follow Daniel's pattern and not only confess our sins, but also the sins of our nation:

> 3 So I gave my attention to the Lord God to seek Him by prayer and supplications, with

fasting, sackcloth, and ashes.

4 And I prayed to the Lord my God and confessed and said, "Alas, O Lord, the great and awesome God, who keeps His covenant and lovingkindness for those who love Him and keep His commandments,

5 We have sinned, committed iniquity, acted wickedly, and rebelled, even turning aside from Thy commandments and ordinances.

6 "Moreover, we have not listened to Thy servants the prophets, who spoke in Thy name to our kings, our princes, our fathers, and all the people of the land.

7 "Righteousness belongs to Thee, O Lord, but to us open shame, as it is this day--to the men of Judah, the inhabitants of Jerusalem, and all Israel, those who are nearby and those who are far away in all the countries to which Thou hast driven them, because of their unfaithful deeds which they have committed against Thee.

8 "Open shame belongs to us, O Lord, to our kings, our princes, and our fathers, because we have sinned against Thee.

9 "To the Lord our God belong compassion and forgiveness, for we have rebelled against Him;

10 nor have we obeyed the voice of the Lord our God, to walk in His teachings which He set before us through His servants the prophets. . . .

20 Now while I was speaking and praying, and confessing my sin and the sin of my people Israel, and presenting my supplication before the Lord my God in behalf of the holy mountain of my God, . . .

--Daniel 9

4. Thanksgiving

What a joyful thing it is to thank the Lord for all of His goodness to us, for we know that every good and perfect gift comes from Him (James 1:17). We can thank Him for our country, our home, our health, our food, each loved one who is dear to us, and the long, long list of things that normally we thank the Lord for once a year, at Thanksgiving time. Perhaps we should follow Paul's admonition:

> 2 Devote yourselves to prayer, keeping alert in it with an attitude of thanksgiving; . . .
>
> --Colossians 4

We know it is God's will for us to keep giving thanks to the Lord:

> 16 Rejoice always;
> 17 pray without ceasing;
> 18 in everything give thanks; for this is God's will for you in Christ Jesus.
>
> --1 Thessalonians 5

5. Authorities

We know that we are to pray for the authorities that are over us, because the Scriptures command it:

> 1 First of all, then, I urge that entreaties and prayers, petitions and thanksgivings, be made on behalf of all men,
> 2 for kings and all who are in authority, in order that we may lead a tranquil and quiet life in all godliness and dignity.
>
> --1 Timothy 2

> 12 But we request of you, brethren, that you appreciate those who diligently labor among you, and have charge over you in the Lord and give you instruction,
> 13 and that you esteem them very highly in love because of their work. Live in peace with one another.
>
> --1 Thessalonians 5

I believe praying for the authorities over you means all authorities, whether they be spiritual or civil. The list would include:

The chief executive of your nation
The national legislative bodies
The chief executive of the state or province
The legislative bodies of the state or province
The county authorities
The mayor of the city
The city council
The policemen
The military forces
The government regulatory bodies
The post office
National and international leaders of your church organization
The local leaders of your church
Any other Christian who is in spiritual authority over you

We should pray for all of these people and their own personal relationship with God through Jesus Christ and that their personal lives would be pure, just and have integrity. We should pray that in all the decisions they have to make, they would be in the center of God's will. We can pray for their personal health and safety. We can pray for their emotional well-being, their marriages and their families.

6. L = Leaders

In this five minutes, you could pray for those in leadership positions who do not have direct authority over you. Here we would include many world leaders in the secular realm and also leaders in the Christian realm.

One of the reasons to pray for these people is because the decisions that they make can affect your life. Some of the world leaders that you might want to pray for would include:

The President of the United States*
The President of the Soviet Union
The Prime Minister of England

The Chancellor of Germany
The Prime Minister of Japan
The Premier of Red China
The Prime Minister of Canada
The Prime Minister of Israel
The President of Egypt
The President of Syria
The President of Jordan
The President of Lebanon
The King of Saudi Arabia
The head of Iran
*He is included here for those living outside the U.S.

In addition to these world leaders, there are others, like the head of the PLO and the head of Afghanistan, that the Lord could bring to your mind. Certainly the heads of all of the Latin American nations, including Cuba, right now are making very vital decisions that could affect your life.

In addition, the Christian leaders of the world are in need of our prayers. Some of the ones that come to mind--but it certainly is not an exhaustive list--would include:

Pat Robertson	Jimmy Swaggart
Jim Bakker	James Robison
Billy Graham	Dave Wilkerson
Oral Roberts	Lorne Sanny
Demos Shakarian	Lorne Cunningham
The Pope	Jerry Falwell

The list could go on and on and include many of those with national television ministries and pastors of large churches around the world. You should include those that the Holy Spirit lays on your heart to pray for.

All these men who truly know Jesus Christ as their Savior and are in world Christian leadership positions deeply need our prayers that they would be protected from the attacks of Satan and that they would remain true to Christ and His truth and have the boldness to proclaim it loudly, in spite of the satanic opposition that will come.

7. L = Lost

Here I am thinking primarily of those who are lost that you know personally. This may be lost people that you really care about, such as your friends, those at work and your relatives. However, it would also include the lost ones who are your enemies and someday might even be persecuting you:

> 44 "But I say to you, love your enemies, and pray for those who persecute you
> 45 in order that you may be sons of your Father who is in heaven; for He causes His sun to rise on the evil and the good, and sends rain on the righteous and the unrighteous.
> 46 "For if you love those who love you, what reward have you? Do not even the tax-gatherers do the same? . . ."
>
> --Matthew 6

I believe that many Christians pray for the lost in an incorrect manner. There are a few things that God has voluntarily restricted Himself from doing. For example, He will not lie. Another thing He has said He will not do is force Himself into anyone's life. Thus, when we pray to God, "Save Mr. or Mrs. So-and-so," we are asking God to do something that He has already said that He would not do. However, there are many legitimate things we can pray for concerning the lost. We can pray that the Holy Spirit will convict them of sin and righteousness and judgment:

> 7 "But I tell you the truth, it is to your advantage that I go away; for if I do not go away, the Helper shall not come to you; but if I go, I will send Him to you.
> 8 "And He, when He comes, will convict the world concerning sin, and righteousness, and

judgment; . . ."

--John 16

We can pray that God would remove the blinders that Satan has placed on their eyes:

3 And even if our gospel is veiled, it is veiled to those who are perishing,
4 in whose case the god of this world has blinded the minds of the unbelieving, that they might not see the light of the gospel of the glory of Christ, who is the image of God.

--2 Corinthians 4

We can also pray that all Christians who come in contact with that individual would be sensitive to the guidance of the Holy Spirit and would say to him the things about Christ that he needs to hear. We can pray that God would bring a Christian or a radio or television program to him to which he would really respond. I believe that God will answer these prayers.

However, after the cross, there is not a single instance in the New Testament where any lost individual is prayed for specifically that he would be saved. If we stick with the Bible pattern and what the Bible tells us to do, we will be far better off and we will see much more results of our prayers for the lost.

If you do not have enough lost people that you are concerned about to take up a full five minutes, then ask the Lord earnestly to bring lost people into contact with you, so that you can share the love of Christ with them.

8. P = Personal

In this five-minute segment, you can share with the Lord all of your personal needs, including those of your family. The Lord wants to meet your needs so that your joy may be full:

24 "Until now you have asked for nothing in My name; ask, and you will receive, that your

joy may be made full. . . ."

--John 16

Your personal needs may be emotional, financial, spiritual, or physical. He wants to heal you, to care for you and to make you full of joy. He loves you. Keep on asking and you will receive!

Earlier in this chapter, we quoted part of Psalm 103, which says that the Lord "heals all your diseases" and "redeems your life from the pit" (vs. 3-4), among other wonderful things. Isn't that great! Praise the Lord! He is the One who heals all our diseases and meets all our needs.

9. O = Other Christians

In this five-minute segment, you can pray for other Christians in your own church (or fellowship), missionaries, Christians that you have been close to in times past who live other places now, Christians in other countries where there is war or persecution, Christians in prison in Communist countries and any other Christians that the Lord might bring to your mind. It is commanded that we pray for all the Christians:

> **18 With all prayer and petition pray at all times in the Spirit, and with this in view, be on the alert with all perseverance and petition for all saints, . . .**

--Ephesians 6

Do you think your prayers for Christians in Communist prisons will help them? Of course you and I believe that, because we believe in the power of prayer. This also means, though, that your lack of prayer will hurt them. Many of those Christians over there are counting on the prayers of free Christians.

What we need is a deeper love for all Christians everywhere. If we have a deep love for them, then we cannot help praying for them:

> 11 Now may our God and Father Himself and Jesus our Lord direct our way to you;
> 12 and may the Lord cause you to increase and abound in love for one another, and for all men, just as we also do for you;
> 13 so that He may establish your hearts unblamable in holiness before our God and Father at the coming of our Lord Jesus with all His saints.
>
> --1 Thessalonians 3

As far as things to pray for concerning missionaries, here is a partial list:

Their language study
Their time in prayer
Their time in the Scriptures
That they would not be discouraged
That the Holy Spirit would guide them as to who to talk to
That the Holy Spirit would guide them as to how to spend their time
That the Holy Spirit would go before and prepare the hearts of those they will minister to
That they will remain healthy
That they will be filled with the Holy Spirit
That they will be able to help new Christians to grow
For their financial needs and support

The list could go on and on. Of course the Holy Spirit will show you what to pray for them and the other Christians that He brings to your mind.

10. W = World

It is said that the soldiers in Napoleon's army carried a map of the world in their knapsack. It was on Napoleon's heart to conquer the world and what was on his heart, they wanted to be on their hearts. We know that God loves the world. He loved us so much that He sent His very own Son, Jesus Christ, to die for the world. Therefore, we should pray for the world. It should be on our hearts, like it is on God's heart. Carry a map of the world in the "knapsack" of your heart.

One of the things that you can pray about during this five minutes is some of the news items that you hear on the evening news or read in the newspapers. If there is an earthquake, a hurricane or a flood, you can pray for the victims there and their physical needs. You can pray that God will use this tragedy to bring them closer to Himself through Jesus Christ. Specific international meetings and decisions could be bathed in prayer.

One thing I like to do is to take a continent each day and concentrate on that continent. You can pray for the lost there, the governments, their food, and so forth. You could rotate the continents, taking a day each on:

North America
South America
Europe
Africa
Asia and the Orient
Australia and the Islands

11. E = End Times

Concerning the end times, much prayer needs to go into your own personal preparation: what would God have you to do as an individual, as a family, and as a body of believers to prepare for the end times? This preparation could be spiritual, emotional, financial, social and/or physical. He will show you what you should do to get ready for the days ahead.

We need to pray for the masses of Christians who are "playing ostrich" and are assuming that things are going to be beautiful and that they will be yanked out before any trouble hits planet Earth. We need to pray that they would become aware that we are going to go through tough times and that the Lord would wake them up and then, after getting their attention, would show them what they should do to get ready.

Pray for Christian leaders, that they would be open to the Lord on truth concerning the end times.

You can pray for end-times ministries, such as Omega Ministries, that are trying to help alert the body of Christ and to help them get ready. You could pray for these ministries' outreach to be expanded, that the finances would come in to support that expanded outreach and that the leaders of any end-times ministry would be very, very sensitive to the Holy Spirit and totally controlled by Him.

Praying for the end times is something that Jesus asked us to do:

> 34 "Be on guard, that your hearts may not be weighted down with dissipation and drunkenness and the worries of life, and that day come on you suddenly like a trap;
> 35 for it will come upon all those who dwell on the face of all the earth.
> 36 "But keep on the alert at all times, praying in order that you may have strength to escape all these things that are about to take place, and to stand before the Son of Man.".
> --Luke 21

> 42 "Therefore be on the alert, for you do not know which day your Lord is coming.
> 43 "But be sure of this, that if the head of the house had known at what time of the night the thief was coming, he would have been on the alert and would not have allowed his house to be broken into.
> 44 "For this reason you be ready too; for the Son of Man is coming at an hour when you do not think He will.
> 45 "Who then is the faithful and sensible slave whom his master put in charge of his household to give them their food at the proper time?

46 "Blessed is that slave whom his master finds so doing when he comes.
47 "Truly I say to you, that he will put him in charge of all his possessions. . . ."

--Matthew 24

12. R = Rest

I like to end an hour of prayer with five minutes of quietness. This gives the Lord a chance to speak clearly to me and to guide me. Let your soul wait in silence:

1 My soul waits in silence for God only;
From Him is my salvation.

--Psalm 62

31 Yet those who wait for the Lord
Will gain new strength;
They will mount up with wings like eagles,
They will run and not get tired,
They will walk and not become weary.

--Isaiah 40

As we wait quietly on the Lord, He can show us new things and give us special guidance. He loves you and is far more eager to show you His will than you are to learn it.

JOIN THE DAWN PATROL

As the verse above said, they that wait upon the Lord shall renew their strength, and I believe we could say "they that spend an hour with the Lord" will renew their strength. We also know that times of refreshing come from the presence of the Lord:

19 "Repent therefore and return, that your sins may be wiped away, in order that times of refreshing may come from the presence of the Lord; . . ."

--Acts 3

If you need your strength renewed and you need to be refreshed, I would encourage you to regularly spend an hour with the Lord in prayer. If you do not take the time, then you are cheating yourself out of the refreshment and the strength that you could use.

I would now like to address some things on a very practical level concerning spending an hour in prayer with the Lord. I would suggest that you don't change anything in your life or your routine, except to simply set your alarm one hour earlier. Then spend that extra hour in the morning in prayer with the Lord. You may have to quietly slip out of bed and even go into the bathroom to spend your hour with the Lord. You may have to whisper your songs and praises rather than shout them, but they can be just as joyful and just as effective.

In God's army, I believe He is calling for volunteers to THE DAWN PATROL: those who, like Jesus, will get up a while before dawn and spend time in prayer. The spiritual battles and spiritual war that lie ahead are going to be won by people in their bedrooms, their bathrooms or their closets, on their knees in prayer. The time to learn how to use the weapon of prayer is now, before the major battle begins.

Another thing I would like to suggest is that you initially aim to have this hour on THE DAWN PATROL just five days a week. The weekend schedules for most people are so chaotic, it is very difficult to maintain a regular schedule. If the Lord can expand the hour into the weekend, great, but you might want to start with just the five days.

Another suggestion, so that you don't wind up feeling guilty, is that you do not make this commitment to THE DAWN PATROL on a permanent basis. Initially make it for a month or even just a week. Then renew the commitment at the end of that time frame. I would like to encourage you to make it for this current month. My feeling is that if you do this for a month, you will be eager to continue it.

The final suggestion is that you in no way make this a legalistic thing in your life. The twelve items of "PAC TALL POWER" are just a suggestion and a starting place. Soon the Holy Spirit may have you deviate from those. If you continue to use PAC TALL POWER, you will find that some of the segments require praying longer than five minutes and some of them less. On some days, there will be very little to pray for in some of the areas and you will be led to spend the time interceding for something.

There will also be times of travel and holidays when the Lord would not have you spend that hour on THE DAWN PATROL. (Of course, we certainly don't want the exceptions to become the rule.) If you are going to be a volunteer for THE DAWN PATROL, then about 90 to 95 percent of the working days should see you up an hour early and "about your Father's business."

There seems to be something significant about 5:00 a.m. I know many men and women of God whom He has led to start their prayer time at that hour. They follow it with a time of Bible reading.

This covenant is purely between you and God. However, sometimes it helps to share such a commitment with someone else. You can share with your spouse or a close friend or, if you like, you can drop a note to me to indicate your commitment to join THE DAWN PATROL for a month (you will find my address at the back of the book). It will take a little something extra on your part to become part of THE DAWN PATROL, but it took a little something extra for Gideon's 300 soldiers, too. Try it and remember, "You have not, because you ask not:"

> **2b You do not have because you do not ask.**
> **3 You ask and do not receive, because you ask with wrong motives, so that you may spend it on your pleasures.**
>
> --James 4

All across this nation and the world, God is calling His people to prayer and to a more intimate relationship with Himself. God may have been speaking to your heart about this need. "Today if you hear His voice, do not harden your hearts" (Hebrews 4:7b). If He is calling you to rise early and pray, heed His voice and be encouraged that there are others who hear the call who will be joining you on THE DAWN PATROL.

SUMMARY AND CONCLUSION

I realize this has been a rather long chapter, but prayer was so vitally important in the life of our Savior that I believe He wants it to be vitally important in our lives too. For this reason, I trust you will forgive me for the length of this chapter.

We have seen that Christ prayed fervently, alone with God and very likely at least an hour a day. If He felt the need for extended times of prayer with the Father, certainly we have the same need. His prayer life was evidently pleasing to God and God answered His prayers.

We saw that there are a number of requirements that Christ laid down for us to have our prayers answered. In addition to the things mentioned in the previous paragraph, we have seen that we need to:

1. Pray in Jesus' Name
2. Pray believing
3. Pray in His will
4. Pray without iniquity in our heart
5. Pray without unforgiveness in our heart
6. Pray with a right motive
7. Pray not as a friend of the world
8. Pray continuously--"keep on praying"
9. Pray with obedience to God

Then to help you spend an hour in prayer daily, we suggested that you might want to use the "PAC-TALL-POWER" outline, at least as a starting place and an encouragement. The Holy Spirit will take over as you begin this and will lead you to pray in different and exciting directions. You don't want to make this a legalistic pattern, for then it will be dead. But as you pray in the Spirit and allow Him to use this as a guide, He will make it alive and refreshing.

However you do it, I know that if you earnestly desire to become like Jesus and to have your prayer life become like His, God will help you change your prayer life into the kind of prayer life that will be pleasing to Him.

In the morning, after you pray, your heart is ready and open to receive from the Father through the Scriptures. What a joyful way to begin the day!

5
KNOWING THE SCRIPTURES LIKE HE DID

Evidently Jesus knew the Scriptures very well. If we are going to be like Him, then we too should know the Scriptures very well.

Christ's knowledge of the Scriptures is found portrayed repeatedly in the Gospels. One place is after He had been raised from the dead:

> 27 And beginning with Moses and with all the prophets, He explained to them the things concerning Himself in all the Scriptures . . .
>
> 32 And they said to one another, "Were not our hearts burning within us while He was speaking to us on the road, while He was explaining the Scriptures to us?" . . .
>
> 44 Now He said to them, "These are My words which I spoke to you while I was still with you, that all things which are written about Me in the Law of Moses and the Prophets and the Psalms must be fulfilled."
> 45 Then He opened their minds to understand the Scriptures, . . .
>
> --Luke 24

Here we see that Jesus not only knew the Scriptures but understood them and was able to explain them to others. He was also conscious of what the Scriptures said about Him and that those Scriptures must be fulfilled:

Matthew 22:29 - you should know the scriptures so you do not err.

54 "How then shall the Scriptures be fulfilled, that it must happen this way?"
55 At that time Jesus said to the multitudes, "Have you come out with swords and clubs to arrest Me as against a robber? Every day I used to sit in the temple teaching and you did not seize Me.
56 "But all this has taken place that the Scriptures of the prophets may be fulfilled." Then all the disciples left Him and fled.

--Matthew 26

Jesus actually went beyond just knowing the Scriptures. He taught that people made errors because they did not understand the Scriptures:

29 Jesus answered and said unto them, Ye do err, not knowing the Scriptures, nor the power of God.

--Matthew 22:29, KJV

24 And Jesus answering said unto them, Do ye not therefore err, because ye know not the Scriptures, neither the power of God?

--Mark 12, KJV

In both of these Scriptures Christ pointed out that they were in error, or they were mistaken, because they did not understand the Scriptures. Incidentally, understanding the Scriptures is what will keep us from error at the end of this age.

Jesus was even amazed that some of the people did not read the Scriptures and know what was in them. For example:

42 Jesus said to them, "Did you never read in the Scriptures,

'THE STONE WHICH THE BUILDERS
REJECTED,
THIS BECAME THE CHIEF CORNER
stone;
THIS CAME ABOUT FROM THE LORD,

AND IT IS MARVELOUS IN OUR EYES'?
--Matthew 21: 42

I can almost see Jesus shaking His head when He asked them, "Didn't you ever read this in the Scriptures?" It was amazing to Him that they had not read it. Thus we see Jesus placing tremendous importance on the Scriptures, on knowing what they say and on understanding them.

THE DISCIPLES KNEW AND USED THE SCRIPTURES

From the vast number of times that Paul quotes from the Scriptures, it is obvious that he knew them well and used them readily. We will give just a few verses that give an indication of this:

> 2 And according to Paul's custom, he went to them, and for three Sabbaths reasoned with them from the Scriptures, . . .
>
> --Acts 17

> 1 Paul, a bond-servant of Christ Jesus, called as an apostle, set apart for the gospel of God,
> 2 which He promised beforehand through His prophets in the holy Scriptures, . . .
>
> --Romans 1

> 3 For what does the Scripture say? "AND ABRAHAM BELIEVED GOD, AND IT WAS RECKONED TO HIM AS RIGHTEOUSNESS."
>
> --Romans 4

> 17 For the Scripture says to Pharaoh, "FOR THIS VERY PURPOSE I RAISED YOU UP, TO DEMONSTRATE MY POWER IN YOU, AND THAT MY NAME MIGHT BE PROCLAIMED THROUGHOUT THE WHOLE EARTH."
>
> --Romans 9

11 For the Scripture says, "WHOEVER BELIEVES IN HIM WILL NOT BE DISAPPOINTED."

--Romans 10

8 And the Scripture, foreseeing that God would justify the Gentiles by faith, preached the gospel beforehand to Abraham, saying, "ALL THE NATIONS SHALL BE BLESSED IN YOU."

--Galatians 3

30 But what does the Scripture say?
"CAST OUT THE BONDWOMAN AND HER SON,
FOR THE SON OF THE BONDWOMAN SHALL NOT BE AN HEIR WITH THE SON OF THE FREE WOMAN."

--Galatians 4

3 For I delivered to you as of first importance what I also received, that Christ died for our sins according to the Scriptures,
4 and that He was buried, and that He was raised on the third day according to the Scriptures, . . .

--1 Corinthians 15

In addition to Paul, many of the other outstanding men of God in the New Testament made significant use of the Scriptures, such as Apollos, an Alexandrian who became a Christian under the ministry of Priscilla and Aquilla:

27 And when he wanted to go across to Achaia, the brethren encouraged him and wrote to the disciples to welcome him; and when he had arrived, he helped greatly those who had believed through grace;
28 for he powerfully refuted the Jews in public, demonstrating by the Scriptures that Jesus was the Christ.

--Acts 18

We know that the Christians in Berea searched the Scriptures daily. They didn't do this "occasionally," but we are told they searched the Scriptures every single day. This was their safety net. They wanted to see if what was being taught matched with what the Scriptures said:

> **11 Now these were more noble-minded than those in Thessalonica, for they received the word with great eagerness, examining the Scriptures daily, to see whether these things were so.**
>
> --Acts 17

The Scriptures are still our safety net today, regardless of what teacher, preacher or minister you are listening to or reading. You need to go back to the Scriptures personally, like the Bereans did, and check out whether or not what is being taught matches with what the Scriptures say.

Knowing the Scriptures has so many wonderful benefits; no wonder Satan wants to keep us away from them:

> **7 The law of the LORD is perfect,**
> **restoring the soul;**
> **The testimony of the LORD is sure,**
> **making wise the simple.**
> **8 The precepts of the LORD are right,**
> **rejoicing the heart;**
> **The commandment of the LORD is pure,**
> **enlightening the eyes.**
> **9 The fear of the LORD is clean, enduring**
> **forever;**
> **The judgments of the LORD are true;**
> **they are righteous altogether.**
> **10 They are more desirable than gold, yes,**
> **than much fine gold;**
> **Sweeter also than honey and the drippings**
> **of the honeycomb.**
> **11 Moreover, by them Thy servant is**
> **warned;**
> **In keeping them there is great**

reward. . . .

14 Let the words of my mouth and the meditation of my heart
Be acceptable in Thy sight,
O LORD, my rock and my Redeemer.

--Psalm 19

Praise the Lord that we can meditate on the Scriptures. However, most Christians do not know what meditation on the Scriptures is all about.

MEDITATION ON THE SCRIPTURES

Meditation today is almost a bad word in some Christian circles. Many of the cult religions advocate and practice meditation. Christians have a right to be opposed to this. However, the people in the Bible were meditating on the Scriptures long before many of these cults ever existed. Joshua's first command to the children of Israel was along this line:

> **8 "This book of the law shall not depart from your mouth, but you shall meditate on it day and night, so that you may be careful to do according to all that is written in it; for then you will make your way prosperous, and then you will have success. . . ."**
>
> --Joshua 1

He commanded them to meditate on the Scriptures day and night and if they would do that, then they would be prosperous and have success. The same idea is repeated in the very first Psalm. In talking about a righteous man, David says:

2 But his delight is in the law of the LORD,
And in His law he meditates day and night.
3 And he will be like a tree firmly planted by streams of water,
Which yields it fruit in its season,

And its leaf does not wither;
And in whatever he does, he prospers.
--Psalm 1

According to this, a righteous man delights in the Scriptures, meditates on them day and night and whatever he does prospers.

In Psalm 119, all verses except two really talk about the Scriptures. In it we are encouraged to meditate on them:

15 I will meditate on Thy precepts,
And regard Thy ways. . . .

23 Even though princes sit and talk against me,
Thy servant meditates on Thy statutes. . . .

48 And I shall lift up my hands to Thy commandments,
Which I love;
And I will meditate on Thy statutes. . . .

78 May the arrogant be ashamed, for they subvert me with a lie;
But I shall meditate on Thy precepts. . . .

97 O how I love Thy law!
It is my meditation all the day. . . .

99 I have more insight than all my teachers,
For Thy testimonies are my meditation.
--Psalm 119

Since so much emphasis is placed on meditating on the Scriptures, we ought to examine what meditation really is.

To meditate on the Scriptures means to focus your thoughts on a passage from the Scriptures, to reflect on it, to ponder over it. This enables you to gain understanding and allows an opportunity for scriptural principles to soak into your life.

> 3 My mouth will speak wisdom;
> And the meditation of my heart will be understanding.
>
> --Psalm 49

I like to think of meditation on Scriptures as taking a passage--whether it be a single verse, a paragraph or even a complete chapter--and going over it again and again, "squeezing it" or "milking it" to get all of the "nourishment" out of it. While you do this, ask the Holy Spirit to reveal to you the hidden truths that are in those verses. In this way it becomes food for the soul.

MEMORIZATION OF THE SCRIPTURES

It is interesting to note that in the days of the New Testament, when they did not have Bibles to carry around, the only way they had of carrying the Scriptures with them was through memorization. The reason that almost every time Jesus taught He was able to quote from the Old Testament was that He had memorized large amounts of the Scriptures.

Evidently, He also trained His disciples this way, because on the day of Pentecost Peter quoted five verses from Joel 2, four verses from Psalm 16, and one verse from Psalm 110. After the Holy Spirit fell upon them, Peter obviously did not have an opportunity to run and get all these scrolls from the synagogue before he began speaking. He evidently had memorized these verses, plus much more of the Scriptures. We see this type of memorization repeated by Paul and others in the New Testament.

Even though we have Bibles today, the memorization of Scripture, which was so important to Jesus and the apostles, should be just as important to us. There may be a time of persecution or imprisonment ahead, when we will not have access to Bibles. No one can take from us the verses that we have memorized. The Holy Spirit will be able to use those Scriptures for our spiritual food, and to strengthen and encourage us.

It has been said that memorization is like walking across the lawn. If you walk across it once, the grass lies down and springs back up, but if you keep walking across it daily, in exactly the same place, pretty soon a path appears. When you repeat a memory verse to yourself once, it is like the first trip across the lawn. You must review it and review it and review it, before it becomes a "path" in your memory. A good rule of thumb is that you need to review a verse every day for at least two months before you have it for sure.

In memorizing you should say the reference both before you repeat the verse and after it. You should also be sure that you memorize letter perfect, because we do not want to take liberties with the word of God.

With a long passage, it is good to memorize a phrase at a time, gradually adding additional phrases. For example if you are memorizing John 16:33 out of the KING JAMES VERSION, you might start this way:

> --John 16:33
> These things have I spoken unto you,
> --John 16:33

> --John 16:33
> These things have I spoken unto you, that in me you might have peace.
> --John 16:33

> --John 16:33
> These things have I spoken unto you, that in me you might have peace. In the world you will have tribulation;
> --John 16:33

> --John 16:33
> These things have I spoken unto you, that in me you might have peace. In the world you will have tribulation; but be of good cheer; I have overcome the world.
> --John 16:33

You might want to pray about possibly setting a goal for yourself of memorizing so many verses per week or per month. If you read through the Scriptures and the Holy Spirit makes alive a verse or two, merely copying down and accumulating those verses can be a beginning help to memorizing them. Many of the Christian bookstores have little blank cards about the size of a calling card that you can use to type or write out your verses. Some people prefer to use plain 3x5 cards, since it gives them a bit more room and will still fit in a purse or pocket conveniently.

Whatever comes in the future, the verses that you have memorized will remain in your heart.

Meditation may involve memory. Unfortunately, one can memorize a verse without ever meditating on it. Hopefully, the two can go hand in hand; you meditate so much on a verse that you wind up memorizing it! That way it will not be something that you just memorized by rote, but it will be a vital, living part of your soul and your being.

When we have our mind filled with the Scriptures, even our subconscious mind is positively influenced. This will affect even our words because "out of the abundance of the heart, the mouth speaks" (Matthew 12:34, NKJV). It also will influence our will, and we will be more likely to trust and obey the Master.

STUDYING THE SCRIPTURES

Whereas meditation is primarily food for our own souls, study is usually designed to give understanding, so that we are able to teach others. Many pastors and teachers only study and never meditate. Many students in Bible schools and seminaries only study and never meditate. There is no promise of prosperity for your soul if you study, only if you meditate on the Scriptures. However, study is important:

> **15 Study to shew thyself approved unto God, a workman that needeth not to be ashamed, rightly dividing the word of truth.**
>
> --II Timothy 2, KJV

This tells us that we are to study the Scriptures so that we rightly (accurately) are able to handle the word of truth. We must take the Scriptures as a whole, of course, and not just take isolated bits here and there. Studying takes time, energy and effort, but the rewards are worth it. According to this verse in II Timothy, one of the rewards is to be approved of God.

READING THE SCRIPTURES

Many people study the Scriptures in Bible study groups and so forth. Very few Christians really meditate on the Scriptures which, of necessity, must be done alone. The third big area is reading the Scriptures; many Christians really do not do enough of this.

This reading can be group reading or individual reading. Imagine what a surprise your Sunday school class or home Bible study group would have if you came in sometime and said that you were not going to have a lesson this time, but you simply were going to read the Scriptures, and you then sat there and read chapter after chapter for an hour. Try it sometime. You will be amazed at what a blessing it will be. All the way through the Old and New Testaments, we have this public reading of the Scriptures, since they did not have individual Bibles but, at best, had only one copy. Here are a few of the places that talk about this:

> **7 Then he took the book of the covenant and read it in the hearing of the people; and they said, "All that the LORD has spoken we will do, and we will be obedient!"**
>
> **--Exodus 24**

> **11 when all Israel comes to appear before the LORD your God at the place which He will choose, you shall read this law in front of all Israel in their hearing.**
>
> **--Deuteronomy 31**

34 Then afterward he read all the words of the law, the blessing and the curse, according to all that is written in the book of the law.
35 There was not a word of all that Moses had commanded which Joshua did not read before all the assembly of Israel with the women and the little ones and the strangers who were living among them.

--Joshua 8

2 And the king went up to the house of the LORD and all the men of Judah and all the inhabitants of Jerusalem with him, and the priests and the prophets and all the people, both small and great; and he read in their hearing all the words of the book of the covenant, which was found in the house of the LORD.

--2 Kings 23

8 And they read from the book, from the law of God, translating to give the sense so that they understood the reading.

--Nehemiah 8

3 While they stood in their place, they read from the book of the law of the LORD their God for a fourth of the day; and for another fourth they confessed and worshiped the LORD their God.

--Nehemiah 9

16 And when this letter is read among you, have it also read in the church of the Laodiceans; and you, for your part read my letter that is coming from Laodicea.

--Colossians 4

27 I adjure you by the Lord to have this letter read to all the brethren.

--1 Thessalonians 5

Here we see that all the way through the Bible, the Scriptures were read out loud in a group. In those days it was the only way it could occur, since there were no printing presses and any copies had to be handmade. Thus, there were very few copies of the Scriptures for people to read. Even at that, Jesus was amazed when people had not read the Scriptures:

> 3 But He said to them, "Have you not read what David did, when he became hungry, he and his companions; . . .
>
> 5 "Or have you not read in the Law, that on the Sabbath the priests in the temple break the Sabbath, and are innocent? . . ."
>
> --Matthew 12

> 4 And He answered and said, "Have you not read, that He who created them from the beginning MADE THEM MALE AND FEMALE,
>
> --Matthew 19

> 16 and said to Him, "Do You hear what these are saying?" And Jesus said to them, "Yes; have you never read 'OUT OF THE MOUTH OF INFANTS AND NURSING BABES THOU HAS PREPARED PRAISE FOR THYSELF'?"
>
> --Matthew 21

> 42 Jesus said to them, "Did you never read in the Scriptures,
>
> 'THE STONE WHICH THE BUILDERS
> REJECTED,
> THIS BECAME THE CHIEF CORNER stone;
> THIS CAME ABOUT FROM THE LORD,
> AND IT IS MARVELOUS IN OUR
> EYES'? . . ."
>
> --Matthew 21

There are many treasures in the Bible, but it may have been a long time since your eyes have actually read them, if ever. When Jesus comes back and asks you if you have ever read "such and such," hopefully you will be able to answer with a very positive "yes."

To help you in this, I would like to present the OMEGA READING PLAN. It is a fantastic way for you to personally read through the Bible, plus some, in a year, and it takes only twenty minutes a day. The OMEGA READING PLAN is copyrighted (1983) by Omega Ministries and is used here by permission:

OMEGA READING PLAN

The OMEGA READING PLAN is an exciting new way to read the Bible! In it, you will go through the four Gospels, Psalms, and Proverbs twice during the year. The Gospels are spread out so you do not read all four of them in a row. If you ask a group of Christians which they emphasize the most in their reading and studying, the Gospels or the Epistles, 85 percent of them will say "the Epistles." In the OMEGA READING PLAN we change this balance and we read through the Gospels twice during the year. This helps us read more about what Jesus was like, so we can become like Him.

In addition, you read the rest of the New Testament and the Old Testament. However, you read the Old Testament not in the sequence in which the books are found in the Bible, but in the sequence in which the events occurred. For example, Daniel and Ezekiel wrote during the Babylonian captivity. Ezra came back from that captivity to rebuild the temple. Therefore, in the OMEGA READING PLAN, you read Daniel, then Ezekiel, then Ezra. You will find that the Old Testament will come alive as these books are placed in their proper chronological sequence. Try it--you'll love it!

Suggestion For Use Of The Omega Reading Plan

START AT ANY TIME: You can start the OMEGA READING PLAN at any time during the year. Simply start on today's date and use this plan faithfully for the next twelve months, and you will have completed the circle. Thus, anytime is fine to get additional copies to give to your friends, Sunday school class, members of the church, or anyone else you care about.

IF YOU MISS A DAY: Sometimes emergencies or other events will cause you to miss a day in your Bible reading. We would strongly suggest that you not go back the next day and try to read two days' worth. If you take this approach, you can get progressively further behind. Satan will use this to discourage you and it soon becomes easy to give up the entire thing. What we do suggest is that if you do miss a day, simply skip that day in your Bible reading. Then if, on some weekend, you have some extra time, you can go back and read any of the days that you missed.

WRITE DOWN KEY VERSES: In the blank space to the right of the Old Testament reading, you can write down a key verse from that day's reading that God made particularly alive to your heart. If it is a verse(s) that you think God wants you to meditate on or to memorize, then you could put some special mark beside that verse.

All Scripture Is Profitable

The Bible says that all Scripture is inspired by God and is profitable:

> **16 All scripture is given by inspiration of God, and is profitable for doctrine, for reproof, for correction, for instruction in righteousness: . . .**
>
> **--II Timothy 3, KJV**

This verse says that all Scripture is profitable for one of four things. To help you understand what these four things really mean, let's look at them in plain English. Doctrine means something that you are to believe. Reproof means something that you are to stop doing. Correction means something that you are to do better. Instruction in righteousness means something that you are to start doing. Thus, all Scripture that you will read in the OMEGA READING PLAN is profitable for one of these four things:

1. Something to believe
2. Something to stop doing
3. Something to do better
4. Something to start doing

After you have read your daily reading, we would encourage you to pause and ask God what there is in the passages that you read for that day that He wants you to believe, that He wants you to stop doing, that He wants you to start doing, and that He wants you to do better. As you pray that prayer, the Scriptures will work their way into your life and into your behavior. It is also a good idea to pray at the beginning, before doing your daily reading, to ask God to have the Holy Spirit teach you and show you the meanings of the Scriptures. By praying at the beginning and the end, your Bible reading will be vital, alive and will change your life.

Make A Commitment

Many of us need to actually take an overt action and make a commitment to God; this tends to help us stick to our guns. For your convenience, below is a commitment that you can make to God in connection with the OMEGA READING PLAN.

> *Father God, I believe that you want me to read the Bible through during the next twelve months. I am committing to do that and trusting your Holy Spirit to teach me*

new and exciting things as I read the Scriptures. Help me to set aside time every day to spend with you and to read the Holy Scriptures. In Jesus' name, I make this commitment.

Signed: Ann Eveler *Date:* april 6, 1987

Additional Copies Of Omega Reading Plan

Omega Ministries has the OMEGA READING PLAN printed up in leaflet form, for ease in keeping it inside your Bible. If two or more members of your family wish to use the OMEGA READING PLAN, you may wish to get additional copies or you may wish to get enough copies for your Sunday school class or even your entire church.

If you would like copies, they are $.50 for the first one and $.25 for any additional ones. For large orders of 100 copies or more, they are $.20 apiece. Please send your check and request to:

Omega Ministries
P.O. Box 1788
Medford, OR 97501

JANUARY 19____

	1	Ps 1	Matt 1	Gen 1-2	
	2	Ps 2	Matt 2	Gen 3-4	
	3	Ps 3	Matt 3	Gen 5-6	
	4	Ps 4	Matt 4	Gen 7-8	
	5	Ps 5	Matt 5	Gen 9-10	
	6	Ps 6	Matt 6	Gen 11-12	
	7	Ps 7	Matt 7	Gen 13-14	
	8	Ps 8	Matt 8	Gen 15-16	
	9	Ps 9	Matt 9	Gen 17-18	
	10	Ps 10	Matt 10	Gen 19-20	
	11	Ps 11	Matt 11	Gen 21-22	
	12	Ps 12	Matt 12	Gen 23-24	
	13	Ps 13	Matt 13	Gen 25-26	
	14	Ps 14	Matt 14	Gen 27-28	
	15	Ps 15	Matt 15	Gen 29-30	
	16	Ps 16	Matt 16	Gen 31-32	
	17	Ps 17	Matt 17	Gen 33-34	
	18	Ps 18	Matt 18	Gen 35-36	
	19	Ps 19	Matt 19	Gen 37-38	
	20	Ps 20	Matt 20	Gen 39-40	
	21	Ps 21	Matt 21	Gen 41-42	
	22	Ps 22	Matt 22	Gen 43-44	
	23	Ps 23	Matt 23	Gen 45-46	
	24	Ps 24	Matt 24	Gen 47-48	
	25	Ps 25	Matt 25	Gen 49-50	
	26	Ps 26	Matt 26	Ex 1-2	
	27	Ps 27	Matt 27	Ex 3-4	
	28	Ps 28	Matt 28	Ex 5-6	
	29	Ps 29	Acts 1	Ex 7-8	
	30	Ps 30	Acts 2	Ex 9-10	
	31	Ps 31	Acts 3	Ex 11-12	

FEBRUARY 19____

__	1	Ps 32	Acts 4	Ex 13-14	________
__	2	Ps 33	Acts 5	Ex 15-16	________
__	3	Ps 34	Acts 6	Ex 17-18	________
__	4	Ps 35	Acts 7	Ex 19-20	________
__	5	Ps 36	Acts 8	Ex 21-22	________
__	6	Ps 37	Acts 9	Ex 23-24	________
__	7	Ps 38	Acts 10	Ex 25-26	________
__	8	Ps 39	Acts 11	Ex 27-28	________
__	9	Ps 40	Acts 12	Ex 29-30	________
__	10	Ps 41	Acts 13	Ex 31-32	________
__	11	Ps 42	Acts 14	Ex 33-34	________
__	12	Ps 43	Acts 15	Ex 35-36	________
__	13	Ps 44	Acts 16	Ex 37-38	________
__	14	Ps 45	Acts 17	Ex 39-40	________
__	15	Ps 46	Acts 18	Lev 1-3	________
__	16	Ps 47	Acts 19	Lev 4-5	________
__	17	Ps 48	Acts 20	Lev 6-7	________
__	18	Ps 49	Acts 21	Lev 8-9	________
__	19	Ps 50	Acts 22	Lev 10-11	________
__	20	Ps 51	Acts 23	Lev 12-13	________
__	21	Ps 52	Acts 24	Lev 14-15	________
__	22	Ps 53	Acts 25	Lev 16-17	________
__	23	Ps 54	Acts 26	Lev 18-19	________
__	24	Ps 55	Acts 27	Lev 20-21	________
__	25	Ps 56	Acts 28	Lev 22-23	________
__	26	Ps 57	Mark 1	Lev 24-25	________
__	27	Ps 58	Mark 2	Lev 26-27	________
__	28	Ps 59	Mark 3	Num 1-2	________

MARCH 19____

__	1	Ps 60	Mark 4	Num 3-4	________
__	2	Ps 61	Mark 5	Num 5-6	________
__	3	Ps 62	Mark 6	Num 7-8	________
__	4	Ps 63	Mark 7	Num 9-10	________
__	5	Ps 64	Mark 8	Num 11-12	________
__	6	Ps 65	Mark 9	Num 13-14	________
__	7	Ps 66	Mark 10	Num 15-16	________
__	8	Ps 67	Mark 11	Num 17-18	________
__	9	Ps 68	Mark 12	Num 19-20	________
__	10	Ps 69	Mark 13	Num 21-22	________
__	11	Ps 70	Mark 14	Num 23-24	________
__	12	Ps 71	Mark 15	Num 25-26	________
__	13	Ps 72	Mark 16	Num 27-28	________
__	14	Ps 73	Rom 1	Num 29-30	________
__	15	Ps 74	Rom 2	Num 31-32	________
__	16	Ps 75	Rom 3	Num 33-34	________
__	17	Ps 76	Rom 4	Num 35-36	________
__	18	Ps 77	Rom 5	Deut 1-2	________
__	19	Ps 78	Rom 6	Deut 3-4	________
__	20	Ps 79	Rom 7	Deut 5-6	________
__	21	Ps 80	Rom 8	Deut 7-8	________
__	22	Ps 81	Rom 9	Deut 9-10	________
__	23	Ps 82	Rom 10	Deut 11-12	________
__	24	Ps 83	Rom 11	Deut 13-14	________
__	25	Ps 84	Rom 12	Deut 15-16	________
__	26	Ps 85	Rom 13	Deut 17-18	________
__	27	Ps 86	Rom 14	Deut 19-20	________
__	28	Ps 87	Rom 15	Deut 21-22	________
__	29	Ps 88	Rom 16	Deut 23-24	________
__	30	Ps 89	Luke 1	Deut 25	________
__	31	Ps 90	Luke 2	Deut 26-27	________

6
YOU WILL BE HOLY

I am assuming that you still yearn to become like Jesus Christ in every way. We are now going to look at some of the characteristics of Jesus that will also become characteristics of us as we press on toward the goal of becoming like Jesus Christ.

One of the things the Scriptures say on many occasions is that Jesus was holy. Let's look at some verses from several of the Gospels to verify this:

> 35 And the angel answered and said to her, "The Holy Spirit will come upon you, and the power of the Most High will overshadow you; and for that reason the holy offspring shall be called the Son of God. . . ."
>
> --Luke 1

> 69 "And we have believed and have come to know that You are the Holy One of God."
>
> --John 6

> 24 saying, "What do we have to do with You, Jesus of Nazareth? Have You come to destroy us? I know who You are--the Holy One of God!"
>
> --Mark 1

If Jesus was holy and we desire to be like Him and to be holy, we need to see what the Bible's definition of holy really is. One of the troubles with some of the concepts that we will cover in this chapter, and in the next few chapters, is that our definitions today have wandered very far afield from the true Bible definitions.

If someone were to tell you that a certain individual or a certain object was holy, what would immediately come to your mind? Perhaps you would envisage some rare object from an ancient church or perhaps even a relic of Christ's day and age. Some people may even have the image or idea of holy objects as something to be worshiped. Perhaps in thinking of a holy individual you would think of a monk in a monastery who would spend all day praying. From where did you get these ideas? Perhaps you got them from movies, from fiction stories or from what others have said. Now let's turn and find out what the true Bible definition of "holy" is.

HOLINESS IS SANCTIFICATION

As we begin to look at what holiness is, I would like to ask you to accept temporarily the definition that I will give you, and then we will look at the biblical evidence that backs it up. As far as I am concerned, being "holy" and being "sanctified" are identical in the Bible. This is borne out by many of the current translations of the Bible, but a layman's definition of holiness and sanctification is this:

> **To be holy, or sanctified, means to be withdrawn from the unclean and set apart for God's exclusive use.**

As an example of this, the articles of furniture, in the tabernacle, such as the lampstand, were holy. They were set apart for God's exclusive use and were not used for any unclean purpose. That does not mean that they were always doing something "religious." The lampstand may have been taken outside to be cleaned, or it may have been packed away for moving, but it was always ready and available when God wanted to use it to light the holy place. It was never used for an unclean purpose, such as providing light for an orgy or a dinner where everyone overate. (To overeat means to eat more than the Lord wants you to eat, thus stepping over the boundary into gluttony, which is just as sinful as taking part in an orgy. We overeat, not because we are hungry, but because it tastes good, which is lust of the flesh.) It was set apart for God's exclusive use and for no unclean use.

The nation of Israel in the Old Testament is called a "holy nation," and, as such, they were to separate themselves from unclean things:

> 44 'For I am the LORD your God. Consecrate yourselves therefore, and be holy; for I am holy. And you shall not make yourselves unclean with any of the swarming things that swarm on the earth.
>
> 45 'For I am the LORD, who brought you up from the land of Egypt, to be your God; thus you shall be holy for I am holy.'"
>
> 46 This is the law regarding the animal, and the bird, and every living thing that moves in the waters, and everything that swarms on the earth,
>
> 47 to make a distinction between the unclean and the clean, and between the edible creature and the creature which is not to be eaten.
>
> --Leviticus 11

We find a similar definition of holiness and sanctification later in Leviticus:

> 24 'Hence I have said to you, "You are to possess their land, and I Myself will give it to you to possess it, a land flowing with milk and honey." I am the LORD your God, who has separated you from the peoples.
>
> 25 'You are therefore to make a distinction between the clean animal and the unclean, and between the unclean bird and the clean; and you shall not make yourselves detestable by animal or by bird or by anything that creeps on the ground, which I have separated for you as unclean.
>
> 26 'Thus you are to be holy to Me, for I the LORD am holy; and I have set you apart from the

peoples to be Mine. . . .'

--Leviticus 20

In addition to the nation of Israel being holy, we find many other things in the Old Testament that are holy, such as garments, places, offerings, and the Sabbath:

29 "And the holy garments of Aaron shall be for his sons after him, that in them they may be anointed and ordained.
30 "For seven days the one of his sons who is priest in his stead shall put them on when he enters the tent of meeting to minister in the holy place.
31 "And you shall take the ram of ordination and boil its flesh in a holy place.
32 "And Aaron and his sons shall eat the flesh of the ram, and the bread that is in the basket, at the doorway of the tent of meeting. . . ."

--Exodus 29

23 'And when you enter the land and plant all kinds of trees for food, then you shall count their fruit as forbidden. Three years it shall be forbidden to you; it shall not be eaten.
24 'But in the fourth year all its fruit shall be holy, an offering of praise to the LORD. . . .'

--Leviticus 19

8 Then the LORD spoke to Aaron, "Now behold, I myself have given you charge of My offerings, even all the holy gifts of the sons of Israel, I have given them to you as portion, and to your sons as a perpetual allotment.
9 "This shall be yours from the most holy gifts, reserved from the fire; every offering of theirs, even every grain offering and every sin offering and every guilt offering, which they shall render to Me, shall be most holy for you and for your sons.

--Numbers 18

In addition to these things, we see that water can be holy, a meeting (convocation) can be holy, oil can be holy and so can a temple or a mountain be holy:

> 17 and the priest shall take holy water in an earthenware vessel; and he shall take some of the dust that is on the floor of the tabernacle and put it into the water.
>
> --Numbers 5

> 26 'Also on the day of the first fruits, when you present a new grain offering to the LORD in your Feast of Weeks, you shall have a holy convocation; you shall do no laborious work. . . .'
>
> --Numbers 28

> 25 'And the congregation shall deliver the manslayer from the hand of the blood avenger, and the congregation shall restore him to his city of refuge to which he fled; and he shall live in it until the death of the high priest who was anointed with the holy oil. . . .'
>
> --Numbers 35

> 4 I was crying to the LORD with my voice,
> And He answered me from His holy mountain.
>
> --Psalm 3

> 4 The LORD is in His holy temple; the LORD'S throne is in heaven;
> His eyes behold, His eyelids test the sons of men.
>
> --Psalm 11

Is your definition of what is holy beginning to expand? If you or your church has a bottle of oil that you use to anoint people, it is indeed holy oil. If you have a building that is set aside for the meeting place of God's people, it is a holy building. When you give a tithe or an offering, it is a holy gift to the Lord.

It is sanctified, and set apart for His exclusive use, never again to be used for unclean purposes.

That is not to say that once an object, a nation or an individual has been dedicated--or set apart for God's exclusive use--rebellion and sin cannot come in and cause that individual or nation to act unholy again. The nation of Israel is a classic example of this. We have seen that they were called a holy nation; however, they went whoring after unclean things and, thus, became unholy and, as a result, experienced the wrath of God. God does not like it at all if something causes one of His holy objects to be put to unholy use. For example, if some unqualified person even touched the ark of the covenant, which had been sanctified as holy unto God, God killed him instantly (1 Chronicles 13:9, 10).

I wonder if God looks at things the same way today? I wonder what He would think about a church who would use their holy building for unholy activities? I wonder what He would think about pastors and Christian leaders who use the exposure and glamour of their holy position to seduce women? I believe He looks at those things in the same way that He always has, as abominations, displeasing in His sight. One of the ways He shows His displeasure today is to remove His anointing, blessing and the power of the Holy Spirit from such an individual or group.

I believe it would be a good idea if we started calling our anointing oil "holy oil" and some of our church meeting places "holy buildings." This would cause us to be careful not to use those things in any way that might be considered unclean.

Don't get me wrong. The church is the body of believers; it is never a building. Some churches meet in rented buildings, such as a school. Other churches own a building set aside exclusively for their meetings. If they dedicate and anoint that building to God, then that church meets in a "holy building" or a "holy sanctuary."

I believe the Lord wants me to digress a bit on this subject. When I was the lay pastor of Catalina Bible Church, some of the members wanted to buy a building for the church to meet in. I felt strongly that we should only rent. The church during the first two centuries met in houses and did not own their own buildings. After Constantine made Christianity the official religion of the Roman empire, in the third century, Christianity began to go downhill. One of the two principal reasons for this decline was that the "church" began to own property. Eventually you had a huge church or cathedral in the midst of a poverty-striken village. To me, this was not the picture or essence of what Christ taught.

I have seen churches spiritually ruined by a building program. The new building became a source of pride. The believers invited their friends, not to come to see Jesus, but to come to see the beautiful new building! So you see, I am not strongly in favor of churches owning their own buildings. However, if God does lead a body of believers (a church) to own a building, I do feel that it should be a "holy building," anointed with oil and dedicated to God's exclusive use.

PERSONAL HOLINESS

As we turn from buildings, objects and nations to individuals, including you and me, we need to recognize that there were holy individuals in the first century:

> 1 Therefore, holy brethren, partakers of a heavenly calling, consider Jesus, the Apostle and High Priest of our confession.
>
> --Hebrews 3

Next, I would like to ask you a question. Would you like to see God? Whether now or in eternity, would you like to see God? I'm sure your answer, like mine, is a definite YES. Did you realize that there is something that could cause you not to see God:

> 14 Follow peace with all men, and holiness, without which no man shall see the Lord: . . .
>
> --Hebrews 12, KJV

> **14 Pursue peace with all men, and the sanctification without which no one will see the Lord.**
> **--Hebrews 12, NAS**

Just as an aside, you might note that the KING JAMES VERSION uses the word "holiness" and the NEW AMERICAN STANDARD uses "sanctification." This is just another indication of the equivalency of these two English words. They both mean "set apart for God's exclusive use."

Turning back to the main thought of Hebrews 12:14, did you realize that without holiness you and I cannot see God? Let that soak in for a minute. This is not my idea, but according to the Scriptures, without being holy, we cannot see God. This puts an incredible importance on becoming holy, like Jesus was holy.

The following verses from 1 Peter 1 explicitly command us to be holy, like the "Holy One" who called us:

> **14 As obedient children, do not be conformed to the former lusts which were yours in your ignorance,**
> **15 but like the Holy One who called you, be holy yourselves also in all your behavior;**
> **16 because it is written, "YOU SHALL BE HOLY, FOR I AM HOLY."**

I believe there is a fresh stirring of the Holy Spirit within the body of Christ for Christians to become holy. However, this new holiness movement is not going to be anything like the holiness movement that occurred at the beginning of the century. In those days, people were expected to dress a certain way, behave a certain way, not wear makeup, and many such things. It was very legalistic and the rules were established by men; thus, they were dead laws and put people in bondage.

I believe the new call of the Holy Spirit to personal holiness is going to have life and set men free. If you and I are both holy, set apart for God's exclusive use, He may direct you in one way and me in another. The uses to which God chose to put the holy altar for blood sacrifices and the holy table of showbread were different. They were each to be used in the way in which God wanted them to be used. Holiness is not the same for all.

God may lead me to do one thing and it would be holy, but if you were to do the same thing, it would not be holy, and vice versa. Much of what we consider sin does not come from the Bible but from our own environment.

A classic example of this is the following. Shortly after World War II, Intervarsity Christian Fellowship had a world conference in France. In those days Christian women in Europe, no matter how liberal, didn't wear lipstick. When the American girls arrived wearing lipstick, all the European girls rushed up to Stacy Woods, then president of Intervarsity Christian Fellowship, and asked him if these American girls were Christians, because they were wearing lipstick. He explained to them that in America that was okay.

Then the first evening the banquet began, and of course they served wine with the meal, because in Europe everyone drank wine with meals, even Christians, no matter how conservative. Immediately after the banquet, all of the American girls rushed up to Stacy Woods and asked him if these Europeans were Christians, because they were drinking wine.

Each of these groups were being obedient to God and were pleasing Him. The Europeans were abstaining from lipstick because they felt God wanted them to do so, and the American girls were abstaining from wine because they felt God wanted them to abstain. The problem comes when we try to force on other people that which God has led us to do. What we are really doing is trying to play God in other peoples' lives, and that is one of the most horrible forms of pride and blasphemy. Paul dealt with this in depth when he wrote to the Romans:

> **1 Now accept the one who is weak in faith, but not for the purpose of passing judgment on his opinions.**

2 One man has faith that he may eat all things, but he who is weak eats vegetables only.
3 Let not him who eats regard with contempt him who does not eat, and let not him who does not eat judge him who eats, for God has accepted him.
4 Who are you to judge the servant of another? To his own master he stands or falls; and stand he will, for the Lord is able to make him stand.

--Romans 14

This passage of Scripture deals with eating meat. Some meat was sacrificed in pagan temples and was sold on the market place along with meat that had not been sacrificed. There were some Christians (those weak in the faith or new Christians) who abstained from eating all meat, in case they might accidentally get some that had been sacrificed to an idol. Some stronger Christians felt that it was fine to eat any meat. If both groups had let it rest there everything would have been fine.

However, those who were not eating meat judged those who were eating meat, thinking they were out of the will of God. Those who ate meat tended to regard with contempt those who had the "ridiculous idea" that they should not eat any meat. They each were trying to impose on each other how God was leading them.

I have seen the same thing happen over and over again in the body of Christ today. To one Christian God has given the liberty to drink wine. Sometimes that individual is almost evangelistic in his attempts to loosen up other Christians who do not drink wine to try to get them to realize that it is not a sin. On the other hand, I have known many Christians who were staunchly against drinking wine, who "looked down their spiritual noses" at those Christians who did drink wine, considering them as loose, immoral, or carnal Christians and treating them with contempt. How sad for both groups! As Paul says in verse 4 of the preceding passage, we should not regard one another with contempt, because each of us has to answer to our

Master, Jesus Christ. Let us read on about what Paul had to say to the Romans:

> 5 One man regards one day above another, another regards every day alike. Let each man be fully convinced in his own mind.
>
> 6 He who observes the day, observes it for the Lord, and he who eats, does so for the Lord, for he gives thanks to God; and he who eats not, for the Lord he does not eat, and gives thanks to God.
>
> 7 For not one of us lives for himself, and not one dies for himself;
>
> 8 for if we live, we live for the Lord, or if we die, we die for the Lord; therefore whether we live or die, we are the Lord's.
>
> 9 For to this end Christ died and lived again, that He might be Lord both of the dead and of the living.
>
> 10 But you, why do you judge your brother? Or you again, why do you regard your brother with contempt? For we shall all stand before the judgment seat of God.
>
> --Romans 14

In his letter to the Romans, Paul next deals with a similar problem to that of eating meat. Some Christians were celebrating special days (such as Christmas) and other Christians counted all days alike. If each had been doing this as unto the Lord and had left alone others whom God had led differently, that would have been fine. However, contention comes when we try to force the way that God is leading us onto other Christians. We must not attempt to "play God" in the lives of others; we must allow the Holy Spirit to lead them, even if it is in ways that are contradictory to how God is leading us and, in our eyes, might even seem to be sin.

We each have the liberty in Christ to not be bound by someone else's rules and regulations, but to follow whatever the Holy Spirit leads us to do. However, we should never let that liberty lead us into sin:

> **13 For you were called to freedom, brethren; only do not turn your freedom into an opportunity for the flesh, but through love serve one another.**
> **--Galatians 5**

Paul tells us that all things are lawful (1 Corinthians 10:23) and that nothing is unclean in itself, which is certainly true. However, we must not let the freedom we have, to follow whatever the Holy Spirit leads us to do, lead us into sin. If we are holy--set apart for God's exclusive use and removed from unclean things--then the Holy Spirit can lead us as He wills, and it will never result in sin.

Thus, we conclude that being holy has nothing to do with how we dress, what we eat or what days we observe. Our personal holiness means that we are dedicated and set apart to be used by God, whenever and however He chooses. Some evening, I may think that I would like to go to church, but there is a special on television that I want to see. If seeing that special is my sole reason for staying home, it is likely that doing so would be an unholy act. On the other hand, God could lead someone else to stay home and watch that same special, while He might lead me to go to the church function. We both must do what God tells us to do.

A HOLY BODY

In considering our own personal holiness, we need to realize that God expects our bodies to be holy. Paul points this out so beautifully in Romans:

> **1 I urge you therefore, brethren, by the mercies of God, to present your bodies a living and holy sacrifice, acceptable to God, which is your spiritual service of worship.**
> **--Romans 12**

This verse says that we are to present our bodies to be a holy sacrifice. We will talk more later in this chapter about presenting our bodies, but the main thing we want to do here is to realize that God expects our bodies to be holy. He expects them to be separated from unclean things and set apart for His exclusive use.

One problem we Christians have is that we don't like to call sin sin and we don't like to call unholiness unholy. If we are plagued by the sin of gluttony and are overweight, our bodies are not glorifying God and our bodies could not be classified as holy. Yet overweight Christians never say that they have a sin problem in overeating or that they have a problem with gluttony. Instead of calling it sin, they call it a "tendency." They say that they have a tendency to overeat.

My wife feeds me well with nutritious food in the right amounts at meal times. My overweight problem was because of my 3:00 snack time. I felt that I had worked hard during the day and deserved a nice snack in the afternoon. It was when I stopped calling it my "snack break" and started calling it my "sin break" that the problem began to be solved.

This certainly is true in other areas. Some Christians say they have a tendency to drink too much, or that they have a tendency to spend too much time watching television, or that they have a tendency to spend too much time on their hobbies. Others might have a tendency to seek affection and sex from someone other than their spouse. Others might have a tendency to tell little white lies or a tendency to lose their temper. As long as we think of these things as "tendencies," we will not confess them as sin, repent, be cleansed of them and dedicate our bodies as holy unto God.

The solution, of course, is to see these things as God sees them, as unholy and sinful acts, and to repent of them, turn from them and dedicate our bodies once and for all as holy unto God.

A HOLY DAY EACH WEEK

God commanded the Old Testament saints to have a holy day each week--a day during which they were to totally separate themselves from anything unclean and devote the day exclusively to Him. This command is in numerous places throughout the Old Testament. One of these is:

> **2 "For six days work may be done, but on the seventh day you shall have a holy day, a sabbath of complete rest to the LORD; whoever does any work on it shall be put to death.**
>
> **3 "You shall not kindle a fire in any of your dwellings on the sabbath day."**
>
> **--Exodus 35**

Even though we are not under the Old Testament law, God set up a sabbath day because it was on His heart, it would please Him, and it would be beneficial for the people. We do not want to be legalistic about it, but I believe this is still on God's heart.

It does not matter if you want to consider the sabbath as Saturday, which it is, or make Sunday your holy day. Either way you need to have one day each week, according to the Scriptures, that you make a holy day. Many of us need to ask ourselves when was the last time we really had a holy day. When was the last time we really had an entire day separated totally from anything unclean and set aside exclusively for the Lord's use. Many Christians may have never had such a day, or at best it was a long, long time ago.

You and I need to ask God if we should have a holy day each week and, if He says "yes" (and I suspect He will), then we need to totally reserve one day each week for God and separate ourselves from anything that is unclean. Perhaps we should watch no television at all on that day. If we follow the biblical pattern, we will certainly do no work, including putting in the garden and so forth. In the Old Testament, the women did all of the cooking the day before the sabbath (they could not light a fire on the sabbath), so on the sabbath there was not even the work of cooking to be done. I am not trying to lay down any rules or put us under the Old Testament law. However, I do think it is wisdom for us to go to God and find out what His desire is concerning us having a holy day each week.

HOW DO WE BECOME SANCTIFIED AND HOLY?

Again, as we are seeking to become like Jesus Christ, the answer to **how** we become sanctified might well lie in the way Jesus Himself was sanctified or made holy. Let's take a look at how He became sanctified:

> **19 "And for their sakes I sanctify Myself, that they themselves also may be sanctified in truth. . . "**
>
> **--John 17**

This verse tells us that Jesus sanctified Himself. Someone else didn't do it. God didn't do it. Jesus **Himself** sanctified Himself. The Bible also tells us that we are to do a similar thing:

> **21 Therefore, if a man cleanses himself from these things, he will be a vessel for honor, sanctified, useful to the Master, prepared for every good work.**
>
> **22 Now flee from youthful lusts, and pursue righteousness, faith, love and peace, with those who call on the Lord from a pure heart.**
>
> **23 But refuse foolish and ignorant speculations, knowing that they produce quarrels.**
>
> **24 And the Lord's bond-servant must not be quarrelsome, but be kind to all, able to teach, patient when wronged,**
>
> **25 with gentleness correcting those who are in opposition, if perhaps God may grant them repentance leading to the knowledge of the truth,**
>
> **26 and they may come to their senses and escape from the snare of the devil, having been held captive by him to do his will.**
>
> **--2 Timothy 2**

This passage says that we are to cleanse ourselves (from unclean things) and sanctify ourselves. Then verses 22-26 give us some of the things that will follow. We will flee from lust; we will pursue righteousness, faith, love and peace; we will refuse foolish speculations and quarrels; and we will be kind, patient, gentle and able to teach. These things will be a result of our becoming holy (sanctified); they are not a prerequisite to sanctifying ourselves. This idea of separating ourselves and "touching not the unclean things" is also found in Paul's second letter to the church of Corinth.

> **16 Or what agreement has the temple of God with idols? For we are the temple of the living God; just as God said,**
> **"I WILL DWELL IN THEM AND WALK AMONG THEM;**
> **AND I WILL BE THEIR GOD, AND THEY SHALL BE MY PEOPLE.**
> **17 "Therefore, COME OUT FROM THEIR MIDST AND BE SEPARATE," says the Lord.**
> **"AND DO NOT TOUCH WHAT IS UNCLEAN;**
> **And I will welcome you.**
> **18 "And I will be a father to you,**
> **And you shall be sons and daughters to Me,"**
> **Says the Lord Almighty.**
> --2 Corinthians 6

I believe the Lord would have us pause here for a moment and discuss the meaning of "unclean." While in the Old Testament many things were considered unclean, such as certain foods, we know from Acts 10 that all foods have been cleansed by God for our use. We also know, however, that just because all things are lawful to us, that does not mean that we are to indulge in all things without discrimination. Paul gives us counsel on this in 1 Corinthians:

> **23 All things are lawful, but not all things are profitable. All things are lawful, but not all things edify.**

24 Let no one seek his own good, but that of his neighbor. . . .

31 Whether, then, you eat or drink or whatever you do, do all to the glory of God.

--1 Corinthians 10

Paul gives us the key to the discernment we must exercise. The key is given in verse 31, wherein we are called to "do all to the glory of God."

Under the Law of Moses, God declared great classes of things, actions as well as foods, to be unclean. But in the freedom of Christ Jesus, all things are lawful. What then is "unclean"? Unclean is anything which is not profitable to the Gospel, does not edify the body of Christ, or, in short, anything which does not glorify God.

Do you see how God, in His infinite wisdom and mercy, has helped us over the biggest stumbling block of them all, our reasoning, rational minds? We are admonished not to "lean to our own understanding" (Proverbs 3:5,6), yet the law left us no alternative. Now, through the freedom granted us by the cross, we can instead depend on the Lord to guide us at every turn. With His Spirit within us, we can discern what glorifies Him in our lives from moment to moment and, thus, know for certain what is "clean" and what is not, for us. Praise God!

Now we come to the act of sanctification itself. (There are other aspects of sanctification that appear to be a process, but we must leave those for another book.) In the Old Testament, when an object was to be sanctified (to become holy), they anointed it with holy oil as an act of dedication of that object to God for His exclusive use. This was also true of individuals. For example, when they anointed Aaron for the high priesthood, they poured oil on his head and it ran down over his beard and the hem of his garment:

4 "Then you shall bring Aaron and his sons to the doorway of the tent of meeting, and wash them with water. . . .

7 "Then you shall take the anointing oil, and pour it on his head and anoint him. . . ."

--Exodus 29

23 "Take also for yourself the finest of spices: of flowing myrrh five hundred shekels, and of fragrant cinnamon half as much, two hundred and fifty, and of fragrant cane two hundred and fifty,
24 and of cassia five hundred, according to the shekel of the sanctuary, and of olive oil a hin.
25 "And you shall make of these a holy anointing oil, a perfume mixture, the work of a perfumer; it shall be a holy anointing oil.
26 "And with it you shall anoint the tent of meeting and the ark of the testimony,
27 and the table and all its utensils, and the lampstand and its utensils, and the altar of incense,
28 and the altar of burnt offering and all its utensils, and the laver and its stand.
29 "You shall also consecrate them, that they may be most holy; whatever touches them shall be holy.
30 "And you shall speak to the sons of Israel, saying, 'This shall be a holy anointing oil to Me throughout your generations. . . .'"

--Exodus 30

Let's see if we can get a picture of this. There was a mixture of perfume-type spices and olive oil, which became a holy anointing oil. The tent of the tabernacle, the objects in the tabernacle, and Aaron and his sons were anointed with this holy oil to consecrate them or to make them holy.

After Aaron was anointed with oil, and made holy, it was very important for him to obey God:

7 "You shall not even go out from the doorway of the tent of meeting, lest you die; for the LORD'S anointing oil is upon you." So they did

according to the word of Moses.
8 The LORD then spoke to Aaron, saying,
9 "Do not drink wine or strong drink, neither you nor your sons with you, when you come into the tent of meeting, so that you may not die--it is a perpetual statute throughout your generations--
10 and so as to make a distinction between the holy and the profane, and between the unclean and the clean,
11 and so as to teach the sons of Israel all the statutes which the LORD has spoken to them through Moses."

--Leviticus 10

The Bible tells us that we are to sanctify ourselves. In order to make this act of sanctifying yourself more real to you, it may even be that the Lord would like you to get alone with Him and actually anoint yourself with holy oil. As you do this, you could tell the Lord that with this act you are consecrating yourself to Him, or setting yourself apart to be holy unto Him. If you wanted to follow the biblical example as closely as possible, you might even want to stand in a bathtub, shower, or outside and actually pour a bit of this oil on your head.

However it is done, I believe there needs to come a point in time at which, once and for all, you dedicate yourself to be holy to God. The same concept of a "once-and-for-all dedication" is also the essence of Paul's urging in this verse, which we read earlier, about presenting our bodies:

1 I urge you therefore, brethren, by the mercies of God, to present your bodies a living and holy sacrifice, acceptable to God, which is your spiritual service of worship.

--Romans 12

The tense of the Greek word used in this verse means to present our bodies once and for all as a living sacrifice. When we sanctify ourselves (and remember, Jesus sanctified Himself), there is a once-and-for-all commitment to be holy to God. Once we make that commitment, we no longer belong to ourselves and we cannot even take "vacations" to do whatever we want to do, if it is unclean (sin).

There is a verse that would be good to memorize in connection with this. It points out that we are to cleanse ourselves and to become holy:

> **1 Therefore, having these promises, beloved, let us cleanse ourselves from all defilement of flesh and spirit, perfecting holiness in the fear of God.**
>
> **--2 Corinthians 7**

ANOINTING OTHER THINGS

Anointing yourself with oil is not necessary for you to become holy. However, I believe that that one act can really help to seal the covenant in your own heart. In addition to yourself, there may be other things that you wish to anoint and make holy. As we saw earlier, many things in the Old Testament were anointed with holy oil and set apart as holy unto God.

You may want to anoint your automobile and set it apart as holy. If an unmarried person were to do this, this would mean that there could be no lustful or promiscuous sexual activities going on in that holy automobile. For a family, it could well mean that there could no longer be all the fighting and bickering that sometimes goes on in cars.

There may be other things that you own, such as a boat, a camper, a motorhome or even a bed, that have in times past been used for unholy purposes. The Lord may lead you to anoint these with holy oil and set them aside as holy unto God.

There is one area that I have really had to pray about seriously, and perhaps you will too. What changes would you make if you were to anoint your stereo (or record player) and your television set with holy oil and dedicate them as holy unto God. What difference would it make in what television programs we watched on that television set, if it were truly a **holy** television set. This might be the solution for those Christians who are television addicts. A holy television set would certainly cut down on the amount of television an individual could watch. In talking about a Holy God, Habbakuk said that His eyes were too pure to look on wickedness with favor:

> 12 Art Thou not from everlasting,
> O LORD, my God, my Holy One?
> We will not die.
> Thou, O LORD, has appointed them to judge:
> And Thou, O Rock, hast established them to correct.
> 13 Thine eyes are too pure to approve evil,
> And Thou canst not look on wickedness with favor. . . .
>
> --Habakkuk 1

This is not to say that the Lord may not occasionally tell you to watch a television series or special to be aware of that which the world is observing. However, if we are eagerly looking forward to some television programs that depict evil with favor, then perhaps that is not a holy act and our televion set is being used as an unholy instrument.

One good thing to do might be to anoint your house and dedicate it as holy to the Lord first, and then go through the house anointing the various things that God tells you to anoint. If we are going to be holy individuals, we need to have our dwellings, our television sets and all of the major things that we own set apart also for God's exclusive use.

SUMMARY AND CONCLUSION

We have seen that Jesus was holy or sanctified. This means that He was set apart for God's exclusive use and was removed from unclean things. There evidently was a point in time when He made this act of dedication and consecration to Father God.

Being holy is commanded, not just suggested to us. We are "to be holy as God is holy" (1 Peter 1:15,16). It is also important because, without being holy (sanctified), we cannot see God.

If we have a burning desire to become like Jesus Christ, then this would include becoming holy, because He indeed was holy.

7
YOU CAN BE PURE

I don't know what God is doing with you as you read this book, but God is really working me over as I'm writing it. After writing about being holy, I began to wonder what was left. Then the Lord showed me that there was more, much more that we need to look at as we press toward our goal of becoming like Jesus Christ.

Another thing we can observe about Jesus is that He is pure. We also read that if our hope is fixed on Him, we will purify ourselves:

> 2 Beloved, now we are children of God, and it has not appeared as yet what we shall be. We know that, when He appears, we shall be like Him, because we shall see Him just as He is.
> 3 And everyone who has this hope fixed on Him purifies himself, just as He is pure.
> --1 John 3

Do you have your hope fixed on Jesus? I have my hope on Him. The Scriptures tell us that if this is true, then you and I will purify ourselves, just as Jesus is pure.

WHAT DOES IT MEAN TO BE PURE?

As I began to search the Scriptures to see the Bible's definition of "pure," I got confused. I looked up the word pure in a concordance based on the KING JAMES VERSION. When I looked up the Scriptures listed there in the NEW AMERICAN STANDARD BIBLE, the word "pure" was frequently translated "clear." For example:

> **20 And thou shalt command the children of Israel, that they bring thee pure oil olive beaten for the light, to cause the lamp to burn always.**
>
> --Exodus 27, KJV

> **20 "And you shall charge the sons of Israel, that they bring you clear oil of beaten olives for the light, to make a lamp burn continually. . ."**
>
> --Exodus 27, NAS

I began to ponder the relationship between pure and clear. Evidently, after you squeezed the oil from olives, not only would you have the olive oil, but you would also have some sediment suspended in the oil, minute particles of the olives themselves. If you strained the oil repeatedly to remove all those contaminants, then it would be pure or clear olive oil.

A similar concept is found in the refining of gold. When we talk about pure gold, this means without any contaminants in it:

> **6 And he made a mercy seat of pure gold, two and a half cubits long, and one and a half cubits wide.**
>
> --Exodus 37

To purify gold in Christ's day, the gold was heated repeatedly and had the impurities skimmed off the top, until the goldsmith could see his reflection on the surface of the gold.

Even today, the gold that is traded on the world market is all .995 fine. That means that there is only .005 of any contaminants in those gold bars or coins; that is essentially gold without any impurities. I have seen molten gold poured into bricks in South Africa, and the final purification of the gold is with fire. The impurities are burnt away. Perhaps the baptism of fire for Christians will do a similar thing with any impurities in our lives.

We can conclude that a biblical definition of pure would be this:

Pure means clean and clear of contaminants.

For us to be pure, as Jesus was, does this mean that our bodies are "clear and clean of any contaminants"? I do not believe so; otherwise we would have to live in a totally sterile environment, and Jesus certainly didn't live in that kind of environment. (By this, I don't mean that we are not to strive for "physical purity" and good health through a nutritious diet and adequate exercise. I do believe that is pleasing to the Lord too, but I feel there is a much deeper meaning of "purity.")

In emphasizing that it was internal purity, that He was teaching, not external, Jesus had this to say:

> 1 And the Pharisees and some of the scribes gathered together around Him when they had come from Jerusalem,
> 2 and had seen that some of His disciples were eating their bread with impure hands, that is, unwashed. . . .
>
> 14 And after He called the multitude to Him again, He began saying to them, "Listen to Me, all of you, and understand:
> 15 there is nothing outside the man which going into him can defile him; but the things which proceed out of the man are what defile the man. . . .
>
> 18 And He said to them, "Are you so lacking in understanding also? Do you not understand that whatever goes into the man from outside cannot defile him;
> 19 because it does not go into his heart, but

> into his stomach, and is eliminated?" (Thus He declared all foods clean.)
> 20 And He was saying, "That which proceeds out of the man, that is what defiles the man.
> 21 "For from within, out of the heart of men, proceed the evil thoughts, fornications, thefts, murders, adulteries,
> 22 deeds of coveting and wickedness, as well as deceit, sensuality, envy, slander, pride and foolishness.
> 23 "All these evil things proceed from within and defile the man."
>
> --Mark 7

The purity that we are talking about in this chapter is purity of heart. It is spiritual purity.

BE PURE IN HEART

Perhaps the goal of writing this book is a similar goal to what Paul had in writing to Timothy:

> 5 But the goal of our instruction is love from a pure heart and a good conscience and a sincere faith.
>
> --1 Timothy 1

Paul wanted Timothy to have love, but only from a pure heart--a heart that was free from contamination.

Let us turn back to the question we addressed in the previous chapter, that of seeing God. According to the Bible, there are several requirements that Christians have to meet before they can "see God." I believe that many Christians who are walking casually through the Christian life, assuming that they are going to see God, are going to be very disappointed. As we saw in the last chapter, being holy is one requirement for seeing God; another is this:

> 8 "Blessed are the pure in heart, for they shall see God. . . ."
>
> --Matthew 5

Here we see that those who are "pure in heart" shall see God. I have gone to charismatic meetings where they sang a chorus that goes like this:

> Blessed are they which do hunger and thirst
> after righteousness for they shall be
> filled.
> Blessed are they which do hunger and thirst
> after righteousness.
> Blessed are the merciful, for they shall obtain
> mercy.
> Blessed are the pure in heart, for they shall
> see God.

They keep increasing the tempo with each repetition of the song until they are singing it so fast that they are really just mumbling the words. I wonder if some of those precious Christians truly realize the significance of the words that they are singing. "Blessed are the pure in heart, for they shall see God." There may be some of them there without a pure heart, who are simply rattling off the words of the song, not realizing that because of their impure heart, they are not going to see God. (Remember, this is not my idea, this is what the Scriptures say.)

Let's go back to the main thought. What does it really mean to have a pure heart, a clean heart, a heart without contamination? To help us understand this, we need to step back and take at broader view. The basic intent of our heart determines what we think, and what we think determines what we say. Thus, our words are a mirror of what is in our heart. Do angry words come out of our mouth? Do selfish words come out of our mouth? Do unclean suggestions, jokes and stories come out of our mouth? If we have impure, contaminated things coming out of our mouth, what does that tell us about our heart?

I believe that if our heart were pure, like the heart of Jesus, then our words would be pure and clear of contamination by the filth of this world.

Perhaps we should cry to the Lord with the same prayer as David:

> 10 Create in me a clean heart, O God,
> And renew a steadfast spirit within me.
> 11 Do not cast me away from Thy presence,
> And do not take Thy Holy Spirit from me.
> 12 Restore to me the joy of Thy salvation,
> And sustain me with a willing spirit.
> 13 Then I will teach transgressors Thy ways,
> And sinners will be converted to Thee.
>
> --Psalm 51

As we pray that prayer and our heart becomes clean and pure, we will see it reflected in our words. When our words change, we can know that our heart has changed also.

HOW DO WE BECOME PURE IN HEART?

We have already looked at one way to become pure in heart; that is to pray, asking God for that clean heart.

In addition to praying, there is something else that we need to do. We find this in the book of James, which was most likely written by James, the brother of Jesus (Mark 6:3). Having grown up with Jesus, and having spent more time with Him even than the disciples, James would have had a special insight into the character of Jesus and His heart's desire for God's people. Let's read what James had to say about believers who were friendly with the world and the pleasures the world has to offer:

> 3 You ask and do not receive, because you ask with wrong motives, so that you may spend it on your pleasures.
>
> 4 You adulteresses, do you not know that friendship with the world is hostility toward God?

Therefore whoever wishes to be a friend of the world makes himself an enemy of God.

5 Or do you think that the Scripture speaks to no purpose: "He jealously desires the Spirit which He has made to dwell in us"?

6 But He gives a greater grace. Therefore it says, "GOD IS OPPOSED TO THE PROUD, BUT GIVES GRACE TO THE HUMBLE."

--James 4

James encourages us to pray with right motives, not to be a friend of the world and to be humble before Almighty God. However, the real solution James gives is in the next few verses:

7 Submit therefore to God. Resist the devil and he will flee from you.

8 Draw near to God and He will draw near to you. Cleanse your hands, you sinners; and purify your hearts, you double-minded.

9 Be miserable and mourn and weep; let your laughter be turned into mourning, and your joy to gloom.

10 Humble yourselves in the presence of the Lord, and He will exalt you.

--James 4

I would like to call particular attention to verses 7 and 8. Verse 7, says that we are to submit ourselves to God and are to resist Satan. If we do those two things, we are promised that Satan will flee from us.

Verse 8 is the real key to a pure heart. We are to draw near to God, (a holy, pure God) and He will draw near to us. We are to cleanse our hands and purify our hearts. No one else is going to do it for us. God is not going to come in with a lightening bolt and miraculously cause it to happen. He asks **us** to cleanse our hands and to purify our hearts. We are to cleanse our hands from the things of the world that we have been dabbling in or holding onto. We are to remove any contaminants or anything unclean from our hearts to make them pure.

A Christian brother I know had a sin problem with buying pornographic magazines. He prayed and asked God to remove that problem from him. God told him, "No. You are to be delivered by your own right arm. You are to take dominion over that right arm and no longer let it buy those magazines." As this brother did as God had directed him, he no longer bought those magazines and was delivered from that sin. He actively cleansed his hands and purified his heart.

Once we have cleansed ourselves, when any temptation from Satan comes along, threatening to contaminate our hearts, we must resist with all of our might, so that we can retain a pure heart.

If we do mess up and commit a sin, immediately we are to confess it:

> **9 If we confess our sins, He is faithful and righteous to forgive us our sins and to cleanse us from all unrighteousness.**
>
> --1 John 1

The minute we confess our sin, God promises that He will be faithful to forgive us the sin that we confessed (assuming we confess all known sin as sin). After He does that, He will cleanse us from all unrighteousness--He will cleanse us from the things that contaminate us of which we are not even aware. This way we can walk with a pure heart before Him.

WITHOUT SPOT OR WRINKLE

Jesus Christ desires that the church be without spot or wrinkle, that she be holy and blameless. Since the church is composed of individual believers, this means that He desires that individual believers have no spot or wrinkle, but rather be holy and blameless:

> **27 that He might present to Himself the church in all her glory, having no spot or wrinkle or any**

> such thing; but that she should be holy and blameless.
>
> --Ephesians 5

I have to ask myself if I have any spot, wrinkle or blemish. If I answer "Yes," this means that I am not pure. This means that there are areas in my life that need a fresh touch and need to become like Jesus Christ. I need to be pure like Him.

How does one get rid of spots? By washing. How does one get rid of wrinkles? By ironing (that is, with heat and pressure). Getting rid of spots and wrinkles requires energy and effort. Getting rid of impurities requires straining (for olive oil) and melting (for gold). If we yearn to be without spot or wrinkle, then we need the Lord to crush us, sift us, strain us and even purify us with fire.

There is a terrible misconception going around in Christendom today. Some people have the idea that when Jesus Christ comes back, we are going to be made instantly perfect, instantly pure, instantly holy. I do not find that concept to be consistent with the Scriptures. If that were true, there would be no need for us to press on to become like Jesus Christ in this life. All we would need to do would be to wait for the rapture. I believe that concept of instant perfection is a false teaching.

When Jesus Christ comes back, we will receive our new resurrected bodies, but our spirits will still need refining. Paul points this out in talking about the judgment seat of Christ:

> 11 For no man can lay a foundation other than the one which is laid, which is Jesus Christ.
>
> 12 Now if any man builds upon the foundation with gold, silver, precious stones, wood, hay, straw,
>
> 13 each man's work will become evident; for the day will show it, because it is to be revealed with fire; and the fire itself will test the quality of each man's work.

14 If any man's work which he has built upon it remains, he shall receive a reward.

15 If any man's work is burned up, he shall suffer loss; but he himself shall be saved, yet so as through fire.

--1 Corinthians 3

The purification that is not done while we are down here on the earth will be done in the millennium at the judgment seat of Christ, but without reward. It is far better to do it now, here on the earth, where we can do it in private, alone with the Lord, than to have the purification done in public, before Jesus Christ and the millions of Old Testament saints and New Testament believers.

Christ is calling those who are holy and blameless, those who are without spot or wrinkle, to be His bride. As I pointed out in my book, YOU CAN OVERCOME, not all Christians are going to be part of the bride of Christ, only those who are bondslaves of God. (Don't let this concept cause you to stumble. Just "put it on the shelf" until you have read YOU CAN OVERCOME).

What we are saying is that the bride of Christ is indeed going to be pure and holy, without spot or wrinkle. This life is the time during which we are either going to qualify to be one of the Christians who are part of the bride of Christ, or we are not. Now is the time to purify our lives of all "spots and wrinkles."

NOT I, BUT CHRIST LIVES IN ME

One of the reasons for my emphasizing some of the things that God expects us to do, is that most Christians are "sitting back in their easy chairs," expecting God to do it all. We have a primary responsibility in these areas of becoming holy and pure.

Even though God expects us to take the responsibility to sanctify ourselves and to cleanse ourselves, becoming like Christ ultimately is not a set of things that we do or don't do. It involves our entire being. However, the concept of becoming like Christ is so vast that I don't think any of us could really grasp it if we took it as a giant whole. Of necessity, we must look at it piece by piece, in order to be able to grasp what He was like and to let Him deal with those things in our lives so that we move on to become like Jesus.

In the end, you cannot in your own strength become like Jesus Christ. It must be Jesus Christ Who lives His life out through you:

> **20 "I have been crucified with Christ; and it is no longer I who live, but Christ lives in me; and the life which I now live in the flesh I live by faith in the Son of God, who loved me and delivered Himself up for me. . . ."**
>
> **--Galatians 2**

Even though it is Christ living through us, we certainly are not devoid of responsibility. Christ expects us to do our part, which includes sanctifying ourselves (making ourselves holy) and purifying ourselves for His glory.

SUMMARY AND CONCLUSION

We have seen that Jesus was pure. If we yearn to be like Him, we too will want to be pure. We saw that this purity really meant purity of heart.

As we cleanse ourselves with the only known solvent for our sins, the precious blood of Jesus, it washes us clean and makes us as white as snow in God's eyes. Then it is our responsibility to resist Satan and temptations with every fiber of our being. The victory will be ours! Satan must flee from us, when we resist him in the authority of Jesus Christ and protected by His mighty name.

In those cases when we do blow it and sin, we must learn to immediately confess that sin, turn away from it and ask God to cleanse us from it and from all unrighteousness. By doing this, we can walk as a

Christian with a pure heart. We can become like Jesus! He will help us as we move in this direction. Christ will live out His life through us if we let Him, and if we have no reservations. He really will!

8
SEEK HIS RIGHTEOUSNESS

There is no doubt that Jesus Christ was righteous. The Bible tells us this many places:

> 19 And while he was sitting on the judgment seat, his wife sent to him, saying, "Have nothing to do with that righteous Man; for last night I suffered greatly in a dream because of Him."
>
> --Matthew 27

Since Jesus Christ was righteous--and we have already seen that we **can** become like Christ, if we pursue it with all of our heart--then we too should seek to be righteous, shouldn't we?

But what does it really mean to be righteous? Many people talk about being righteous, and many Christians have had this as a vague, lofty goal, even from their youth. For example, when we read or quote the 23rd Psalm, we are proclaiming that the Lord is leading us in paths of righteousness:

> 1 The Lord is my shepherd,
> I shall not want.
> 2 He makes me lie down in green pastures;
> He leads me beside quiet waters.
> 3 He restores my soul;
> He guides me in the paths of
> righteousness
> For His name's sake.
>
> --Psalm 23

We "say" that we want to be led in the paths of righteousness, but Christ took that even further. He promised us that we would have the necessities of life--enough to eat, clothing to put on, and a place to stay--if we did two things. Do you know what those two things are? Christ did not promise us any luxuries, but He did promise us the necessities of life, if we would do the two things found in this passage:

> 25 "For this reason I say to you, do not be anxious for your life, as to what you shall eat, or what you shall drink; nor for your body, as to what you shall put on. Is not life more than food, and the body than clothing?
> 26 "Look at the birds of the air, that they do not sow, neither do they reap, nor gather into barns, and yet your heavenly Father feeds them. Are you not worth much more than they?
> 27 "And which of you by being anxious can add a single cubit to his life's span?
> 28 "And why are you anxious about clothing? Observe how the lilies of the field grow; they do not toil nor do they spin,
> 29 yet I say to you that even Solomon in all his glory did not clothe himself like one of these.
> 30 "But if God so arrays the grass of the field, which is alive today and tomorrow is thrown into the furnace, will He not much more do so for you, O men of little faith?
> 31 "Do not be anxious then, saying, 'What shall we eat?' or 'What shall we drink?' or 'With what shall we clothe ourselves?'
> 32 "For all these things the Gentiles eagerly seek; for your heavenly Father knows that you need all these things.
> 33 "But seek first His kingdom and His righteousness; and all these things shall be added to you. . . ."
>
> --Matthew 6

We will have the necessities of life if we seek first:

1. God's kingdom
2. And His righteousness (to be righteous like Him)

If you were to ask most Christians what it means to seek first the kingdom of God, they could probably give you a fairly good answer. It would probably go something like this: "Seek first to let God be the king of your life and to rule over you." However, if you then were to ask what it means to "seek first His righteousness," you would get an incredible variety of answers. I have heard answers to that question such as:

1. "To be in a right relationship with God."
2. "To be pure."
3. "To obey the ten commandments."

The list could go on and on. Of all the concepts in the Bible, by and large, Christians have the poorest idea of what righteousness is. If they do not know what righteousness is, how could they possibly be seeking it first?

Not only should we seek after righteousness; according to Jesus, we should actually hunger and thirst after righteousness:

> **6 "Blessed are those who hunger and thirst for righteousness, for they shall be satisfied...."**
> --Matthew 5

We are supposed to hunger and thirst after righteousness. You and I need to ask ourselves if we really are hungering and thirsting to be righteous.

Jesus further said in the beatitudes that we would receive a blessing if we were persecuted for a particular thing. We would not receive a blessing if we were persecuted for disobeying the laws of the land or for doing or saying bad things. There is only one thing mentioned in the beatitudes for which we could be persecuted and receive a blessing from the Lord. That is being persecuted for righteousness:

> 10 "Blessed are those who have been persecuted for the sake of righteousness, for theirs is the kingdom of heaven.
>
> 11 "Blessed are you when men cast insults at you, and persecute you, and say all kinds of evil against you falsely, on account of Me.
>
> 12 "Rejoice, and be glad, for your reward in heaven is great, for so they persecuted the prophets who were before you. . . ."
>
> --Matthew 5

Did you also realize that righteousness is a requirement for entering the kingdom of heaven? The Pharisees were quite righteous men, even though they missed and rejected God's own Son. They kept the Old Testament Law, including the ten commandments and, in that sense, they were righteous and blameless. But the righteousness after which we are to seek and hunger must be even more than that:

> 20 "For I say to you, that unless your righteousness surpasses that of the scribes and Pharisees, you shall not enter the kingdom of heaven. . . ."
>
> --Matthew 5

You might want to reread that verse and let it soak into your spirit. These are not my words; these are the words of Jesus. Our righteousness must exceed the righteousness of the Pharisees or you and I cannot enter the kingdom of heaven.

In order to discover what righteousness truly is, I would ask you to do what we have done in other chapters: that is to erase the blackboard of your mind of any preconceived ideas about what righteousness is and take a fresh look at the Scriptures to see what they indicate righteousness really means.

RIGHTEOUSNESS THROUGHOUT THE SCRIPTURES

Before we look at an actual definition of righteousness, we need to review some of the

Scriptures which show us that righteousness has been a critical thing from the very beginning.

For example, in talking about the end of this age, Daniel said that there are going to be some people who will have insight--I believe special insight from God--and here is what they are going to do:

> **3 "And those who have insight will shine brightly like the brightness of the expanse of heaven, and those who lead the many to righteousness, like the stars forever and ever. . . ."**
>
> **--Daniel 12**

There are going to be those who will lead many to righteousness. Of course they are first going to have to be righteous themselves. You and I can yearn to be one of those with insight who will have the joy and privilege of leading many into righteousness.

Would you like to have a lot of income? Most likely your answer is "yes." However, if you had to choose between a great income and righteousness, which would you choose? Solomon, one of the wisest men who ever lived, had this to say:

> **8 Better is a little with righteousness**
> **Than great income with injustice.**
>
> **--Proverbs 16**

Here we get the beginnings of a definition of righteousness; we see that it is the opposite of injustice, which is justice.

Luke gives us more insight as to what righteousness is. It is walking blameless and obeying the Lord. In speaking of Zacharias and Elizabeth, he said:

> **6 And they were both righteous in the sight of God, walking blameless in all the commandments and requirements of the Lord.**
>
> **--Luke 1**

Another interesting thing is that the Lord is going to repay each of us for our righteousness or lack of righteousness. David had this to say:

> 23 "And the LORD will repay each man for his righteousness and his faithfulness; for the LORD delivered you into my hand today, but I refused to stretch out my hand against the LORD'S anointed. . . ."
>
> --1 Samuel 26

> 21 "The LORD has rewarded me according to
> my righteousness;
> According to the cleanness of my hands
> He has recompensed me.
> 22 "For I have kept the ways of the LORD,
> And have not acted wickedly against my
> God.
> 23 "For all His ordinances were before me;
> And as for His statutes, I did not
> depart from them.
> 24 "I was also blameless toward Him,
> And I kept myself from my iniquity.
> 25 "Therefore the LORD has recompensed me
> according to my righteousness,
> According to my cleanness before His
> eyes. . . ."
>
> --2 Samuel 22

In these two passages, we see that the Lord is going to reward the righteous according to their righteousness. Again we begin to see a little more of the definition of righteousness, because of the parallel construction of Hebrew poetry. In verses 21 and 25, we see that righteousness is the same thing as having clean hands. In verse 22, we see that it is also keeping the ways of the Lord and not acting wickedly. The main thing I want to emphasize here, however, is that God will eventually pay back every man according to his righteousness.

The Bible lists many rewards of the righteous. Here are a few:

15 The eyes of the LORD are toward the
righteous,
And His ears are open to their cry.
16 The face of the LORD is against
evildoers,
To cut off the memory of them from the
earth,
17 The righteous cry and the LORD hears,
And delivers them out of all their
troubles.
18 The LORD is near to the brokenhearted,
And saves those who are crushed in
spirit.
19 Many are the afflictions of the
righteous;
But the LORD delivers him out of them
all.

--Psalm 34

Also in Psalms we find additional rewards for the righteous:

11 Light is sown like seed for the righteous,
And gladness for the upright in heart.
12 Be glad in the Lord, you righteous ones;
And give thanks to His holy name.

--Psalm 97

As you read the Scriptures, you will run across many passages that speak of the Lord's love, concern and rewards for the righteous. Let's now move on in our search for the Bible's definition of "righteousness."

RIGHTEOUSNESS AND JUDGMENT

Righteousness is frequently connected in the Bible to judgment. A "righteous judge" is one who always makes the "right" decisions. We know that God is such a judge:

8 And He will judge the world in righteousness;

He will execute judgment for the peoples
with equity.

--Psalm 9

Let me just share with you a few other verses that connect "justice" and "judging" to righteousness:

4 But with righteousness He will judge the
poor,
And decide with fairness for the afflicted
of the earth; . . .

--Isaiah 11

1 "Thus says the LORD,
Preserve justice, and do righteousness,
For My salvation is about to come
And My righteousness to be
revealed. . . ."

--Isaiah 56

5 "Behold, the days are coming," declares
the LORD,
"When I shall raise up for David a righteous Branch;
And He will reign as king and act wisely
And do justice and righteousness in the
land. . . ."

--Jeremiah 23

11 And I saw heaven opened; and behold, a white horse, and He who sat upon it is called Faithful and True; and in righteousness He judges and wages war.

--Revelation 19

We have just taken a sampling of verses here. In this last verse out of Revelation 19, it is interesting that Jesus judges in righteousness and He also wages war in righteousness. You can also see from all these verses that righteousness is very closely connected to judgment and justice.

WHAT IS RIGHTEOUSNESS?

Up until now, we have just skirted around the issue. Now we need to look at righteousness directly to see if we can determine from the Scriptures what it really is.

Let's begin with what it is not. We saw earlier, in Proverbs 16:8, that righteousness was not injustice. We saw in 2 Samuel 22 that righteousness was not being wicked. We find out from the writing of James that the anger of man is not a part of righteousness:

> **19 This you know, my beloved brethren. But let everyone be quick to hear, slow to speak and slow to anger;**
> **20 for the anger of man does not achieve the righteousness of God.**
>
> --James 1

In his second letter to the church at Corinth, Paul tells us that righteousness and lawlessness (not obeying the law) are also opposites:

> **14 Do not be bound together with unbelievers; for what partnership have righteousness and lawlessness, or what fellowship has light with darkness?**
>
> **--2 Corinthians 6**

So we know several things that righteousness is not: it is not being unjust, not being wicked, not being angry and not disobeying the law. It is avoiding those acts that would not please God, that would not glorify God, and that would not be in keeping with God's desires and commandments.

We should yearn to be cleansed of all unrighteousness. God will cleanse us if we confess these unrighteous acts as sin and ask His forgiveness:

> **9 If we confess our sins, He is faithful and righteous to forgive us our sins and to cleanse us from all unrighteousness.**
>
> **--1 John 1**

Now let's turn to the positive side and see what the Scriptures have to say about what righteousness is. I believe you will quickly find that righteousness is something we do:

> **9 "Blessed be the LORD your God who delighted in you to set you on the throne of Israel; because the LORD loved Israel forever, therefore He made you king, to do justice and righteousness."**
>
> **--1 Kings 10**

This verse is referring to Solomon and God is letting him know that he wants him to do justice and to do righteousness. This concept was repeated in a verse we looked at earlier:

> **1 Thus says the LORD,**
> **"Preserve justice, and do righteousness,**
> **For My salvation is about to come**
> **And My righteousness to be**
> **revealed. . . ."**
>
> **--Isaiah 56**

Here again we are told to do righteousness. If this be so, let's look at some of the things that a righteous man is supposed to do, as found in Ezekiel:

> **4 "Behold, all souls are Mine; the soul of the father as well as the soul of the son is Mine. The soul who sins will die.**
>
> **5 "But if a man is righteous, and practices justice and righteousness,**
>
> **6 and does not eat at the mountain shrines or lift up his eyes to the idols of the house of Israel, or defile his neighbor's wife, or approach a woman during her menstrual period--**
>
> **7 if a man does not oppress anyone, but restores to the debtor his pledge, does not commit robbery, but gives his bread to the hungry, and covers the naked with clothing,**
>
> **8 if he does not lend money on interest or**

take increase, if he keeps his hand from iniquity, and executes true justice between man and man,
9 if he walks in My statutes and My ordinances so as to deal faithfully--he is righteous and will surely live," declares the Lord GOD.

--Ezekiel 18

In this passage that God gave to Ezekiel, we see that a righteous man **practices** justice and **practices** righteousness. He doesn't defile (have sex with) his neighbor's wife, nor even his own wife during her menstrual period. Verse 7 says that he does not oppress anyone, he pays his debts, he does not rob, and he gives bread to the hungry and clothing to the naked.

Verses 8 and 9 say that he does not lend money at interest. (In Old Testament times, this was so that someone would not wind up owning another individual because of the way interest compounds. One could be forced into becoming an indentured servant if he couldn't pay his debts.) A righteous man keeps his hand from iniquity, he executes true justice and he walks in God's statutes and ordinances faithfully. That is quite a tall order, isn't it? Does this mean that he keeps all of God's commandments? Let us see:

172 Let my tongue sing of Thy word,
For all Thy commandments are righteousness.

--Psalm 119

Here David tells us that every single commandment of the Lord is a righteous commandment; therefore, a righteous man would obey them.

I believe that Psalm 15 is also talking about righteous men. It speaks of those who are going to abide in the tent of the Lord (tabernacle with Him) and dwell on His holy hill (Mount Zion) during the millennium:

1 O LORD, who may abide in Thy tent?
Who may dwell on Thy holy hill?

2 He who walks with integrity, and works righteousness,
And speaks truth in his heart.
3 He does not slander with his tongue,
Nor does evil to his neighbor,
Nor takes up a reproach against his friend;
4 In whose eyes a reprobate is despised,
But who honors those who fear the LORD;
He swears to his own hurt, and does not change;
5 He does not put out his money at interest,
Nor does he take a bribe against the innocent.
He who does these things will never be shaken.

--Psalm 15

You might want to read those verses again slowly. Psalm 15 all by itself would be quite a standard of living. What we are talking about here really is a disciplined life. In fact, the word disciple, which we will examine further in a later chapter, has its root in "discipline." Do you remember that the last one of the fruits of the Spirit listed is "self-control" (Galatians 5:22,23). Very few Christians are really disciplined and self-controlled. This is something that I think God wants to begin doing more in all of us. He wants us to exercise our self-control, to cleanse ourselves and to lead a disciplined life. Do you realize what the end result of discipline is? . . .

11 All discipline for the moment seems not to be joyful, but sorrowful; yet to those who have been trained by it, afterwards it yields the peaceful fruit of righteousness.

--Hebrews 12

Did you read that! The end result of a disciplined life, a self-controlled life, will be the "peaceful fruit of righteousness." Hallelujah!

Let me see if I can pull together what we have examined and come up with a layman's definition of righteousness:

"RIGHTEOUSNESS IS DOING THE RIGHT THING"

Let me amplify on what I mean by that. If there is a judgment situation, a righteous man does the right thing by people, even if it is to his disadvantage. If there is a temptation to do something evil or wicked to someone, he refrains and does the right thing instead. If there is a decision wherein he has to make a judgment, say, between two of his children, he would put favoritism aside and would always do the right thing in God's eyes. If one always does the right thing, then one will actually keep God's commandments. Doing the right thing requires discipline, because we are often tempted to do either the easy thing or the thing that would work out to our advantage.

To help you understand that it is possible to obey the commandments of God and still not be doing what is "right," we need to turn to the teachings of Jesus.

> **23 "Woe to you, scribes and Pharisees, hypocrites! For you tithe mint and dill and cummin, and have neglected the weightier provisions of the law: justice and mercy and faithfulness; but these are the things you should have done without neglecting the others. . . .**
>
> **28 "Even so you too outwardly appear righteous to men, but inwardly you are full of hypocrisy and lawlessness. . . ."**
>
> --Matthew 23

The scribes and Pharisees lived by the law yet, according to Jesus, their righteousness was shallow. You might note that He says they neglected "justice" (a word used in connection with righteousness, as we have seen) and they were full of "lawlessness" (unrighteousness). Let's read further:

6 And He said to them, "Rightly did Isaiah prophesy of you hypocrites, as it is written,

'THIS PEOPLE HONORS ME WITH THEIR LIPS,
BUT THEIR HEART IS FAR AWAY FROM ME.
7 BUT IN VAIN DO THEY WORSHIP ME,
TEACHING AS DOCTRINES THE PRECEPTS OF MEN.'

8 "Neglecting the commandment of God, you hold to the tradition of men."

9 He was also saying to them, "You nicely set aside the commandment of God in order to keep your tradition.

10 "For Moses said, 'HONOR YOUR FATHER AND YOUR MOTHER'; and, 'HE WHO SPEAKS EVIL OF FATHER OR MOTHER, LET HIM BE PUT TO DEATH';

11 but you say, 'If a man says to his father or his mother, anything of mine you might have been helped by is Corban (that is to say, given to God),'

12 you no longer permit him to do anything for his father or his mother;

13 thus invalidating the word of God by your tradition which you have handed down; and you do many things such as that."

--Mark 7

What Jesus was saying here was that God wanted them to honor their fathers and mothers and to take care of them. However, the Pharisees, and other Jews of that day, could say that all that they had was "given to God" (even though it still remained in their home and they were using it). Then they could say to their mothers and fathers: "I don't have anything to give you; I've given it all to God."

Jesus very bluntly told them that on the external side they may be legalistically obeying the law of God, but they were not doing "the right thing"--they were not being righteous.

In contrast, Jesus did the right thing (was righteous) in all that He did. There was no law saying that He had to be baptized, but He was baptized so that He could fulfill all righteousness:

> **14 But John tried to prevent Him, saying, "I have need to be baptized by You, and do You come to me?"**
> **15 But Jesus answering said to him, "Permit it at this time; for in this way it is fitting for us to fulfill all righteousness." Then he permitted Him.**
> --Matthew 3

Righteousness is doing what is "right," what is God's will, even if it is over and above the commandments. Just as an aside, Jesus commanded us to be baptized in water (after we believe in Him). He was baptized in water to fulfill righteousness. A Christian should be baptized for the same reason. But back to our main thought.

We need to examine our hearts to see if there is anyone by whom we are not doing the right thing. We may be feeding and clothing our children, but neglecting their spiritual training or not spending quality time with them. Is that doing the right thing by them?

Our spouse may have needs that we should be meeting, but we are not, for some small reason. Is that right? We may be teaching a Bible class or Sunday school class and be preparing half-heartedly; we may be doing poorly the things in our church that God has asked us to do. We may not be tithing--always with some "good" excuse; whatever the excuse, it is still robbing God and we know that robbing is not right (not righteous).

We could examine our relationships with our neighbors, our fellow workers, or with employees of the grocery store, gas station, and drug store we frequent. We could even examine our "relationship" with those driving other cars on the streets and highways. God wants us to do the right thing by each of those precious people for whom Christ died.

As we hunger and thirst after righteousness, we are seeking to do the right thing by everyone and by God. This is what Paul encouraged Timothy to do:

> 6 But godliness actually is a means of great gain, when accompanied by contentment.
> 7 For we have brought nothing into the world, so we cannot take anything out of it either.
> 8 And if we have food and covering, with these we shall be content.
> 9 But those who want to get rich fall into temptation and a snare and many foolish and harmful desires which plunge men into ruin and destruction.
> 10 For the love of money is a root of all sorts of evil, and some by longing for it have wandered away from the faith, and pierced themselves with many a pang.
> 11 But flee from these things, you man of God; and pursue righteousness, godliness, faith, love, perseverance and gentleness.
>
> --1 Timothy 6

Paul is encouraging Timothy to flee from the love of money and the other temptations and to **pursue** righteousness and the other characteristics of Jesus Christ. He is really telling him to become like Jesus Christ. If you take Paul's advice and pursue righteousness, do you know the wonderful thing that happens?

> 9 The way of the wicked is an abomination
> to the LORD,
> But He loves him who pursues
> righteousness.
>
> --Proverbs 15

Did you get that? God **loves** those who pursue righteousness. How it must please our heavenly Father when we sincerely and zealously pursue righteousness!

TWO WAYS TO HAVE RIGHTEOUSNESS

There are two basic ways that we can seek to have righteousness (to do the right thing). The first way is that we can rely on ourself and our own good deeds. This is called "self-righteousness."

We see many examples of self-righteousness in the Bible. One of the primary examples would be the Pharisees in the New Testament. They had a righteousness, but it was purely of self. They were trying to "pull themselves up by their own bootstraps" to eternal life, and it was not working. Paul spoke of them:

> 3 For not knowing about God's righteousness, and seeking to establish their own, they did not subject themselves to the righteousness of God.
>
> --Romans 10

Another example is the rich young ruler. He was keeping all the commandments, but he was far from having eternal life:

> 16 And behold, one came to Him and said, "Teacher, what good thing shall I do that I may obtain eternal life?"
> 17 And He said to him, "Why are you asking Me about what is good? There is only One who is good; but if you wish to enter into life, keep the commandments."
> 18 He said to Him, "Which ones?" And Jesus said, "YOU SHALL NOT COMMIT MURDER; YOU SHALL NOT COMMIT ADULTERY; YOU SHALL NOT STEAL; YOU SHALL NOT BEAR FALSE WITNESS;
> 19 HONOR YOUR FATHER AND MOTHER; and YOU SHALL LOVE YOUR NEIGHBOR AS YOURSELF."
> 20 The young man said to Him, "All these things I have kept; what am I still lacking?"
> 21 Jesus said to him, "If you wish to be complete, go and sell your possessions and give to

> the poor, and you shall have treasure in heaven; and come, follow Me."
>
> 22 But when the young man heard this statement, he went away grieved; for he was one who owned much property.
>
> --Matthew 19

Unfortunately, we see many self-righteous people in the world today. They are good, moral, ethical people, who contribute to the Red Cross and community chests, and who get involved in all sorts of campaigns to help cure diseases and to help the poor and the hungry. Yet these people often are trying to do "good" without Jesus Christ and, thus, all of their righteousness is "self-righteousness." Unfortunately all of this type of righteousness is like filthy rags in God's sight (Isaiah 64:6).

Much of this self-righteousness is to impress other people, and Christ warns against this:

> 1 "Beware of practicing your righteousness before men to be noticed by them; otherwise you have no reward with your Father who is in heaven.
>
> 2 "When therefore you give alms, do not sound a trumpet before you, as the hypocrites do in the synagogues and in the streets, that they may be honored by men. Truly I say to you, they have their reward in full. . . .
>
> 5 "And when you pray, you are not to be as the hypocrites; for they love to stand and pray in the synagogues and on the street corners, in order to be seen by men. Truly I say to you, they have their reward in full. . . .
>
> 16 "And whenever you fast, do not put on a gloomy face as the hypocrites do, for they neglect their appearance, in order to be seen fasting by men. Truly I say to you, they have their reward in full. . . ."
>
> --Matthew 6

Here we see three things that Christ included in righteousness: giving tithes and offerings (alms), praying and fasting. However, He warns us not to practice this righteousness before men because if we do, we have already gotten all the reward we will ever have for it, because this is not pleasing to the Father. (You might want to reread the entire chapter of Matthew 6 for the details of this.)

Many people--including the Hebrews in the land of Palestine, whom I love so much--are trying to achieve righteousness through obeying the law, and it can never be done:

> **21 "I do not nullify the grace of God; for if righteousness comes through the Law, then Christ died needlessly."**
>
> **--Galatians 2**

Here the Bible tells us that righteousness cannot côme through obeying the law alone. We need something more. Praise God that the verse right before that tells us how to have the righteousness that pleases God:

> **20 "I have been crucified with Christ; and it is no longer I who live, but Christ lives in me; and the life which I now live in the flesh I live by faith in the Son of God, who loved me, and delivered Himself up for me. . . ."**
>
> **--Galatians 2**

We quoted this verse in the last chapter too and, as we saw there, it is not I who live, but Christ lives in Me! I am not the one doing the right thing; it is Christ in me who does the right (righteous) thing. I can never brag or boast about the "right things" that I do, because it is not I who do them; it is Jesus Himself.

Jesus always did the right thing by everyone. We may do some of the same things that we would have done were we trying to be righteous on our own (self-righteous). However, our motivation and power is not our own, but it is Christ. We have been created afresh to be righteous men and women of God:

> 20 But you did not learn Christ in this way,
> 21 if indeed you have heard Him and have been taught in Him, just as truth is in Jesus,
> 22 that, in reference to your former manner of life, you lay aside the old self, which is being corrupted in accordance with the lusts of deceit,
> 23 and that you be renewed in the spirit of your mind,
> 24 and put on the new self, which in the likeness of God has been created in righteousness and holiness of the truth.
>
> --Ephesians 4

Isn't that a wonderful passage of Scripture? Our old self is dead and our old self-righteousness is gone and worthless. However--praise God--we have been renewed in our spirit and in our mind. We have put on a new self in the likeness of God--in the likeness of His Son, Jesus Christ. We have been created anew to walk in righteousness and holiness! We could not do it, the law could not do it, but Jesus can do it in us!

The righteousness that God puts inside us causes us always to do the right thing, if we allow the Holy Spirit to control us. Thus, it is His works, not ours.

Many of you will remember from Romans 4 that Abraham believed God and it was counted unto him as righteousness. The faith of Abraham was not a dead, empty faith. It caused Abraham to obey God:

> 2 For if Abraham was justified by works, he has something to boast about; but not before God.
> 3 For what does the Scripture say? "AND ABRAHAM BELIEVED GOD, AND IT WAS RECKONED TO HIM AS RIGHTEOUSNESS."
>
> --Romans 4

Jesus became sin for us so that something beautiful might happen to you and me:

20 Therefore, we are ambassadors for Christ, as though God were entreating through us; we beg you on behalf of Christ, be reconciled to God.
21 He made Him who knew no sin to be sin on our behalf, that we might become the righteousness of God in Him.

--2 Corinthians 5

We cannot increase the harvest of our righteousness, but God can. I'm so glad that it doesn't depend on us. It depends only on our willingness:

10 Now He who supplies seed to the sower and bread for food, will supply and multiply your seed for sowing and increase the harvest of your righteousness;
11 you will be enriched in everything for all liberality, which through us is producing thanksgiving to God.

--2 Corinthians 9

To close this humble writing on righteousness, I would like to quote from the Scriptures a prayer that Paul was praying for the Christians in Philippi. Let's you and I pray this prayer for each other:

9 And this I pray, that your love may abound still more and more in real knowledge and all discernment,
10 so that you may approve the things that are excellent, in order to be sincere and blameless until the day of Christ;
11 having been filled with the fruit of righteousness which comes through Jesus Christ, to the glory and praise of God.

--Philippians 1

Another good prayer for righteousness is found in Luke:

74 To grant us that we, being delivered
from the hand of our enemies,

Might serve Him without fear,
75 In holiness and righteousness before Him all our days.

--Luke 1

As we do righteousness, which means we will do the right thing, it will produce a bountiful, fruitful harvest and it all comes through Jesus Christ to the glory and praise of God!

Make no mistake. If we are going to become like Jesus and be sincere and blameless in the day of Christ, we will indeed do the right thing and be righteous. Yet it is not our power that is able to achieve this. It is the power of Jesus living in us!

SUMMARY AND CONCLUSION

When I first wrote this book, this chapter was not included. I had wanted to include it, but I knew it would be a very difficult subject to write on clearly. After I dictated the last chapter of the book, the Lord commanded me to go back and write this chapter on righteousness. By far, it was the most difficult chapter in the entire book for me to write.

We know that Jesus was righteous: He always did the right thing. He always obeyed God and He always did the right thing by other people, even though He did not always "please" other people. As we yearn to be like Jesus, we too will yearn to be righteous.

We have seen that God will reward according to our righteousness. That includes us Christians, who have varying degrees of righteousness. We are to seek righteousness first; we are to hunger and thirst after righteousness; we are to pursue righteousness with all of our heart. If we do this, the Bible tells us that God will love us and will satisfy and fill us.

As we seek to do the right thing, we cannot do it in our own energy and strength, nor can we take credit for it. The only way we can be truly righteous is to die to self and to let Jesus Christ live in us. If we allow Him to live out His life through us, then we will indeed be righteous.

Think for a moment what a great football player you would be if you had an O.J. Simpson living inside you. Think what a great composer you might be if you had a Tchaikovsky living inside you. Imagine what a wise man or woman you would be if you had King Solomon living inside you.

Just pause for a moment and imagine what you would be like if you had a Jesus Christ living inside you. Praise God! We do have Jesus Christ living inside us. What He wants to do is to make us like Himself and conform us to His image, so that we will be pure, holy and righteous all the days of our lives.

You might say: "Jim, if we were all those things, wouldn't we just about be perfect?" The answer is, "Yes, we would be." Do you think we can be perfect like Jesus? Could it be that God wants this of us?

9
CAN WE BE PERFECT?

Just about everyone would agree that Jesus was perfect. But did you realize that there are four other men in the Bible who were also said to be perfect? Let's look at those four perfect men, in order to see what being "perfect" really means. Most of us have a very incorrect idea of what it means when the Bible says someone was perfect. To find out the truth, we will examine these men one at a time.

NOAH WAS PERFECT

We are all familiar with the story of Noah and the flood. But do you remember what he did after the flood was over?

> 20 Then Noah began farming and planted a vineyard.
> 21 And he drank of the wine and became drunk, and uncovered himself inside his tent.
> --Genesis 9

Here the Bible says that after the flood was over, Noah planted a vineyard, evidently made wine, and then got drunk. Thus, we would have to conclude that Noah was not sinless. However, the Bible says he was perfect:

> 9 These are the generations of Noah: Noah was a just man and perfect in his generations, and Noah walked with God.
>
> --Genesis 6, KJV

DAVID WAS PERFECT

We are all aware of some of the many sins of David, such as having a man killed so that he could take the man's wife for his own wife (2 Samuel 11:2-27). Yet the Bible says David was perfect:

> 4 For it came to pass, when Solomon was old, that his wives turned away his heart after other gods: and his heart was not perfect with the LORD his God, as was the heart of David his father.
>
> --1 Kings 11, KJV

> 3 And he walked in all the sins of his father, which he had done before him: and his heart was not perfect with the LORD his God, as the heart of David his father.
>
> --1 Kings 15, KJV

These two verses tell us that David was perfect in his heart.

ASA WAS PERFECT

One of the descendants of David was Asa. He reigned over Judah for forty-one years. (Even though the following Scripture says that David was his father, he was actually his great-great-grandfather.) Let's read what the Scriptures have to say about Asa:

> 9 And in the twentieth year of Jeroboam king of Israel reigned Asa over Judah.
>
> 10 And forty and one years reigned he in Jerusalem. And his mother's name was Maachah, the daughter of Abishalom.

11 And Asa did that which was right in the eyes of the LORD, as did David his father.
12 And he took away the sodomites out of the land, and removed all the idols that his fathers had made.
13 And also Maachah his mother, even her he removed from being queen, because she had made an idol in a grove; and Asa destroyed her idol, and burnt it by the brook Kidron.
14 But the high places were not removed: nevertheless Asa's heart was perfect with the LORD all his days.

--1 Kings 15, KJV

Just as in David's case, with Asa we see that his heart was perfect.

JOB WAS PERFECT

Job evidently lived about the time of Abraham, perhaps a little earlier. We are all familiar with the trials and tribulations that God allowed Satan to bring upon Job. But did you realize that the Bible says Job was perfect?

8 And the LORD said unto Satan, Hast thou considered my servant Job, that there is none like him in the earth, a perfect and an upright man, one that feareth God, and escheweth evil?

--Job 1, KJV

WHAT DOES IT MEAN TO BE PERFECT?

There are probably other men in the Bible who were perfect, but we have looked at the four that the Bible explicitly says were perfect.

However, we must ask ourselves if all four of them were sinless. The answer is no. We know that each of them had sinned ("for all have sinned and fall short of the glory of God"--Romans 3:23), and yet the Bible says they were perfect. The perfection was not of their actions; it was of their hearts.

I like to think of it this way. Suppose I were cleaning out a garage and an eight-year-old boy came by and wanted to help me sweep the garage floor, and suppose I allowed him to do that. Would he do a "perfect" job of sweeping the floor? No, he wouldn't. There would probably be dust left in the corners, along the edges and possibly even spots in the middle of the floor. However, the question we must ask is whether his heart was perfect? The answer likely is yes. His performance might not be perfect, but his heart could be perfect. That is so important for us to remember. Praise be to God who also looks at our hearts and not at our performance:

> **7 But the LORD said to Samuel, "Do not look at his appearance or at the height of his stature, because I have rejected him; for God sees not as man sees, for man looks at the outward appearance, but the LORD looks at the heart."**
>
> **--1 Samuel 16**

Aren't you glad that God looks at our hearts as a loving heavenly Father?

We should do the same thing, in our dealings with others. For example, when a child is trying to be helpful by bringing a pitcher of milk to the table, but he trips and spills the milk, his performance is poor, but his heart is probably perfect. We have to be careful in situations like that to look at the heart of an individual.

A husband may have things scattered all over some area of the house and he knows just where everything is. The wife, wanting to be a good wife, cleans up the house and neatly stacks all these things someplace. Unfortunately, some husbands would be upset when they could not find what they wanted. Was the wife's heart perfect in this instance? Yes, she was trying to be helpful, even though her performance did not happen to please her husband. At times like that, husbands need to pause and ask God to show them the intent of their wife's heart.

So when we are talking about being perfect, we are talking about our hearts being perfect, even though our actions may be far from perfect and we still may make mistakes. I have done a long detailed study on David's life, especially looking at anything that would reveal his heart. The thing that jumps out from the pages of the Scriptures over and over again is that before David did something, he almost always "inquired of the Lord." He really wanted to do God's will. Oh, that you and I might have a heart like David's, so that at the end of our lives God might say that we too had a "perfect heart"!

CAN WE REALLY BE PERFECT?

In pursuing the answer to the question, "Can we really be perfect," we must first ask ourselves if Jesus would command us to do anything that was impossible for us to do. I do not think that our Savior would ever be unreasonable. He certainly would not ask us to do something that was impossible for us to achieve. Yet, He commanded us to be perfect:

> **48 "Therefore you are to be perfect, as your heavenly Father is perfect. . . ."**
>
> **--Matthew 5**

The command of Jesus to be perfect is just as much a command as the command to love your neighbor or not to commit adultery. Many of these other commands we try to obey, and yet the command to be perfect we simply ignore. It is not right to pick and choose which commandments we will accept. I believe we should really pursue trying to obey all of the commands that Jesus gave us, including His command to be perfect. Many of the other commands will naturally be obeyed, as our hearts become perfect.

There is another way for us to look at becoming perfect (becoming like Jesus). Most of us are familiar with the five-fold ministries outlined in Ephesians. Do you realize why these gifts were given? Let's take a look:

11 And he gave some, apostles; and some, prophets; and some, evangelists; and some, pastors and teachers;
12 For the perfecting of the saints, for the work of the ministry, for the edifying of the body of Christ:
13 Till we all come in the unity of the faith, and of the knowledge of the Son of God, unto a perfect man, unto the measure of the stature of the fulness of Christ: . . .

--Ephesians 4, KJV

Verse 12 says that these gifts were given for the perfecting of the saints--to make the saints (the believers) perfect. Then verse 13 so beautifully amplifies this, saying that this perfecting will continue until we become "a perfect man, unto the measure of the stature of the fulness of Christ." These five ministries should help us until we become perfect and we become like Jesus Christ.

There will be many apostles, prophets, evangelists and teachers traveling around and some perhaps even coming into your church or onto your television screen. One test to see whether or not an individual is indeed a true apostle, prophet, evangelist, pastor or teacher is whether you (and the other believers in your church) are more perfect after that person leaves than before he came. Ask yourself if your heart is really and truly more perfect after experiencing his ministry.

We see that God wants His people to be perfect and that is why He gave the five-fold ministries. If those who exercise the five-fold ministries were doing their job properly, we would have vast numbers of perfect Christians or at least Christians moving towards perfection and the fulness of Christ. Christians would become like Jesus.

THE PROCESS OF BECOMING PERFECT

Becoming perfect is not easy. It frequently involves trials and testings that purge out of your life those things that are displeasing to God:

> 2 Consider it all joy, my brethren, when you encounter various trials,
>
> 3 knowing that the testing of your faith produces endurance.
>
> 4 And let endurance have its perfect result, that you may be perfect and complete, lacking in nothing.
>
> --James 1

According to verse 4 in this passage, the end result of trials and testings is that you will be "perfect and complete, lacking in nothing." Do you feel that describes you? Are you perfect? Are you complete? Are you lacking in nothing? That is what God wants you to be. Ask Him for it and it will happen, although the process may be a bit painful, but only for a short while. We can forget the pain in looking for the joy that is set before us. In his first letter, Peter points out that suffering may be involved in becoming perfect:

> 6 Humble yourselves, therefore, under the mighty hand of God, that He may exalt you at the proper time,
>
> 7 casting all your anxiety upon Him, because He cares for you.
>
> 8 Be of sober spirit, be on the alert. Your adversary, the devil, prowls about like a roaring lion, seeking someone to devour.
>
> 9 But resist him, firm in your faith, knowing that the same experiences of suffering are being accomplished by your brethren who are in the world.
>
> 10 And after you have suffered for a little while, the God of all grace, who called you to His eternal glory in Christ, will Himself perfect, confirm, strengthen and establish you.
>
> --1 Peter 5

Please read that last verse again, and let the Holy Spirit make it alive to you. Is the suffering that will happen on the way worth it?

We need to leave elementary teachings and press on to perfection:

> **1 Therefore, leaving the discussion of the elementary principles of Christ, let us go on to perfection, not laying again the foundation of repentance from dead works and from faith toward God,**
> **2 of the doctrine of baptisms, of laying on of hands, of resurrection of the dead, and of eternal judgment.**
> **3 And this we will do if God permits.**
> **--Hebrews 6, NKJV**

In verse 1, the NEW AMERICAN STANDARD translates it as "elementary teaching." As we press on to perfection, we leave behind the six things that Hebrews 6 lists as elementary teachings:

1. Repentance from dead works
2. Faith toward God (the faith message)
3. Doctrine of baptisms (water and Holy Spirit)
4. Laying on of hands (for healing and for ministry)
5. Resurrection of the dead (miracles and rapture)
6. Eternal judgment (judgment seat of Christ)

There are so many ministers and organizations who still are stuck in these "elementary teachings." But God wants you and me to go beyond these and to move into perfection.

Another thing we need to do is to pray to be perfect. We find that Epaphras was praying for the Christians back in Colossae to be perfect:

> **12 Epaphras, who is one of your number, a bondslave of Jesus Christ, sends you his greetings, always laboring earnestly for you in his prayers, that you may stand perfect and fully**

assured in all the will of God.

--Colossians 4

Epaphras was praying that the precious brothers and sisters that he had left back home would be perfect. Do you think that might be a good prayer for you to pray for the brothers and sisters in your own church or fellowship? Do you think that it also might be a legitimate prayer that we could pray for ourselves? Yes, indeed! We need to be praying that we will have a perfect heart before God.

A PERFECT HEART BRINGS PERFECT THOUGHTS

There are many wonderful results of having a perfect heart. One of these is that our thoughts will come under the control of Christ. From the following Scripture, we know that "the intents of our heart" and "our thoughts" are two totally separate things:

> **12 For the word of God is living and active and sharper than any two-edged sword, and piercing as far as the division of soul and spirit, of both joints and marrow, and able to judge the thoughts and intentions of the heart.**
>
> **--Hebrews 4**

We also know that thoughts come from the heart. Matthew tells us that evil thoughts come from the heart:

> **19 "For out of the heart come evil thoughts, murders, adulteries, fornications, thefts, false witness, slanders. . . ."**
>
> **--Matthew 15**

We also know that good thoughts come from the heart. As our heart becomes perfect, our thoughts--which come out of that heart--will begin to be more and more pleasing to Christ:

5 We are destroying speculations and every lofty thing raised up against the knowledge of God, and we are taking every thought captive to the obedience of Christ, . . .

--2 Corinthians 10

This verse in 2 Corinthians 10 says that Paul and the people traveling with him were actually taking every thought captive and bringing it under the obedience of Christ. How do we go about bringing every thought captive to the obedience of Christ? The key is found in Paul's letter to the believers in Philippi:

8 Finally, brethren, whatever is true, whatever is honorable, whatever is right, whatever is pure, whatever is lovely, whatever is of good repute, if there is any excellence and if anything worthy of praise, let your mind dwell on these things.

--Philippians 4

As we fix our mind on things that are wonderful, clean, pure and edifying, our thought life will be brought under the control of Christ, and we will become more and more like Him. We know that whatever we think about is what we are going to become:

7 For as he thinketh in his heart, so is he:

--Proverbs 23a, KJV

If we want to become like Jesus we are going to need to think about Him and about good things, just as Jesus did.

When we watch prime time television, what are we thinking about? We are thinking the thoughts that the people on the screen are projecting. Do you think these would match with Philippians 4:8? Are the thoughts that you are thinking, while you are watching television, beautiful, clean, pure and worthy of praise? Probably not. That time might be better spent reading the Scriptures, Christian books or something that would focus your mind on Christ, rather than the things of the world. If we are thinking the thoughts of prime time television, what are we going to become like? We are going to become like the people on the screen, because as we think in our hearts, so we become.

What we watch is the food that we are giving to our souls. Our mouths feed our bodies. Our eyes and ears feed our souls. If we are going to become perfect and become like Jesus, we must feed our souls pure, clean, excellent spiritual food, especially during our free time, which is in the evenings, for most people.

Many Christians have eliminated physical junk food from their diets. Isn't it time that we eliminated the "spiritual junk food" that we consume with our eyes and ears? It is far more harmful to us than anything physical. Jesus told us this:

> 18 And He said to them, "Are you so lacking in understanding also? Do you not understand that whatever goes into the man from outside cannot defile him;
>
> 19 because it does not go into his heart, but into his stomach, and is eliminated?" (Thus He declared all foods clean.)
>
> 20 And He was saying, "That which proceeds out of the man, that is what defiles the man.
>
> 21 "For from within, out of the heart of men, proceed the evil thoughts, fornications, thefts, murders, adulteries,
>
> 22 deeds of coveting and wickedness, as well as deceit, sensuality, envy, slander, pride and foolishness.
>
> 23 "All these evil things proceed from within and defile the man."
>
> --Mark 7

The things we watch, listen to and read go into our hearts and not our stomachs. Just as physical food is stored and then used, so is spiritual food. The spiritual food we see and hear is stored and feeds our hearts and minds. We must carefully guard what goes into our hearts. There are a few, very few, really uplifting movies and television programs. However, I suspect that over 90 percent of what most Christians watch hinders them from having perfect thoughts and being perfect.

GOOD THOUGHTS BRING FORTH GOOD WORDS

We think something before we speak it. Thus, if every thought is captive to the obedience of Christ, our words will be perfect. Our words are so very important. They happen to be one of the major things that Christ is going to judge us on at the judgment seat of Christ:

> **34 ". . . For the mouth speaks out of that which fills the heart. . . .**
>
> **36 "And I say to you, that every careless word that men shall speak, they shall render account for it in the day of judgment.**
> **37 "For by your words you shall be justified, and by your words you shall be condemned."**
>
> --Matthew 12

One beautiful thing about a perfect heart is that it brings forth perfect thoughts which, in turn, cause our words to be ones that will be well pleasing to the Lord Jesus, as He reviews them at the judgment seat of Christ.

SUMMARY AND CONCLUSION

God wants you to be perfect. Jesus commanded it. He gave the five-fold ministry so that Christians could be perfect.

There were at least four men in the Bible whom the Lord says were perfect. Their hearts were perfect, even though their behavior was not necessarily always perfect. Their hearts wanted to do only God's will and things that would please Him.

Satan will try to convince you that you can never become perfect and that you can never become like Jesus Christ. Yet Christ commands us to be perfect and wants us to press on toward it. Whom are you going to believe?

Let us believe God and together press on toward becoming perfect--having a perfect heart. Then we know that our thoughts are going to become perfect and our words will become perfect. In addition to our thoughts and our words, some of the things that we do (our works) will also become perfect and well pleasing to the Lord.

10
THE RIGHTFUL PLACE OF WORKS

Earlier we talked about good works and how some churches, in reality, are preaching salvation by works. We also observed that the charismatics, fundamentalists, and evangelicals have almost swung in the opposite direction and are so intent on preaching Christ as Savior that they have almost made works of no importance. Let's see if we can now bring good works into their rightful place, according to the Scriptures.

Did Jesus do good works? The answer is a definite yes. He fed the hungry, He preached the gospel to the poor, He healed the sick and cast demons out of those who were possessed. These are all good works that He did in relation to believers and unbelievers alike. If we are going to be like Jesus, then we, too, will do good works.

We know that we can never have eternal life by doing good works:

> 8 For by grace you have been saved through faith; and that not of yourselves, it is the gift of God;
> 9 not as a result of works, that no one should boast.
>
> --Ephesians 2

As this Scripture points out, prior to the time when one becomes a Christian, works mean absolutely nothing. They are of no value at all regarding salvation. Good deeds done by an unsaved individual do not gain him any merit with God. They do not take him any closer to having eternal life. However . . .

AFTER SALVATION WORKS BECOME VERY IMPORTANT

In order to help you understand the extreme importance of our works ("deeds" is another name for "works") after salvation, I would like to review the first event that occurs in the millennium. This occurs right after Christ returns to Mount Zion and sets up His throne there. Do you know what it is? Jesus tells us in Matthew:

> **31 "But when the Son of Man comes in His glory, and all the angels with Him, then He will sit on His glorious throne.**
> **32 "And all the nations will be gathered before Him; and He will separate them from one another, as the shepherd separates the sheep from the goats;**
> **33 and He will put the sheep on His right, and the goats on the left.**
> **34 "Then the King will say to those on His right, 'Come, you who are blessed of My Father, inherit the kingdom prepared for you from the foundation of the world.**
> **35 'For I was hungry, and you gave Me something to eat; I was thirsty, and you gave Me drink; I was a stranger, and you invited Me in;**
> **36 naked, and you clothed Me; I was sick, and you visited Me; I was in prison, and you came to Me.'**
> **37 "Then the righteous will answer Him, saying, 'Lord, when did we see You hungry, and feed You, or thirsty, and give You drink?**
> **38 'And when did we see You a stranger, and invite You in, or naked, and clothe You?**
> **39 'And when did we see You sick, or in prison, and come to You?'**
> **40 "And the King will answer and say to**

> **them, 'Truly I say to you, to the extent that you did it to one of these brothers of Mine, even the least of them, you did it to Me.'. . ."**
>
> --Matthew 25

The first thing that happens in the millennium is the judgment seat of Christ. Much later, long after the millennium, there will be a great white throne judgment, at which point every human being will stand before the judgment seat of God the Father. When we Christians stand there, we will be wrapped in the robe of the righteousness of Jesus and God will look at us as perfect.

However, at the very beginning of the millennium, every Christian is going to stand before the judgment seat of Christ. We will stand clothed only in the deeds that we have done. The Holy Spirit told Paul about this judgment seat of Christ. He passed it on to the Christians in Corinth:

> **10 For we must all appear before the judgment seat of Christ, that each one may be recompensed for his deeds in the body, according to what he has done, whether good or bad.**
>
> **--2 Corinthians 5**

Paul is writing to the Christians in Corinth. He says that we must **all** appear before the judgment seat of Christ. That means that **every Christian** is going to appear before the judgment seat of Christ. The second half of this verse tells us what we are going to receive, as we stand before the judgment seat of Christ. It says that we are going to be recompensed (paid back) for what we did when we were in our natural bodies. We will be rewarded either good or bad, depending on our deeds.

In commenting on the place of our works (deeds), I would like to excerpt a section out of my last book, THE COMING CLIMAX OF HISTORY:

> We have to be very careful here. Works, or deeds, have no value before one becomes a

Christian. We know that one cannot be saved because of works:

16 nevertheless knowing that a man is not justified by the works of the Law but through faith in Christ Jesus, even we have believed in Christ Jesus, that we may be justified by faith in Christ, and not by the works of the Law; since by the works of the Law shall no flesh be justified.

--Galatians 2

8 For by grace you have been saved through faith; and that not of yourselves, it is the gift of God;
9 not as a result of works, that no one should boast.

--Ephesians 2

Most born-again Christians realize that we are not saved by works. But many then carry this almost to the other extreme, by belittling works and negating their importance. What these Christians do not realize is that the moment we are born again, by receiving Christ as our personal Savior, the situation concerning "works" flips 180 degrees and our works (deeds) become all-important.

This is a significant point. What are we going to be judged on when we stand before the judgment seat of Christ? We will **not** be judged on whether or not we have received Christ as Savior; that question will be examined by God the Father at the great white throne judgment. If that is not what we are judged on, what are we judged on when we stand before the judgment seat of Christ?

The Bible clearly tells us in 2 Corinthians 5:10 that we will be judged on our deeds, on what we have done. Did we walk in the Spirit? Did we live holy and righteous lives? Did we help the needy? Did we preach the gospel? The list could go on and on to include our family relationships, whether we cheated on our taxes, and every other area of our lives.

As we read earlier, the Bible says that if we have done bad things, we are going to receive retribution for those bad things; if we have done good things, we will receive good payment in return. Living a holy and a righteous life is all-important. The popular idea that we can lead someone in a prayer to receive Christ, and then walk away from them, is a false one. That would be like having a baby and then putting it out in the woods to try to grow up.

We need to help a new Christian to grow up into righteousness. It takes about three minutes to help somebody become born again. But then it takes about three years to help that baby Christian grow up in Christ. If you lead someone to Christ, you then have a responsibility to nourish that baby Christian until he or she has grown up and understands deeper things of the Lord.

Returning specifically to the judgment seat of Christ, we find more details about this in Paul's first letter to the Corinthians:

10 According to the grace of God which was given to me, as a wise master builder I laid a foundation, and another is building upon it. But let each man be careful how he builds upon it.
11 For no man can lay a foundation other than the one which is laid, which is Jesus Christ.
12 Now if any man builds upon the foundation with gold, silver, precious stones, wood, hay, straw,
13 each man's work will become evident; for the day will show it, because it is to be revealed with fire; and the fire itself will test the quality of each man's work.
14 If any man's work which he has built upon it remains, he shall receive a reward.
15 If any man's work is burned up, he shall

suffer loss; but he himself shall be saved, yet so as through fire.

--1 Corinthians 3

In the passage of Scripture above, we see that when we become Christians, Jesus Christ is our foundation and the foundation is empty. After we have received Christ as our Savior, we each build our own building on the precious foundation of Jesus Christ. Verse 13 tells us that it is our "work" that determines what we build on that foundation.

When we stand before the judgment seat of Christ, He is going to apply fire to the building that we have built on His foundation. The good things that we have done, represented by gold and silver, will not be burned up, but will remain, and verse 14 tells us that we will receive a reward for those things. However, the bad things that we have done, or even the neutral things (wasting time), will be burned up and we will "suffer loss." We do not know what that loss or negative payment will be, but I assure you that it is something that we will not want.

In verse 15 of 1 Corinthians 3, we see that if the work that a man has built upon the foundation of Christ is totally burned up, he will be saved "yet so as through fire." In other words, he will be saved, but it will be equivalent to him going through fire. That is not something that we would like at all.

Christ yearns that each Christian build on His precious foundation a valuable building composed of good works. If you are not interested in good works now, believe me, you will be when you stand before the judgment seat of Christ. I would encourage you really to pray about this and to ask God to help you emphasize good works, holiness, and righteousness in your personal life.

Jesus Himself, in no uncertain terms, told you what He was going to judge you on. He said that He was going to pay back (recompense) every man according to his deeds:

27 "For the Son of Man is going to come in the glory of His Father with His angels; and WILL THEN RECOMPENSE EVERY MAN ACCORDING TO HIS DEEDS. . . ."

--Matthew 16

We need to be highly concerned about our deeds. Would your neighbors classify you as a man or woman of good works and good deeds? Not all Christians would be classified that way by their neighbors. Are you concerned for the victims when a natural disaster hits? Are you concerned for the survivors of the families of those who are killed when war breaks out? Are you concerned for the family down the road (whom you do not know) who just lost everything when their house burned down? Are you concerned for the poor and the needy in your community? Are you eager to take the gospel of the kingdom to everyone in your community and to help others take it places where you can not go? Many evangelicals and charismatics are eager to share the gospel, but are really not very concerned about their deeds or their good works.

I gave the following illustration in one of my other books, but it bears repeating here. A number of years ago there was a professor at Dallas Theological Seminary who was also pastor of a church in the suburbs of Dallas. There was a Methodist preacher right down the street and this good pastor had disdain toward the Methodist preacher, because he wasn't really preaching "the gospel."

Then one afternoon there was a tornado alert there in Dallas. Our good evangelical pastor shut down the church office and rushed home to take care of his family. A few days later he found out that while he was home hiding under the kitchen table, the Methodist pastor was calling his parishioners and telling them to bring canned food and clothing to the church so they could distribute it to the victims of the tornado.

This evangelical pastor confessed that God really clobbered him about his lack of concern for other people's needs.

Let me ask you a question. Assuming that both of these men knew Christ as their Savior, when each of them stands before the judgment seat of Christ, which one's works do you think will be gold and silver, in this specific instance? I believe it will be the deeds of the Methodist preacher.

The judgment seat of Christ is no light thing. Christ had this to say about it:

35 "Be dressed in readiness, and keep your lamps alight.
36 "And be like men who are waiting for their master when he returns from the wedding feast, so that they may immediately open the door to him when he comes and knocks.
37 "Blessed are those slaves whom the master shall find on the alert when he comes; truly I say to you, that he will gird himself to serve, and have them recline at the table, and will come up and wait on them.
38 "Whether he comes in the second watch, or even in the third, and finds them so, blessed are those slaves.
39 "And be sure of this, that if the head of the house had known at what hour the thief was coming, he would not have allowed his house to be broken into.
40 "You too, be ready; for the Son of Man is coming at an hour that you do not expect."
41 And Peter said, "Lord, are You addressing this parable to us, or to everyone else as well?"
42 And the Lord said, "Who then is the faithful and sensible steward, whom his master will put in charge of his servants, to give them their rations at the proper time?
43 "Blessed is that slave whom his master finds so doing when he comes.
44 "Truly I say to you, that he will put him in

charge of all his possessions.
45 "But if that slave says in his heart, 'My master will be a long time in coming,' and begins to beat the slaves, both men and women, and to eat and drink and get drunk;
46 the master of that slave will come on a day when he does not expect him, and at an hour he does not know, and will cut him in pieces, and assign him a place with the unbelievers.
47 "And that slave who knew his master's will and did not get ready or act in accord with his will, shall receive many lashes,
48 but the one who did not know it, and committed deeds worthy of a flogging, will receive but a few. And from everyone who has been given much shall much be required; and to whom they entrusted much, of him they will ask all the more. . . ."

--Luke 12

Verse 40 makes it obvious that this is talking about what happens right after Christ comes back. But did you notice verse 46? This parable about the slaves of the master who returns unexpectedly is a depiction of what things will be like when Christ, our Master, returns. If a Christian is not truly following Christ, it says that Christ will "assign him a place with the unbelievers." (We are not sure, but the assignment is probably for the duration of the millennium.) That is very strong and we certainly would not want to be found in that category, so it behooves us to be ready for the Lord's return and to be doing the Father's will.

Do you see what we are trying to say? Now look forward to this next year. You can determine what kind of deeds you are going to do during the next twelve months. Forgetting what lies behind and looking toward what lies ahead, let's press on to full maturity and even perfection in the Lord. May all of your deeds and mine this next year be glorifying to God and to Christ.

May they be gold, silver, and precious stones, built upon the foundation of Jesus.

The Lord encourages us to live the Christian life just one day at a time. One thing that I have found helpful is to ask the Lord, at the end of every day, what I have done that day that He would consider to be building with gold, silver, and precious stones. After He shows me, I ask Him to show me what I have done that day that is wood, hay, and straw. I ask Him to show me the careless words I have spoken and the times when I was not glorifying Him. After He shows me and I repent of those things, I pray earnestly not to be guilty of doing those things during the next day. By taking it a day at a time, the task of building something beautiful on the foundation of Jesus Christ becomes much more attainable.

It is going to be awesome when we stand before the judgment seat of Christ. His eyes will pierce into each man's heart. He will be loving, and yet very firm, because the Bible tells us that He will rule the nations with a rod of iron.

--Omega Publications, p. 235-241

DOING GOOD WORKS

Doing good works is very important, as we have already seen. In fact this is one of the significant reasons the Scriptures were given to us:

> **16 All Scripture is given by inspiration of God, and is profitable for doctrine, for reproof, for correction, for instruction in righteousness:**
> --2 Timothy 3, KJV

We quoted this verse earlier, in Chapter 5. It says that all Scripture is profitable for one of four things. To refresh your memory, let me relist those four things as we redefined them earlier. All Scripture is profitable for one of these four things:

1. Something to believe (doctrine)
2. Something to stop doing (reproof)
3. Something to do better (correction)
4. Something to start doing (instruction in righteousness)

However, verse 16 of 2 Timothy 3 ends with a colon. We need to go on and see what the last half of that sentence says:

> 17 that the man of God may be adequate, equipped for every good work.
>
> --2 Timothy 3

So the reason for the Scriptures is so that you and I will be equipped for good works. There are numerous verses that speak of equipping us for good works. Here is another one:

> 21 Therefore, if a man cleanses himself from these things, he will be a vessel for honor, sanctified, useful to the Master, prepared for every good work.
>
> --2 Timothy 2

We see here that part of the purpose of sanctification and purification is so that we can do good works. If it appears that I am trying to stimulate you to do good works (good deeds), you are absolutely right. But that is a biblical principle:

> 23 Let us hold fast the confession of our hope without wavering, for He who promised is faithful;
> 24 and let us consider how to stimulate one another to love and good deeds, . . .
>
> --Hebrews 10

We should not only do good works, but we should stimulate and encourage one another to do good works (particularly those in our own church or fellowship). In fact, for this very purpose we were created in Christ Jesus:

10 For we are His workmanship, created in Christ Jesus for good works, which God prepared beforehand, that we should walk in them.
--Ephesians 2

WHAT ARE GOOD WORKS?

In the passage we read out of Matthew 25 (verses 31-40) near the beginning of this chapter, Jesus gave us a very good definition of good works. In talking about the judgment seat of Christ, He said that the good works that we will be judged on are things such as:

1. Feeding the hungry
2. Giving a drink to the thirsty
3. Inviting a stranger in
4. Clothing the naked
5. Visiting the sick
6. Visiting those in prison

Every Christian should ask himself the question, "Do I have a real heart for good works?" What do we do when we hear about children starving in another country? Is our heart moved so that we earnestly pray that God will send them food and they will not starve? Do we pray for those people who are raising funds to buy food for those children? Do we pray for the Christians who are among those who are starving to death? Do we ask God if there is anything He wants us to do? If your answer to all of those questions is "yes," then you indeed have a heart for good works.

What is our heart's response when we read of a large area being flooded, leaving thousands homeless? Do we fall on our face before God and pray that those people might find shelter for the night? Do we pray that the children would be comforted and not frightened in their new surroundings? Do we pray for the Christians who have lost their homes and maybe even their churches? Do we pray that they would have adequate food, medical supplies and fresh water to drink?

By and large, Christians have gotten hardened to the tragedies and human needs around us. When one of these things comes to our attention (I believe it is likely God calling it to our attention), He wants us to do something, even if it is just to pray.

Turning from national and international emergencies to your own community, is there a hospital in your community? If so, do you think there are lonely people there, perhaps elderly, who have no one to visit them during visiting hours? Do you think they would appreciate you coming and reading a chapter out of the Bible to them and praying with them (and, if they are open, presenting the gospel to them)?

Is there a jail in your community? When I was first a Christian I went down to the jail in Dallas and preached there one Sunday each month. There were numbers of men who came to know Christ during those services. One was a convicted murderer. After he received Christ, I met with him weekly for Bible study and to encourage him spiritually. When he finally received his sentence, it was death in the electric chair, which was ultimately carried out. His cell mates really teased him about how it felt to have a death sentence. He turned this into an opportunity to witness for Jesus. He told them that they would just throw the switch and he would immediately be in the presence of his Savior. He then asked them how they would feel if they were going to die in an electric chair. Would they be ready to meet God and Jesus Christ?

Are there people like this in the jails in your city who need visiting? Are there hungry and poor who need to be remembered with a basket of food, other than on Christmas and Thanksgiving?

Oh God, give us a heart for good works like Jesus had! When He saw the hungry, His heart went out with love and compassion and He fed them. When He saw the sick, He healed them. When He saw those possessed by demons, His heart went out to them in their horrible bondage and He cast the demons out of them.

You cannot do anything about what you did or did not do yesterday and before that. However, you can do a great deal about tomorrow forward. When you stand before the judgment seat of Christ and He puts His holy fire to your works, what will happen? If from now on you ask God to give you a heart for good works and a sensitivity for the needs of people, He will do it. Then, at least your works during the remainder of this age will not be burned up when they are judged, and Jesus will be well pleased. Did you know that if you do this, you will be a shining light:

> **16 "Let your light shine before men in such a way that they may see your good works, and glorify your Father who is in heaven. . . ."**
>
> --Matthew 5

One thing we must be very careful to do is to be sure that God gets the glory for all of our good works. We can never take credit for our works and our deeds, nor can we be proud of them. We are servants (bondslaves) of God, doing what He tells us to do. There is no such thing as a proud slave. Our good works are a result of Christ living in us, so He and Father God must get all of the glory and praise.

DOING GOD'S WILL

What this chapter on works is really talking about is doing God's will, or what you might call "obedience." Christ was perfectly obedient to the Father and came only to do His will:

> **30 "I can do nothing on My own initiative. As I hear, I judge; and My judgment is just, because I do not seek My own will, but the will of Him who sent Me. . . ."**
>
> --John 5

Since God loves the world and has compassion on the people in the world, if we are going to do His will, like Jesus did, then we too will do good works. Do you want to be a brother or sister of Christ?

34 And looking about on those who were sitting around Him, He said, "Behold, My mother and My brothers!
35 "For whoever does the will of God, he is My brother and sister and mother."

--Mark 3

If we want that close love relationship with Jesus, that close family relationship, then we will do the will of God, which certainly includes doing good works.

WORKS VERSUS RIGHTEOUSNESS

You might ask what the difference is between "doing good works" and "righteousness." That is a question that I had in my own mind for a long time, and I do not have a perfect answer for it. However, I will pass on to you what the Lord has shown me, as I have prayed about it.

As we saw in Chapter 8, righteousness involves doing the right thing by God and by those whom He brings across your path. If you are a judge (even you as a brother or sister judging between two other Christians), then you do the right thing by those who are brought to you. Being righteous means that you do the right thing by your neighbor, your employer, your family, and all those with whom you come into contact.

In righteousness you minister to those who come to you. In doing good works, on the other hand, you go out (under the guidance of the Holy Spirit) and look for people to minister to. You go out "above and beyond the call of duty." You go to a hospital and walk the halls, looking for lonely people who would like to have you read the Bible to them and pray with them. You go to the jails looking for those who would like to truly repent and change the direction of their lives, but who do not have the power. You can give them that power, as you introduce them to Jesus Christ.

Remember, the Pharisees were fairly righteous individuals who kept the Old Testament law, but Christ said that our righteousness has to exceed theirs, if we are going to enter the kingdom of God. I believe that this means we have to go beyond righteousness (dealing justly with those who happen to be involved in our lives) to good works (actively and prayerfully reaching out to help people in need).

The good Samaritan was a truly righteous man who did good works. He stands in golden contrast to the Levite (priest) who was self-righteous and refused to do good works, even when the opportunity presented itself:

> 30 Jesus replied and said, "A certain man was going down from Jerusalem to Jericho; and he fell among robbers, and they stripped him and beat him, and went off leaving him half dead.
>
> 31 "And by chance a certain priest was going down on that road, and when he saw him, he passed by on the other side.
>
> 32 "And likewise a Levite also, when he came to the place and saw him, passed by on the other side.
>
> 33 "But a certain Samaritan, who was on a journey, came upon him; and when he saw him, he felt compassion,
>
> 34 and came to him, and bandaged up his wounds, pouring oil and wine on them; and he put him on his own beast, and brought him to an inn, and took care of him.
>
> 35 "And on the next day he took out two denarii and gave them to the innkeeper and said, 'Take care of him; and whatever more you spend, when I return, I will repay you.'
>
> 36 "Which of these three do you think proved to be a neighbor to the man who fell into the robbers' hands?"
>
> 37 And he said, "The one who showed mercy toward him." And Jesus said to him, "Go and do the same."
>
> --Luke 10

The good Samaritan was moved by compassion and showed mercy, which are characteristics of a righteous man. His righteousness caused him to do the "good works" of binding up the victim's wounds and caring for him.

SUMMARY AND CONCLUSION

We have seen that good works mean nothing before one becomes a Christian. They cannot contribute one iota to our salvation. However, after one becomes a Christian, good works become extremely important. They are one of the major things on which we will be judged when we stand before the judgment seat of Christ.

When we become Christians, everything old and bad is wiped away and we are given the golden foundation of Jesus Christ. At that point in time, we are all created equal. However, each of us builds on that foundation of Jesus Christ with our works (our deeds). Some of us are building junky shacks, and others of us are building golden mansions. At the judgment seat of Christ, Jesus Christ is going to put His holy fire to the house that you and I are building on His foundation. If it remains, we are going to be well rewarded. If it is burned, we will be saved (if we are Christians), though "as through fire."

We need to ask God to give us a tender, loving heart, sensitive to the human needs around us. We need to ask Him to help us to be careful to visit the sick and imprisoned and to be sensitive to the hunger, clothing and shelter needs of those in our community, in our nation and around the world. As we love God with all of our hearts and our neighbor as ourselves, this will happen.

We were created to do good works and we can use the inspired Scriptures to help equip ourselves for those good works. In looking at Christ's example, His good works seemed to flow out naturally from a heart of compassion and love for all people. We can pray that God will give us a heart of compassion, like Jesus had, so that we will be concerned about both the spiritual well-being and the physical needs of people in the world around us, just like Jesus was.

11
FILLED WITH POWER

Everything we have discussed in this book up to now I believe is available to all Christians. However, we are now going to move into some areas of becoming like Christ which require even more supernatural power. I believe God wants all Christians to walk in supernatural power, but something is required on our part for God to be able to entrust us with such power. Christ's healing, casting out of demons, calming the sea and multiplying of food were supernatural acts that could not be achieved with just natural human power.

As we become like Jesus Christ, we too should be able to be used of God to heal, to cast out demons and to do other supernatural acts. Before we get into these areas of ministry in particular, we need to look at how one acquires this supernatural power. This takes us directly to examining a Christian's relationship with the Holy Spirit.

THE TASK OF THE HOLY SPIRIT

There is much confusion in Christian circles today about the Holy Spirit and supernatural power. If you will forgive me, I would like to start at the very beginning and examine the Holy Spirit from ground zero, just to be certain we are all together. We need to look at Who He is, our relationship to Him, and what He does in and through us. Let us first look at the task of the Holy Spirit.

As a prophet, teacher and speaker at conferences, it has always been very difficult for me to give a message on the Holy Spirit. The reason is that the Holy Spirit's task is to glorify Jesus Christ. It is difficult to preach about the Holy Spirit without glorifying the Holy Spirit. Yet if someone gives a message on the Holy Spirit that glorifies the Spirit, it is not of the Spirit; if it were, it would glorify Jesus Christ instead. This is clearly spelled out in John 16:

> **13 "But when He, the Spirit of truth, comes, He will guide you into all the truth; for He will not speak on His own initiative, but whatever He hears, He will speak; and He will disclose to you what is to come.**
> **14 "He shall glorify Me; for He shall take of Mine and shall disclose it to you. . . ."**

I have been to charismatic meetings where the people were so concerned about the gifts of the Spirit, that the Holy Spirit was all they talked about and, I believe, the only One they glorified. The name of Jesus was rarely mentioned. I do not believe a meeting of this type is of the Spirit of God.

Thus, it is my prayer and desire that this chapter, even though speaking about the Holy Spirit and His gifts, be uplifting to our Lord and Savior, Jesus Christ.

WHO OR WHAT IS THE HOLY SPIRIT?

I hate to begin on such an elementary level, but some people think that the Holy Spirit is an "influence, a feeling or a rosy glow." Not so. He is an individual--a person, just like God the Father and Jesus Christ. In fact, Jesus equated the Holy Spirit to Himself:

> **16 "And I will ask the Father, and He will give you another Helper, that He may abide with you forever;**
> **17 that is the Spirit of truth, whom the world**

cannot receive, because it does not behold Him or know Him, but you know Him, because He abides with you, and will be in you. . . ."

--John 14

The word used in verse 16 for "another" means "identical to" or "just like." Literally Christ was saying that when He went away, He would give us someone just like Himself who would be with us forever. We see later in that chapter (verse 26) that the Holy Spirit will teach us all things and bring to our remembrance the things that Christ said. John 16:13 says that the Spirit will guide us.

According to psychologists, to be a "person" one has to have three things:

1. Knowledge
2. Will
3. Feelings

The Scriptures attribute all of these things to the Holy Spirit. Verse 11 of 1 Corinthians 12 tells us that the Holy Spirit gives gifts to Christians **as He wills.** Thus, we know that He has a will. In 1 Corinthians 2:11, we see that only the Holy Spirit knows the thoughts of God. We know from Ephesians 4:30 that we can grieve the Holy Spirit and Romans 15:30 tells us that the Holy Spirit has love. It is apparent that He has feelings, as well as knowledge and a will.

So in every aspect, the Holy Spirit is a person. He is a person without a body. This is why in the earlier days He was called the Holy Ghost: in those days, "ghost" was the term people used for a personality, or a being, without a body. Today "ghost" is reserved for haunted houses and we use the term "spirit" for a person without a body. The Holy Spirit is not limited to being in one place at one time, as Jesus Christ was while He was on earth. In this respect, He is like God the Father; He can be everywhere at once (omnipresent). This beautiful person, the Holy Spirit, Who loves us and cares for us, yearns to teach us about Jesus and to help us become like Him!

OUR BASIC RELATIONSHIP TO THE HOLY SPIRIT

There are three relationships that we have with the Holy Spirit at the time of salvation. They simply occur, whether we want them or not. When we receive Christ as Savior and Lord, we are:

1. Born of the Spirit
2. Sealed of the Spirit
3. Indwelt by the Spirit

We know from the Gospel of John that we must be born of the Holy Spirit, or we cannot enter or even see the kingdom of God.

> 3 Jesus answered and said to him, "Truly, truly, I say to you, unless one is born again, he cannot see the kingdom of God."
> 4 Nicodemus said to Him, "How can a man be born when he is old? He cannot enter a second time into his mother's womb and be born, can he?"
> 5 Jesus answered, "Truly, truly, I say to you, unless one is born of water and the Spirit, he cannot enter into the kingdom of God.
> 6 "That which is born of the flesh is flesh, and that which is born of the Spirit is spirit...."
> --John 3

We see from this passage that when we ask Christ to become our Savior and we are born again, then we are really born of the Spirit.

We are also sealed by the Holy Spirit. There are various types of "sealing." The one that pertains here is like placing a government seal on a document. It is a guarantee-type seal:

> 13 In Him, you also, after listening to the message of truth, the gospel of your salvation--have also believed, you were sealed in Him with the Holy Spirit of promise, . . .
> --Ephesians 1

The third relationship we have with the Holy Spirit is that He comes to dwell within us. This indwelling happens at the time we receive Christ as our personal Savior. If you do not have the Holy Spirit, you do not have a relationship with Jesus Christ, you are not "born again" and, according to the Bible, you are not a son of God.

> 9 However you are not in the flesh but in the Spirit, if indeed the Spirit of God dwells in you. But if anyone does not have the Spirit of Christ, he does not belong to Him.
> 10 And if Christ is in you, though the body is dead because of sin, yet the spirit is alive because of righteousness.
> 11 But if the Spirit of Him who raised Jesus from the dead dwells in you, He who raised Christ Jesus from the dead will also give life to your mortal bodies through His Spirit who indwells you.
> 12 So then, brethren, we are under obligation, not to the flesh, to live according to the flesh--
> 13 for if you are living according to the flesh, you must die; but if by the Spirit you are putting to death the deeds of the body, you will live.
> 14 For all who are being led by the Spirit of God, these are the sons of God.
>
> --Romans 8

In verse 9 we see that if you do not have the Spirit of God dwelling within you, you do not belong to Jesus. Our relationship with the Holy Spirit is one that grows and progresses throughout our Christian lives. One might think that once the Holy Spirit comes to live inside of us, that is all there is. This isn't true; there is more, as we will see in looking at the first apostles.

There is some question as to when the apostles were actually born again. It certainly had to occur after Christ's death and resurrection. After discussing this with many of my dear brothers in Christ, I believe that the apostles' conversion is recorded in John 20:

21 Jesus therefore said to them again, "Peace be with you; as the Father has sent Me, I also send you."

22 And when He had said this, He breathed on them, and said to them, "Receive the Holy Spirit.

23 "If you forgive the sins of any, their sins have been forgiven them; if you retain the sins of any, they have been retained."

At this point in time, the apostles had believed on Jesus Christ as the Son of God and had accepted His resurrection. In these verses, they received the Holy Spirit. (If Jesus commands, "Receive the Holy Spirit," believe me--you receive the Holy Spirit.) In verse 23, Jesus also gave them some measure of spiritual authority. You might think that this was all that they needed, but evidently not; there was more to come, as we will see in a moment.

Many Christians today are living in this realm. They know Christ as their Savior and have the Holy Spirit dwelling inside of them, but they lack evidence of supernatural power.

These first three relationships with the Holy Spirit (born, sealed and indwelt) happen at the time of our salvation. However, there is a fourth relationship with the Holy Spirit that depends on us. Some Christians have this fourth relationship and some do not. However, it is this fourth relationship that is essential if we are to have the supernatural power that God wants us to have.

BEING FILLED WITH THE HOLY SPIRIT

As we have already seen, the disciples received the Holy Spirit in John 20; He came to dwell within them at that point. Yet Jesus later told these same disciples that they needed something in addition to the indwelling of the Holy Spirit:

4 And gathering them together, He commanded them not to leave Jerusalem, but to wait for what the Father had promised, "Which," He

> said, "you heard of from Me;
> 5 for John baptized with water, but you shall be baptized with the Holy Spirit not many days from now." . . .
>
> 8 but you shall receive power when the Holy Spirit has come upon you; and you shall be My witnesses both in Jerusalem, and in all Judea and Samaria, and even to the remotest part of the earth."
>
> --Acts 1

In the verses above, Jesus told the apostles that they needed power and that they would receive this power when the Holy Spirit came upon them, when they were baptized with the Holy Spirit. The fulfillment of this is recorded in the next chapter of Acts:

> 2 And suddenly there came from heaven a noise like a violent, rushing wind, and it filled the whole house where they were sitting.
> 3 And there appeared to them tongues as of fire distributing themselves, and they rested on each one of them.
> 4 And they were all filled with the Holy Spirit and began to speak with other tongues, as the Spirit was giving them utterance.
>
> --Acts 2

We see that these Christians were filled with the Holy Spirit, they received power, and they demonstrated supernatural gifts (speaking in other known but unlearned languages). As we read in Acts 1:5, Christ told the disciples that they would soon be baptized with the Holy Spirit, and this is the fulfillment of that prophecy. Later on in the Book of Acts, many of these same disciples were "filled with the Holy Spirit" on numerous occasions. I use the term "baptized with the Spirit" to refer to the first filling of the Holy Spirit.

Some Christians are strongly against using the term "baptized in the Spirit." I prefer to use the same terms that the Bible uses and I cannot get away from the fact that this is a very biblical term. For example, it is clearly stated that Christ would baptize us with the Holy Spirit:

> **11 "As for me, I baptize you with water for repentance, but He who is coming after me is mightier than I, and I am not fit to remove His sandals; He will baptize you with the Holy Spirit and fire. . . ."**
>
> --Matthew 3

The above Scripture is what John the Baptist had to say about Jesus. As we read earlier in Acts 1:4-5, Jesus Himself told the disciples that they would be "baptized with the Holy Spirit not many days from now."

Since one of the tasks of Jesus was to baptize us with the Holy Spirit, this is why I use that term. But, as I said, I use it to refer to the first infilling of the Holy Spirit.

I was raised as a Methodist and tended to discount (discard is probably a better word) anything concerning being baptized with the Holy Spirit. We thought that those who taught such a thing were trying to say that we needed a "second blessing" and, hence, we tended to look down our noses at them. However, now that I have grown in the Lord, I have discovered that the Bible states clearly that there is indeed a "second blessing." There is something beyond salvation that God wants to give to us and that is the baptism in the Holy Spirit. Let's read further about this:

> **14 Now when the apostles in Jerusalem heard that Samaria had received the word of God, they sent them Peter and John,**
>
> **15 who came down and prayed for them, that they might receive the Holy Spirit.**
>
> **16 For He had not yet fallen upon any of them; they had simply been baptized in the name of the Lord Jesus.**
>
> **17 Then they began laying their hands on them, and they were receiving the Holy Spirit.**
>
> --Acts 8

These verses tell us that people in Samaria had received Jesus Christ and had been baptized in the name of the Lord Jesus. Evidently, though, there was something they still lacked. For this reason, the disciples in Jerusalem sent Peter and John all the way up to Samaria to help them get this thing that they lacked, even though they indeed had believed in Christ.

From Jerusalem to Samaria is very rugged terrain. The journey by foot was long and hard, and it must have taken Peter and John at least a couple of days. Yet they were willing to walk all that distance and risk the dangers of the rugged countryside in order that the believers in Christ in Samaria might receive the baptism of the Holy Spirit. That is how important it was to Peter and John, and they should have known the importance, because they walked and talked and lived with Jesus Christ.

When Peter and John got to Samaria, they prayed for the Christians there and those Christians received the baptism of the Holy Spirit. I believe it is as important for Christians today to be baptized in the Holy Spirit as it was in this incident when Peter and John went to Samaria. Unfortunately, there has been much confusion on the baptism of the Holy Spirit; perhaps I can clear up some of it, as I share with you the things that God has laid on my heart concerning it.

HOW TO BE BAPTIZED IN THE HOLY SPIRIT

The first question that arises is: "How does a Christian know whether or not he has been baptized in the Holy Spirit?" I believe that when a Christian is baptized in the Holy Spirit, something supernatural (unexplainable in human terms) happens to him or through him. The supernatural thing might be seeing a vision; it might be praying for someone and that person is healed; it might be prophesying, singing in the Spirit, performing a miracle, speaking in tongues or something else. I do not believe that it has to be speaking in tongues, although that is the most common manifestation of the baptism of the Holy Spirit.

The Holy Spirit will give each person whatever gift He wants him to have (1 Corinthians 12:1-11), but it will be something miraculous that can't be explained in human terms. If you have never had something supernatural happen to you or through you, there is a good chance that you have not yet been baptized in the Holy Spirit. (Actually I prefer the expression "filled with the Holy Spirit," but "baptized in the Holy Spirit" is more commonly used.)

If you think you might have been baptized in the Holy Spirit but are unsure, I would encourage you to ask God to give you afresh a supernatural confirmation of your baptism in the Holy Spirit.

It would be hard for someone to forget being baptized in water. Being baptized in the Holy Spirit should be an even more memorable event because of supernatural manifestations. Satan is the one who tries to bring doubt and confusion about this.

If you are a Christian and you know that you have not been baptized in the Holy Spirit (you have accepted Jesus Christ as your Lord and Savior and would like the power of God's Spirit operating in your life), the logical question is, how do you receive this? There is much confusion on the subject, which there need not be.

I would like to relate something that happened to me one time when I was ministering at a church in Minnesota. Rarely do I feel impressed of the Holy Spirit, at the end of a message, to give a "come forward" invitation. Even more rarely do I ask for those who want to be baptized in the Holy Spirit to come forward. But on this one particular Sunday, I felt the Lord wanted me to do this. So I asked any of those who would like to receive the baptism of the Holy Spirit to come forward. The pastor suggested that they go into a back room, which they did. I stayed out front and counseled and prayed with a few people and about ten minutes later I went back and joined them in this room.

What I saw there really grieved my spirit. The brother who was trying to help these people receive the baptism of the Spirit was telling them to drop their jaws, to hold up their hands, not to say anything in English, to make sounds and so forth. I thought, "Oh my! There is no way they are going to receive the baptism of the Holy Spirit this way!" So I asked the brother if I could say something. (Since I was the visiting minister, he just about had to say "yes.")

I related to these precious brothers and sisters how I had initially received the baptism of the Holy Spirit. It had occurred a number of years earlier, when I was flying from Houston to Dallas. That particular plane had a compartment up front with eight seats that was totally isolated from the rest of the cabin. I was the only one in this front compartment and I began to pray, as I frequently do on a flight. As I talked to God, I began to tell Him how wonderful, glorious, magnificent and all-powerful He was and to thank Him that He was so holy, pure and righteous. Pretty soon my human words seemed too inadequate to express what I was feeling toward God. I then began what I call "spiritual humming." (I have only heard one other Christian do this since then.) As the pitch of my hum went up, it seemed like it touched God and as the pitch of my hum came down, it was as though it touched my heart. I sat there humming from high notes to low notes, to high notes to low notes, communing with God, praising Him, worshiping Him, and adoring Him in a way that was above and beyond what I could do in English words.

After sharing this experience, I encouraged the people to get their minds off the gifts of the Spirit or speaking in tongues and just to begin to worship and praise God. I told them that when English became totally inadequate to express their adoration, God would take over beyond that.

That evening several of these people came up to me stating that they had received the baptism of the Holy Spirit during the afternoon between the morning and the evening services. I particularly remember one young man who came up to me with tears in his eyes. He said that for eight years he had been seeking the baptism of the Holy Spirit and that every time an invitation was given for those who wanted to receive the baptism of the Spirit, he came forward. Evidently he had been forward literally dozens of times during this eight-year period. However, he had never received the baptism of the Holy Spirit.

With tears rolling down his cheeks, he related to me how, driving home from church that morning after I had shared what God had laid on my heart, he began to praise the Lord and, as his words became inadequate, he began to fluently speak and sing in another tongue. He said that he wanted to jump and dance all over the place and had to pull his car to the side of the road and stop, because he was afraid he would have an accident. He sat there in his car for an hour singing, praising and glorifying God. He said that he was so grateful to me for helping him to get his eyes off the gifts of the Spirit and the baptism of the Holy Spirit and to focus on God and Jesus Christ.

I might relate one other incident about a friend of mine who was a dedicated Christian but had left the church that he had been attending. His daughter started going to an Assembly of God church with a friend of hers. One Sunday morning when he picked her up after church, she had tears in her eyes and she said, "Daddy, this morning I was baptized in the Spirit and spoke in tongues." This really shook up my friend, because he did not believe that those things were for today. He went home and, after lunch, went into his bedroom alone, knelt down beside the bed and began to talk to God. He said: "God, if this is of You, I want it. I want all that you have for me." As he was praying, a glorious light came upon him and he began to praise God in heavenly singing that was not in English.

In other instances in the New Testament, being filled with the Spirit is accompanied by a manifestation of supernatural power in the saints. For example, in Acts 4:31, the believers were filled with the Holy Spirit and began to speak the word of God with boldness. In Acts 7:55-60, Stephen, being full of the Spirit, saw the glory of God and Jesus standing at the right hand of God, and he was able to glorify Christ while being stoned to death. Acts 13:9-11 tells how

Paul, filled with the Spirit, was able to discern a spirit of the devil and cause a man to become blind by his words.

In the Scriptures, we find that almost inevitably the filling with the Holy Spirit caused the individual Christians to exhibit some form of supernatural power (supernatural gift). This filling was also a freeing and exhilarating experience that caused them to praise and worship God in a new and higher way. Acts 2 records that the onlookers thought that the Christians gathered there were drunk. This must have been because they were so uninhibited, free and exuberant. This analogy to being drunk is carried further in Paul's letter to the Ephesians:

> **18 And do not get drunk with wine, for that is dissipation, but be filled with the Spirit,**
> **19 speaking to one another in psalms and hymns and spiritual songs, singing and making melody with your heart to the Lord;**
> **20 always giving thanks for all things in the name of our Lord Jesus Christ to God, even the Father;**
> **21 and be subject to one another in the fear of Christ.**
>
> **--Ephesians 5**

Verse 18 is in the imperative form: "Be filled with the Spirit." This is not a suggestion, but a command. Therefore, not to do so is sin. This filling is something that we can **choose** to allow to happen or not. It is up to us whether or not we yield ourselves to the Holy Spirit, that He might take charge of our minds and bodies in order to glorify Christ in fullness.

The main point here is that supernatural power comes when we are baptized (filled the first time) with the Holy Spirit. Believe me, we are going to need supernatural power in the turbulent days ahead. We need supernatural power to be able to heal, to cast out demons and to perform miracles like Jesus did. If you ask God for the baptism in the Holy Spirit, He will give it to you. The Bible tells us this:

> **13 "If you then, being evil, know how to give good gifts to your children, how much more shall your heavenly Father give the Holy Spirit to those who ask Him?"**
>
> **--Luke 11**

You can be baptized in the Holy Spirit, (filled with the Holy Spirit) right now, as you ask God to baptize you in His Spirit. This can happen wherever you are. God will not withhold His Holy Spirit from you. Ask and receive. ("You do not have because you do not ask"--James 4:2b). Then He will display whtever supernatural gifts He wants you to have and you will receive the power that Jesus promised, supernatural power.

YOU AIN'T SEEN NOTHIN' YET

In the Pentecostal and Charismatic movements, we have seen the gifts of the Holy Spirit restored. The primary gifts that have been exercised in those movements are the gift of tongues, the gift of interpretation, the gift of prophecy, the gift of healing, and, in addition, the casting out of demons. On very rare occasions, there have been instances of food multiplying. However, as the end of this age draws closer, some of the "power gifts" that were exercised by Old Testament prophets are going to be restored to the overcomers, to those who will walk holy and pure before their God.

We are familiar with Elijah calling down fire from heaven to consume the sacrifice, when he was pitted against the prophets of Baal (1 Kings 18:22-39). Also, 2 Kings records how he twice called down fire from heaven to consume a captain with his fifty soldiers. This ability to call down fire from heaven falls within the category of "power gifts."

Also, we see that the prophets in the Old Testament at times exercised control over nature. They would pray and it would stop raining for years and they would pray again and it would start raining. Rivers and the Red Sea would part at their God-controlled command. Water would come out of a rock or they could call down plagues from heaven.

All of these types of power gifts are going to be restored at the end of the age. I believe the two witnesses are simply examples of what the overcomers (the bondslaves of God, the holy ones of God) will be doing and of the power they will have:

> 3 "And I will grant authority to my two witnesses, and they will prophesy for twelve hundred and sixty days, clothed in sackcloth."
>
> 4 These are the two olive trees and the two lampstands that stand before the Lord of the earth.
>
> 5 And if anyone desires to harm them, fire proceeds out of their mouth and devours their enemies; and if anyone would desire to harm them, in this manner he must be killed.
>
> 6 These have the power to shut up the sky, in order that rain may not fall during the days of their prophesying; and they have power over the waters to turn them into blood, and to smite the earth with every plague, as often as they desire.
>
> --Revelation 11

Here we see that at the end of the age, these two witnesses will be able to call forth fire to devour their enemies, to shut up the sky that it might not rain, and to call down plagues upon the earth. God can only give these power gifts to those whom He can trust absolutely. If God were to give this type of power to a Christian who used it in a fleshly way for his own advantage, it would be an abomination to God.

Jesus exercised power over nature and, as we become like Him, I believe we will too (of course, under the control of the Holy Spirit):

> 41 And they became very much afraid and said to one another, "Who then is this, that even the wind and the sea obey Him?"
>
> --Mark 4

The Scriptures contain many other examples of power gifts. We will give just one more here. This is the situation mentioned earlier wherein Paul dealt with a magician:

> **8 But Elymas the magician (for thus his name is translated) was opposing them, seeking to turn the proconsul away from the faith.**
> **9 But Saul, who was also known as Paul, filled with the Holy Spirit, fixed his gaze upon him,**
> **10 and said, "You who are full of all deceit and fraud, you son of the devil, you enemy of all righteousness, will you not cease to make crooked the straight ways of the Lord?**
> **11 "And now, behold, the hand of the Lord is upon you, and you will be blind and not see the sun for a time." And immediately a mist and a darkness fell upon him, and he went about seeking those who would lead him by the hand.**
>
> --Acts 13

I believe that the end result of the new outpouring of the Holy Spirit will include these power gifts. These power gifts will be utilized to achieve God's purposes on the earth and to bring down spiritual strongholds that are set up against God. These will be the weapons of the end-time army that God is raising up.

As the call is going out to the body of Christ to begin to walk pure and holy before God, He is wanting to give you far more supernatural power than you have experienced. But He can only give it to you when He can trust you completely--when you have yielded yourself to Him just as completely.

SUMMARY AND CONCLUSION

We have seen that we have three automatic relationships with the Holy Spirit at the point in time when we receive Jesus Christ as our personal Savior. We are born of the Holy Spirit, we are sealed by the Holy

Spirit, and we are indwelt by the Holy Spirit. Thus, every Christian has the indwelling Holy Spirit. However, that does not mean that every Christian allows the Holy Spirit to control his life or that the power of the Holy Spirit can be exercised through that individual. That depends on the fourth, optional, relationship with the Holy Spirit.

This fourth relationship, being baptized or filled with the Holy Spirit, depends on our yielding ourselves to His control. There is one baptism (the first filling) but there are many fillings. (God has much that He would like to give to His children, but some things can only be given to those who are willing to yield and to receive.) It is when we are filled with the Holy Spirit that we receive supernatural power. This supernatural power can be exhibited in various ways, but something supernatural happens to us or through us when we are baptized in the Holy Spirit.

God wants you to have supernatural power, and you will certainly need it in the turbulent times that will occur as this age draws to a close. You will also need supernatural power if you are going to be like Jesus in healing, casting out demons and performing miracles. These are things for today and God wants to use you in powerful supernatural ways of which you have not even dreamt.

12
GOD CAN USE YOU TO HEAL

The fact that Jesus had a healing ministry is certainly unquestioned. In fact, in the synoptic Gospels He spent about two-thirds of His time healing people and casting demons out of them. If we want to be like Jesus, the question arises, will God also use us to heal people in the name of Christ? I believe the answer is that God will use all of us in this way, but to certain individuals He will give a special gift of healing. Before you accept or reject that conclusion, we need to take a look at healing in the Scriptures, how Jesus healed and how the disciples healed. But first let us briefly look at various types of healings.

DIVINE HEALING VERSUS OTHER HEALINGS

In addition to the type of "healing" that our medical profession in America attempts, there is spiritual healing: such as that practiced by the Christian Scientists; psychic healing, which even includes psychic surgery (which I believe is of an occult nature); and divine healing, which is accomplished by God Almighty and Jesus Christ.

Medical Healing

Concerning medical healing, it is interesting to note that 90-99 percent of all the drugs sold or prescribed have nothing to do with healing. They only treat symptoms and make the patient more comfortable, while the body heals itself. God has created our bodies to be able to heal themselves in an incredible way. Even surgery, to a large extent, can only remove something bad from the body or perhaps reconnect things, but then the body has to heal itself. If the body does not heal itself after the surgery, the patient could be in even worse shape than before.

I have nothing against the medical profession and I feel that Christians should use doctors. We do. But we need to recognize that doctors are not God (although a few doctors I have met seem to think that they are). They can only be of assistance to the body as it actually heals itself. However, doctors can be of real value in helping to bring the body into a state of relaxation or setting it into a condition that will facilitate the healing process.

Spiritual Healing

What many people call spiritual healing, might be better called mental healing. This is where the mind really takes charge of the body. The mind is a very powerful force and it can control the body to a far greater degree than most of us think possible. The mind can make us sick. Many ulcers are generated by the mind transmitting tension to the stomach. Many headaches are created by worry or stress and even paralysis can occur when the mind suffers a great shock and this is its defense mechanism in retreating from the world.

Let's take a simple illustration to help you realize how powerful the mind is. Suppose a prankster placed a rubber snake in his school teacher's desk drawer. When the teacher opens that drawer and sees the snake, her adrenaline starts flowing, her heartbeat increases substantially and other psysiological changes occur, not because there is an actual live snake there, but because her mind tells her body there is a snake there. Do you see how powerful the mind is? It controls the body. This powerful mind can be used as either a channel to cause disease or a channel to cause healing. However, we should realize that this mental (spiritual) healing can, and usually does, occur totally apart from God.

Psychic Healing

Psychic healing is very similar to spiritual (mental) healing, but it is someone else's mind that takes charge of the patient's body, rather than the patient's mind. The occult implications and connections are so great in this type of healing that I believe Christians should avoid it altogether.

Divine Healing

In divine healing, God directly intervenes and not only causes the symptoms to be removed, but also causes the individual's complete health be restored.

This healing is promised by God in the Old Testament:

> **25 "But you shall serve the LORD your God, and He will bless your bread and your water; and I will remove sickness from your midst. . . ."**
>
> --Exodus 23

It is also available to us today:

> **16 "And on the basis of faith in His name, it is the name of Jesus which has strengthened this man whom you see and know; and the faith which comes through Him has given him this perfect health in the presence of you all. . . ."**
>
> --Acts 3

It was divine healing that Jesus exercised and it is divine healing that we exercise, in the name of Jesus Christ, if we are going to be used of God to heal in the same way that God used Jesus to heal. Since it is God Who does the healing, He decides when and where and how divine healing is going to occur. It could occur with or without someone asking Him in prayer. It could happen at a Christian meeting or in a parking lot. If He has a vessel who is completely in tune with Him and obedient to Him, then He can use that vessel as a tool to go to a sick person and instigate the divine healing that God has chosen to do.

For the rest of this chapter when we talk about healing, we will be talking about "divine healing." There are so many examples of healing that we cannot take them all, but I would like to group them into categories.

HOW JESUS HEALED

There is some confusion and disarray today over healing. Some people think that all "faith healing" is quackery and others throng to healing services. Some Christians feel that we should never pray for the sick to be healed but only declare them to be healed with the authority of Christ, while others pray to the Father for healings. Some wonder why one person is healed and another is not, in basically identical situations. There are significant conflicts of belief in the area of healing.

I would like to ask you to erase the "blackboard of your mind" of any prejudices and even experiences concerning healing, and let's start afresh by seeing what the Scriptures have to say on the subject. You may even have been used by God to heal someone, but I would ask you also to come back to neutral for a moment in your thinking, because God may wish to teach you some new things in order to be able to use you in a better and more powerful way in healing.

Now that we have all set our "computers" back to zero and are starting afresh with open minds and hearts, the place to begin is to see how Jesus healed.

Healing In Response To Faith

Faith on the part of the person being healed was frequently a characteristic of Christ's healing ministry, as the following passages show:

> **27 And as Jesus passed on from there, two blind men followed Him, crying out, and saying, "Have mercy on us, Son of David!"**
> **28 And after He had come into the house, the blind men came up to Him, and Jesus said to**

them, "Do you believe that I am able to do this?" They said to Him, "Yes, Lord."
29 Then He touched their eyes, saying, "Be it done to you according to your faith."
30 And their eyes were opened. And Jesus sternly warned them, saying, "See here, let no one know about this!"

--Matthew 9

28 Then Jesus answered and said to her, "O woman, your faith is great; be it done for you as you wish." And her daughter was healed at once.

--Matthew 15

34 And He said to her, "Daughter, your faith has made you well; go in peace, and be healed of your affliction."

--Mark 5

52 And Jesus said to him, "Go your way; your faith has made you well." And immediately he regained his sight and began following Him on the road.

--Mark 10

9 This man was listening to Paul as he spoke, who, when he had fixed his gaze upon him, and had seen that he had faith to be made well,
10 said with a loud voice, "Stand upright on your feet." And he leaped up and began to walk.

--Acts 14

As you can see from this small sampling of verses above, the faith of the person being healed was very important in the healing ministry of Jesus and the early disciples. Perhaps sometimes when a well-meaning Christian takes the initiative to pray for a healing, rather than the sick person taking the initiative, the sick person does not have faith either in God or in that individual (who wants to be used to do the healing) and this is a real hindrance to him receiving his divine healing. In Christ's ministry, the sick people, or someone representing them, almost always came to Jesus and asked for healing. This coming to Him represented an exercising of faith.

I would like to take a couple of other examples wherein faith was involved in the healing, but which also exhibit other aspects of Christ's ministry. The first example is the woman touching the hem of His garment:

> 20 And behold, a woman who had been suffering from a hemorrhage for twelve years, came up behind Him and touched the fringe of His cloak;
> 21 for she was saying to herself, "If I only touch His garment, I shall get well."
> 22 But Jesus turning and seeing her said, "Daughter, take courage; your faith has made you well." And at once the woman was made well.
> --Matthew 9

Here we see that this lady, exercising great faith, simply touched the garment of Jesus, and He told her that her faith had made her well. This evidently happened frequently in His ministry:

> 56 And whenever He entered villages, or cities, or countryside, they were laying the sick in the marketplaces, and entreating Him that they might just touch the fringe of His cloak; and as many as touched it were being cured.
> --Mark 6

This act of touching a cloth rather than the one God was using to do the healing is also found in the ministry of Paul:

> 11 And God was performing extraordinary miracles by the hands of Paul,
> 12 so that handkerchiefs or aprons were even carried from his body to the sick, and the diseases left them and the evil spirits went out.
> --Acts 19

I used to make fun of the idea of someone sending out a "healing cloth," but I now must admit that it has a biblical precedent and evidently God does use it at times, possibly to instill or increase faith in the sick individual.

In several cases the sick people had to show their faith by their actions in order to be healed. One of these situations was with some lepers who were being healed as they obeyed Jesus--as they were going to the priests they were cleansed:

> 12 And as He entered a certain village, ten leprous men who stood at a distance met Him;
> 13 and they raised their voices, saying, "Jesus, Master, have mercy on us!"
> 14 And when He saw them, He said to them, "Go and show yourselves to the priests." And it came about that as they were going, they were cleansed.
>
> --Luke 17

Another example in which faith was a significant factor involved the faith of another individual, rather than that of the sick person himself:

> 5 And when He had entered Capernaum, a centurion came to Him, entreating Him,
> 6 and saying, "Lord, my servant is lying paralyzed at home, suffering great pain."
> 7 And He said to him, "I will come and heal him."
> 8 But the centurion answered and said, "Lord, I am not worthy for You to come under my roof, but just say the word, and my servant will be healed.
> 9 "For I, too, am a man under authority, with soldiers under me; and I say to this one, 'Go!' and he goes, and to another, 'Come!' and he comes, and to my slave, 'Do this!' and he does it."
> 10 Now when Jesus heard this, He marveled, and said to those who were following, "Truly I

say to you, I have not found such great faith with anyone in Israel.
11 "And I say to you, that many shall come from east and west, and recline at the table with Abraham, and Isaac, and Jacob, in the kingdom of heaven;
12 but the sons of the kingdom shall be cast out into the outer darkness; in that place there shall be weeping and gnashing of teeth."
13 And Jesus said to the centurion, "Go your way; let it be done to you as you have believed." And the servant was healed that very hour.
--Matthew 8

Some healing ministries have people stand "in proxy" for a sick person. Looking at this example from Matthew 8, we could conclude that this practice is biblical. However, also according to the example we just read, one of the keys would be that the person standing in proxy would have the faith that the sick person will be healed. Even Jesus was limited in His healing ministry when people had lack of faith (unbelief.) He healed only a "few" of the ones who were sick in His home town:

5 And He could do no miracle there except that He laid His hands upon a few sick people and healed them.
6 And He wondered at their unbelief.
--Mark 6

Healing After The Sin Problem Is Eliminated

Evidently, sometimes a particular sin problem was a hindrance even in the healing ministry of Christ. The sin problem had to be dealt with first before the healing could occur:

2 And many were gathered together, so that there was no longer room, even near the door; and He was speaking the word to them.
3 And they came, bringing to Him a paraly-

tic, carried by four men.
4 And being unable to get to Him because of the crowd, they removed the roof above Him; and when they had dug an opening, they let down the pallet on which the paralytic was lying.
5 And Jesus seeing their faith said to the paralytic, "My son, yours sins are forgiven."
6 But there were some of the scribes sitting there and reasoning in their hearts,
7 "Why does this man speak that way? He is blaspheming; who can forgive sins but God alone?"
8 And immediately Jesus, aware in His spirit that they were reasoning that way within themselves, said to them, "Why are you reasoning about these things in your hearts?
9 "Which is easier, to say to the paralytic, 'Your sins are forgiven'; or to say, 'Arise, and take up your pallet and walk'?
10 "But in order that you may know that the Son of Man has authority on earth to forgive sins"--He said to the paralytic--
11 "I say to you, rise, take up your pallet and go home."
12 And he rose and immediately took up the pallet and went out in the sight of all; so that they were all amazed and were glorifying God, saying, "We have never seen anything like this."
--Mark 2

You notice in this passage that his sins were forgiven first and then the healing took place. In the situation with the man at the pool of Bethesda, we see a caution from Jesus not to sin anymore:

2 Now there is in Jerusalem by the sheep gate a pool, which is called in Hebrew Bethesda, having five porticoes.
3 In these lay a multitude of those who were sick, blind, lame, and withered, waiting for the moving of the waters;
4 for an angel of the Lord went down at certain seasons into the pool, and stirred up the

water; whoever then first, after the stirring up of the water, stepped in was made well from whatever disease with which he was afflicted.

5 And a certain man was there, who had been thirty-eight years in his sickness.

6 When Jesus saw him lying there, and knew that he had already been a long time in that condition, He said to him, "Do you wish to get well?"

7 The sick man answered Him, "Sir, I have no man to put me into the pool when the water is stirred up, but while I am coming, another steps down before me."

8 Jesus said to him, "Arise, take up your pallet, and walk."

9 And immediately the man became well, and took up his pallet and began to walk.

Now it was the Sabbath on that day.

10 Therefore the Jews were saying to him who was cured, "It is the Sabbath, and it is not permissible for you to carry your pallet."

11 But he answered them, "He who made me well was the one who said to me, 'Take up your pallet and walk.'"

12 They asked him, "Who is the man who said to you, 'Take up your pallet, and walk'?"

13 But he who was healed did not know who it was; for Jesus had slipped away while there was a crowd in that place.

14 Afterward Jesus found him in the temple, and said to him, "Behold, you have become well; do not sin anymore, so that nothing worse may befall you."

--John 5

Notice carefully verse 14, wherein Jesus tells the man that he should not sin anymore, lest something worse happen to him. We do not know what that "worse thing" might have been--whether it would have been his old condition returning or something even more terrible--but Christ evidently saw a much stronger connection between sin and healing than we tend to place there today.

This "sin connection" also plays a part in the way that the church is told to heal:

> **14 Is anyone among you sick? Let him call for the elders of the church, and let them pray over him, anointing him with oil in the name of the Lord;**
> **15 and the prayer offered in faith will restore the one who is sick, and the Lord will raise him up, and if he has committed sins, they will be forgiven him.**
> **16 Therefore, confess your sins to one another, and pray for one another, so that you may be healed. The effective prayer of a righteous man can accomplish much.**
> **--James 5**

This passage from James 5 gives us, in command form, the pattern for the normal way that Christians, who belong to a body of believers, are to be healed. It says there that the sick person should take the initiative (which shows his faith) and should ask the elders to anoint him with oil and pray for him. However, confession and forgiveness of sins are also involved. Most people skip verse 16. It says there that if we confess our sins to one another and pray for one another, we are going to be healed!

Let me give you an example of a healing that occurred in this manner. There was a group of believers in Detroit, Michigan who had a small church in a home. One of the members was a blind man, who had been blind for years. At one point in time he came to the elders and asked them to pray for his healing. With fear and trembling, they searched the Scriptures and in James they saw that not only were they to anoint him with oil and pray over him, but they were also to confess their faults and sins one to another. The elders and this blind member met and spent an entire Saturday morning confessing their faults and sins and being cleansed by God. Then in the afternoon, they did as the Scriptures said and anointed the man with oil and prayed. Praise God! His sight was restored!

This normal form of healing (going to the elders) is in keeping with all that we have been saying, because the elders, in a sense, are representing Christ to the other people in the flock. If someone is in a church or a fellowship where the elders cannot or will not anoint him and pray for him if he is sick, then he may be in the wrong fellowship.

It is possible that Christians who seek out traveling "healers," and who are skipping God's normal procedure for dealing with sickness in a body, are cheating themselves out of a healing that would come through their elders. One thing that is "nice" or easy about going to a traveling minister is that the sin problem doesn't have to be dealt with, whereas if the elders (shepherds) were involved, they would know the problems, habits and sins of the sheep and these sins could be dealt with before the anointing, praying and healing took place.

If you are seeking a healing and not getting it, I would suggest that you do these three things:

1. Repent, confess and be cleansed of your sins. (You may need to spend an hour or two with the Lord to let Him show you your heart and condition.)
2. Ask God for more faith; it can be increased.
3. Follow the scriptural pattern and go to the elders in your church.

Another point to consider is that some people say that we should only declare people to be healed in the name of Jesus and that we should never pray for their healing. That is not scriptural, because these verses in James clearly say that we are indeed to pray for the sick. There will be times, however, when the Lord will tell us to exercise His authority and to declare someone to be healed in His name, such as Peter did to the lame man at the temple ("In the name of Jesus Christ of Nazareth rise up and walk"--Acts 3:6, KJV). Both praying and taking authority are equally legitimate.

Talking about dealing with the sin problem in connection with healing takes us to our next subject.

DOES GOD WANT EVERYONE WELL?

Before answering that question directly, we need to look at what the Scriptures say about sin and sickness. Some say that God would never make anyone sick. That is a lovely theory, but it is contrary to the Scriptures. Frequently God sends sickness, pestilence (a form of sickness) or plagues upon people. One example of this is the following:

> **58 "If you are not careful to observe all the words of this law which are written in this book, to fear this honored and awesome name, the Lord your God,**
> **59 then the Lord will bring extraordinary plagues on you and your descendents, even severe and lasting plagues, and miserable and chronic sicknesses.**
> **60 "And He will bring back on you all of the diseases of Egypt of which you were afraid, and they shall cling to you.**
> **61 "Also every sickness and every plague which, not written in the book of this law, the Lord will bring on you until you are destroyed. . . ."**
>
> --Deuteronomy 28

Not all sickness is sent by the Lord because of sin, but some of it is. This is still true, as we find in the New Testament:

> **27 Therefore whoever eats the bread or drinks the cup of the Lord in an unworthy manner, shall be guilty of the body and the blood of the Lord.**
> **28 But let a man examine himself, and so let him eat of the bread and drink of the cup.**
> **29 For he who eats and drinks, eats and drinks judgment to himself, if he does not judge the body rightly.**

30 For this reason many among you are weak and sick and a number sleep.

--1 Corinthians 11

This says that some people are sick (and a few have even died) because of taking communion in an unworthy manner. I do not believe that God caused the sickness to come upon those people, but He has certainly allowed it and evidently is going to continue to allow them to remain sick until they repent and turn from their sin. Does God desire that they turn from their sin and be made well? The answer is obviously "yes." However, if you ask, "Does God desire that they remain in their sin and still be healed," I believe the answer is probably "no." What would you do if a person who was sick because of sin came to you for healing? Should you pray for that individual to be healed? (We need to think about that carefully.)

Today in many circles, the Christians would almost automatically put anyone asking for prayer in the "hot seat" and pray for him or her to be healed. Sometimes nothing would happen, perhaps on occassions like that of the previous paragraph, where that person is persisting in sin and is unrepentant in attitude. Does it glority God for those Christians to pray in such instances and have nothing happen? Returning to our example of Jesus, in such situations, remember He dealt with the sin problem first, and then the person was healed.

By this I am not saying that every time a Christian gets sick or is afflicted it is because he is harboring some sin in his life. Let's look at the example of Job. With God's permission, Satan caused sores to come upon the skin of Job:

6 So the LORD said to Satan, "Behold, he is in your power, only spare his life."

7 Then Satan went out from the presence of the LORD, and smote Job with sore boils from the sole of his foot to the crown of his head.

--Job 2

In Job's case, God did not cause the sores, but He allowed them. He allowed them specifically to test Job. I wish we had time to go into the subject of "testing" in the manner which it deserves, but we find over and over again that God tests righteous men:

> **5 The LORD tests the righteous and the wicked,**
> **And the one who loves violence His soul hates.**
>
> **--Psalm 11**

> **1 Now it came about after these things, that God tested Abraham, and said to him, "Abraham!" And he said, "Here I am."**
> **2 And He said, "Take now your son, your only son, whom you love, Isaac, and go to the land of Moriah; and offer him there as a burnt offering on one of the mountains of which I will tell you."**
>
> **--Genesis 22**

In God's testing and purifing of His righteous people, sometimes--as with Job--God even allows sickness to come upon them. The question is, if we had been there, should we have gone and prayed for Job's healing, or would that have been contrary to God's will?

What it comes down to is that when a situation comes up wherein healing is involved, we should do what Jesus did. He did what the Father told Him to do (the Father's will) in each situation. The Holy Spirit knows if an individual has a sin problem or has no faith. In those cases, if we will allow Him to, the Holy Spirit will tell us how to pray for that individual, and whether or not to pray for his healing. When the Holy Spirit does tell us to pray for an individual to be healed, then we can pray with full confidence that God will heal him, because He will not lead us to do anything that is contrary to His purposes and His will.

In some situations, Christ healed all who came to Him. In others, such as in Nazareth, He healed but a few. In this situation in Capernaum He healed many:

34 And He healed many who were ill with various diseases, and cast out many demons; and He was not permitting the demons to speak, because they knew who He was.
35 And in the early morning, while it was still dark, He arose and went out and departed to a lonely place, and was praying there.
36 And Simon and his companions hunted for Him;
37 and they found Him, and said to Him, "Everyone is looking for You."
38 And He said to them, "Let us go somewhere else to the towns nearby, in order that I may preach there also; for that is what I came out for."
39 And He went into their synagogues throughout all Galilee, preaching and casting out the demons.

--Mark 1

Evidently, there were more people who wanted healing, and they were looking for Jesus. Even though they were coming to Jesus for healing, the Holy Spirit led Him to ignore them and to go on to other towns. The main thing is that Jesus did whatever God told Him to do. If He was led to heal someone, it happened 100 percent of the time.

In his book, JESUS WANTS YOU WELL, C.S. Lovett sums up very well the topic of this section--that is, whether or not God wants everyone well:

> This is sufficient to show that healing is a natural function of the body. God has installed a healing program in the brain via the DNA. But nowhere has He installed any kind of a program that moves in the direction of sickness or disease. The mere fact that the healing program is built into our bodies is proof that God does not want us sick. If he did, He would have designed us differently. Therefore no reader needs be puzzled as to whether or not it is God's will for him to be healed. Jesus wants us well.

Note: I don't mean to imply that God doesn't use sickness. Indeed He does. It is surely His favorite form of discipline. When their bodies are in pain, people tend to get serious with the Lord. It is one time when He really has their undivided attention. And it is a time when they are usually ready to make the changes God wants in their lives. But the point is--**He doesn't send** sickness. He doesn't have to. We bring it on ourselves by the way we react to people and circumstances. It's true that God does manipulate circumstances, but He does **not** attempt to control our reactions to those circumstances. He allows us to act as we choose. But **how** we react, determines whether we stay well or get sick. Once the illness occurs, God is pleased to make the most of it. If His people are to suffer, He wants it to count. But as for **wanting** anyone sick, that is out of the question. His design of the human body is proof that He does not.

--Personal Christianity, P.O. Box 549
Baldwin Park, CA 91706, p. 34

COMMANDED TO HEAL

Jesus gave the twelve disciples the authority to heal and to cast out demons, and then He commanded them to go out and use that authority, as He sent them out:

1 And having summoned His twelve disciples, He gave them authority over unclean spirits, to cast them out, and to heal every kind of disease and every kind of sickness. . . .

7 "And as you go, preach, saying, 'The kingdom of heaven is at hand.'
8 "Heal the sick, raise the dead, cleanse the lepers, cast out demons; freely you received, freely give. . . ."

--Matthew 10

This command to go out and heal was later extended to the seventy who went out two by two. (Luke 10:1-17). Ultimately this authority was given to everyone who would believe in the name of Jesus:

> 15 And He said to them, "Go into all the world and preach the gospel to all creation.
> 16 "He who has believed and has been baptized shall be saved; but he who has disbelieved shall be condemned.
> 17 "And these signs will accompany those who have believed: in My name they will cast out demons, they will speak with new tongues;
> 18 they will pick up serpents, and if they drink any deadly poison, it shall not hurt them; they will lay hands on the sick, and they will recover."
>
> --Mark 16

Verse 17 says these things **will** accompany those who have believed in Jesus' name. Would that include you and me? Have we believed in His name? Of course it would include us! Do those signs accompany you and me? According to this passage, they should. One of the things that Christ said would happen is that we would lay our hands on the sick and they would recover. This would follow the pattern of Jesus, who frequently touched the people whom He healed, as well as speaking to them.

I yearn that all Christians could be used in a healing ministry like that of Jesus. He had compassion when He saw someone sick. He was willing to walk a long distance to have someone healed and to alleviate suffering. However, all that He did was totally under the control of God. I am sure that during the time Christ lived in Palestine, there were many people in the land who were not healed. There were requirements for healing. The people had to come into contact with Jesus in faith and usually had to be willing to have sin eliminated from their lives. Then the channels were opened for God to perform a miracle of divine healing through the hands and words of Jesus.

THE GIFT OF HEALING

Even though we all have authority from Christ to heal, and we should be exercising the authority He has given us out of a heart of love, the Holy Spirit gives an extraordinary "gift of healing" to some, such as Oral Roberts and Kathryn Kuhlman. Peter had this gift:

> 14 And all the more believers in the Lord, multitudes of men and women, were constantly added to their number,
> 15 to such an extent that they even carried the sick out into the streets, and laid them on cots and pallets, so that when Peter came by, at least his shadow might fall on any one of them.
> 16 And also the people from the cities in the vicinity of Jerusalem were coming together, bringing people who were sick or afflicted with unclean spirits; and they were all being healed.
>
> --Acts 5

Paul had this gift and, like Jesus, he laid hands on the sick and they were healed:

> 8 And it came about that the father of Publius was lying in bed afflicted with recurrent fever and dysentery; and Paul went in to see him and after he had prayed, he laid hands on him and healed him.
> 9 And after this had happened, the rest of the people on the island who had diseases were coming to him and getting cured.
>
> --Acts 28

I praise God for people who have this gift and are exercising it; I wish there were more of them. However, Christians should not sit around waiting to be healed by God through such a person. When we encounter a sick person, we need to exercise our authority to heal, if God tells us to do so (and we must be listening). Or if we get sick, we should go to our elders and ask for prayer, just as the Scriptures command us.

One of the men who frequently ministers with me, Jimmy Smith, is a trained concert pianist and opera singer. He has a fantastic gift in the area of music. In addition, he also has a beautiful gift of healing. The Lord will give him many words of knowledge about people's diseases in the congregation and either during the service or at the end of it, he will call out these words and the people receive their healing. The Lord also frequently leads him to pray for someone who is sick, as the sick person requests it, and He will often give subsequent words of knowledge to Jimmy while he is praying for such people.

The Lord has given me a gift in the area of healing that works primarily in connection with words of knowledge. The Lord will let me know during a meeting when He wants to do some healings. Sometimes it is before I speak and sometimes it is afterward. He simply lets me know what He is doing. He will let me know that He is healing someone's right hip, left knee, ears, or whatever it is. As I have traveled and ministered all over the world, it has been a great confirmation that whenever God has given me these words of knowledge and I have been obedient to speak them out, He has always been faithful to heal those people.

In case any of you are not familiar with the operation of this type of gift, let me give you a couple of examples. When I was speaking at a FGBMFI meeting in Minnesota, there was a man there whose left shoulder had been hurting him ever since an injury in World War II. The Lord gave me the word of knowledge about it and as I shared that word, God removed the pain. There was a lady who came to one of our Omega Seminars and, during one meeting, the Lord showed me that He was healing some lady's right leg. I had not realized it, but she had barely been able to hobble into the seminar, holding onto her husband. For the remainder of the seminar she was walking around as well as anyone, ecstatic that the Lord had touched her.

Sometimes the Lord shows me explicitly who the individual is. A beautiful example of this was when I was in the hospital in January, 1984, following a heart attack. Two couples came to visit me, and my wife, Jeani, was there. They wanted to have prayer before they left, so the six of us held hands. A couple of them prayed and then I began to pray. As I was praying, the Lord showed me that one of the ladies had pain in her right shoulder. I began to pray for her, by name, asking the Lord to take away the pain and to heal her shoulder.

My wife and my dear brother, Jim Andrews, were wondering if they had missed something earlier, because they had not heard this lady say anything about any pain in her shoulder. After our prayer time was finished, this sister told us that she had had some trouble with her right shoulder a number of years ago, but it had not bothered her for a couple of years. Then just the previous day, she had reached to get something and her shoulder had begun hurting with sharp pains and it had been hurting ever since. She had been praying silently that some "body ministry" would take place, even as we prayed there in the hospital, but she had no idea that she would be the recipient of God's special healing touch! Praise God that He can tell us where the needs are and can use us as His tools, as He does the healing.

When I have been out ministering, the Lord has rarely led me to pray for anyone for healing. If someone asks me to do so, I always ask God if that is what He wants. If the Lord says, "Yes," then I pray. If the Lord says, "No," it is a bit embarrassing both to me and to the sick person, but I have to tell that individual that I do not feel that I am the one that the Lord wants to pray for his or her healing. That is not to say that the Lord does not want to heal that person; He may indeed, but He may want to use the elders in his church or some other Christian as the initiator of the healing.

At one of the Omega World Conventions, I had to say "no" to a lady who stood up in the meeting and asked me to pray for her. The Lord did not allow me to do so and I had to tell her lovingly that I did not have liberty to pray for her. Jimmy Smith then spoke up and told her to see him at the end of the meeting. It turned out that the Lord had given him a word of knowledge about an evil spirit that was causing the lady's problem. God--using Jimmy--cast away the evil spirit and the lady was set free and healed! You can begin to see how important it is to be obedient to the leading of the Holy Spirit in each specific situation.

Jesus has given us authority over disease and, when we know that we are moving in His will, we can be absolutely assured that healing will take place. Jesus' healing ministry was 100 percent successful and I believe ours should be too, if we are to be like Jesus. I believe our healing ministry will have 100 percent success, if we do not rush out and pray for people in an ill-advised manner, but rather wait for the Holy Spirit to prompt us. That way it is all under His control and Jesus will get all the glory.

As the Holy Spirit begins to do a new thing on the earth, during these end times, I believe we are going to see healings as we have never seen them before. As the full power of Jesus is released through those who are seeking to become like Him, we will see crippled people leap up out of wheel chairs, en masse. When persecution comes, Christians may not have access to doctors or medicines. Divine healing may be the only way to be healed.

DEMONS CAUSE SOME ILLNESSES

Some illnesses are caused by viruses and germs. Other illnesses are caused by our own bad habits of eating the wrong things and/or not getting the proper amount of sleep and exercise. If God were to perform a miraculous healing for some of us, we would simply turn around and make ourselves sick again by our bad habits. Those bad habits (really sin) need to be eliminated before true divine healing can permanently rest upon an individual.

However, as we have already seen in the example of Job, some sicknesses can be caused by Satan or his demon henchmen:

32 And as they were going out, behold, a dumb man, demon-possessed, was brought to Him.
33 And after the demon was cast out, the dumb man spoke; and the multitudes marveled, saying, "Nothing like this was ever seen in Israel."

--Matthew 9

In these verses, we see that this man, who was brought to Jesus, was dumb and it was not a physical abnormality that was causing his problem; it was a demon. In this case, the real road to healing was not a prayer for healing but to cast out the demon. Jesus had the spiritual discernment to know when an illness was caused by demonic forces and when it was not. If we allow the Holy Spirit to control us, He will give us also the discernment to know when evil spirits are present and are causing an illness. Another example of demon-caused illness is found in the following passage:

10 And He was teaching in one of the synagogues on the Sabbath.
11 And behold, there was a woman who for eighteen years had had a sickness caused by a spirit; and she was bent double, and could not straighten up at all.
12 And when Jesus saw her, He called her over and said to her, "Woman, you are freed from your sickness."
13 And he laid His hands upon her; and immediately she was made erect again, and began glorifying God. . . .

16 "And this woman, a daughter of Abraham as she is, whom Satan has bound for eighteen long years, should she not have been released from this bond on the Sabbath day?"

--Luke 13

As you can see here, again there was a physical problem that was caused by a demon (verse 11). In this case, it had lasted for eighteen years.

In our quest to be like Jesus, we now come to the subject of casting out demons like Jesus did.

SUMMARY AND CONCLUSION

The subjects of healing and casting out demons are so interrelated that I have combined the summaries of these two chapters at the end of Chapter 13.

13
YOU HAVE AUTHORITY OVER DEMONS

One of the things that Christ did very often was to set people free from demons. This comprised about one-fourth of His ministry. Some Christians, today, do not even believe that demons exist. Unfortunately, they are at cross-purposes with Jesus, since He definitely believed they were real and even talked to them at times, as we will see.

Some of these demons caused physical illnesses, such as epilepsy, dumbness and walking humpbacked, while others tormented people. Since Jesus Himself said that those physical ailments, at least in those specific cases, were caused by demons in His day, there is no reason to believe that the same thing is not occurring today. If we truly desire to be like Jesus Christ, then we too will want to see people set free from these demons.

James Robison had a deliverance in 1983. This is the way he described it in NEW WINE MAGAZINE (March 1984 issue):

> I would describe the change I've experienced in my life as deliverance from bondage and captivity of the enemy--deliverance from appetites and attitudes that did not express the holiness of God. My mind was so full of thoughts I knew were not of the Holy Spirit. I knew there was somebody in my garden bringing forth poisonous sprouts and weeds. But I didn't understand the nature of spiritual warfare--that the enemy could, in fact, gain ground in a believer's life.

I had been taught to ignore evil spirits and demonic influences ever since I became a Christian; that I couldn't be bothered by the evil one. Yet Jesus taught us to pray for deliverance from the evil one. We're told in Scripture to resist the devil. We're told to test the spirits and to rejoice not only because the spirits are subject to us but also because our names are written in heaven and we have access to God's grace. And through His grace we have overcome the enemy.

Before my deliverance, I knew there was a devil but I didn't realize what the term stronghold meant. I knew I obviously had some strongholds within me but I didn't realize how they got there.

Now I know our fight is not with flesh and blood but with the spiritual powers of darkness. We're in a fight with the devil and all his forces. Yet most people have never been taught about the fight. They've never been taught to suit up with the whole armor of God. They've never been taught where the battlefield is. They think the field is outside, but the field is the human vessel, which is to be possessed with honor and to bring forth fruit a hundredfold; fruit that resembles Jesus--love, joy, peace, and patience. The enemy was in me because God allows the hedge around us to be torn down when we don't bring forth fruit, when we don't abide in the Word.

I didn't realize that I had been so strongly assaulted and harassed by the enemy that he had actually brought portions of my life into captivity. And I had to be delivered. I didn't even believe in deliverance. After all, who would have ever thought that a nationally-known evangelist who had led a million people to Christ needed to be delivered? But I did. I needed to be delivered! If Simon Peter could be influenced by Satan to the point that he savored the things of men rather than of God, and Jesus had to rebuke Satan in him, well, we can certainly be influenced by Satan as well. And I was. I was tormented, and in some areas of my life I was defeated by him.

The Lord set me free and moved me into new life in the Word, so now the Word is not something I go to just for sermons--it's where I go for life and food. And I come away with the life of God and the likeness of Jesus. If we don't come away with that, I suspect we're approaching the Word of God improperly, if not impurely. But when we go to the Word, we should get life--we should get food.

--Integrity Communications
P. O. Box B,
Mobile, AL 36616, p. 7-8

I praise God that James Robison no longer ignores demons and has been delivered from them. I love that brother. But, like him, many Christians ignore demons while others become overly concerned with them and blame every little problem on them. I have found a real lack of agreement in the body of Christ on this subject. Let us put aside our ideas and prejudices and look afresh at what the Scriptures teach about it.

Upon reviewing this chapter, one man of God, whom the Lord beautifully uses to cast out demons, felt that I should place far more emphasis on deliverance than I had in this chapter. Another man of God, Dave Wilkerson, thought there should be a different emphasis. He had this to say:

There are over seventeen sins of the flesh listed in Corinthians including adultery and witchcraft--without any demon activity whatsoever. There is a danger in blaming our lust of the flesh on demonic activity, thereby not dealing with the flesh. The Spirit is revealing to many praying men that this emphasis on demons in the church is going to be totally repudiated by revelation of the final and absolute victory of the cross.

A third man of God felt that the subject of casting out demons is not often taught, nor taught very well when it is, and that the chapter was really great.

All three of these are men whom I respect highly in the Lord, and yet they had a divergence of opinion about how the subject of demons should be treated. You may or may not agree with what is contained in the rest of this chapter. I hope you will love me anyhow and have an open heart in the Lord. However, I would urge you not to discount the rest of this book because you may not completely agree with what is in this chapter. If this chapter bothers you too much, just ignore it and let the Lord use the rest of this book to change your life and help make you more like Jesus Christ.

If you are in the process of becoming like Jesus Christ, I believe you will love me and look past my "seeing this subject through a glass darkly." My sincere desire in this chapter is that Christians would realize the authority that they have over demons, in the name of Jesus Christ, and would utilize that power to get rid of any demons that may be hurting or harassing them or people to whom they minister. I believe we can all agree on that objective.

As we begin to think about casting out demons, we need to remind ourselves that, just as Jesus gave us authority over every illness, He also gave us authority over demons:

> **17 "And these signs will accompany those who have believed: in My name they will cast out demons, they will speak with new tongues;**
> **18 they will pick up serpents, and if they drink any deadly poison, it shall not hurt them; they will lay hands on the sick, and they will recover."**
>
> **--Mark 16**

Here, in verse 17, Jesus said that one of the signs that would accompany those who believe in His name is that they would cast out demons. However, this authority has additional requirements that go with it. To help you understand this, let's see when Christ first gave the twelve disciples authority over demons:

> 1 And having summoned His twelve disciples, He gave them authority over unclean spirits, to cast them out, and to heal every kind of disease and every kind of sickness. . . .
>
> 7 "And as you go, preach, saying, 'The kingdom of heaven is at hand.'
> 8 "Heal the sick, raise the dead, cleanse the lepers, cast out demons; freely you received, freely give. . . ."
>
> --Matthew 10

Jesus gave His disciples this authority, to cast out unclean spirits, prior to His transfiguration, which occurs in the early part of Matthew 17. (You might note in verse 8 that He actually commanded them to cast out demons, as well as to heal. He expected them to exercise the authority He was giving to them.) Now let's read what occurs after the Mount of Transfiguration:

> 14 And when they came to the multitude, a man came up to Him, falling on his knees before Him, and saying,
> 15 "Lord, have mercy on my son, for he is a lunatic, and is very ill; for he often falls into the fire, and often into the water.
> 16 "And I brought him to Your disciples, and they could not cure him."
> 17 And Jesus answered and said, "O unbelieving and perverted generation, how long shall I be with you? How long shall I put up with you? Bring him here to Me."
> 18 And Jesus rebuked him, and the demon came out of him, and the boy was cured at once.
> 19 Then the disciples came to Jesus privately and said, "Why could we not cast it out?"
> 20 And He said to them, "Because of the littleness of your faith; for truly I say to you, if you have faith as a mustard seed, you shall say to this mountain, 'Move from here to there.' and it shall move; and nothing shall be impossible to you.

> **21 "But this kind does not go out except by prayer and fasting."**
>
> **--Matthew 17**

Understand this very clearly. Jesus had given His disciples authority over demons back in Chapter 10 of Matthew, but here in Chapter 17, in verses 15 and 16, we see that the disciples were unable to cast out this strong demon, even though they had already cast out some demons in the name of Christ. The authority alone was not enough in this case. The disciples then asked Jesus why they could not do it and, in answer to that, He pointed out that there are three other requirements, in addition to the authority, to cast out the stronger demons (verses 20-21):

1. Faith
2. Prayer (Fervent prayer)
3. Fasting

This is not my idea, but this is what Jesus told His disciples they needed to do if they wanted to be able to cast out strong demons. God can and has used Christians, who have not really prayed and fasted, to cast out weaker demons. However, they may not realize how much more spiritual power they would have if they would make the sacrifice to pray and fast. Evidently Jesus had an ongoing life of prayer and fasting so that at any time He could cast out the strongest demon or resist Satan.

I have read almost all of the books on the subject of deliverance. I praise God for the men and women of God whom the Lord has used to help alert the body of Christ to the authority that we have over demons and the fact that Christians should be casting out demons today. However, right now I am not talking about the current concept of "deliverance." Let us instead go back to the biblical concept of "casting out of demons" and take our clues entirely from the Scriptures, so we can know how we should take authority over demons and cast them out.

Incidentally, to "cast out" something does not necessarily mean that that something was indwelling (although it could mean that). The most common usage of "cast out" in the Bible means "to cause to leave the presence of," such as Abraham "casting out" Hagar and her son:

> 10 Wherefore she said unto Abraham, Cast out this bondwoman and her son: for the son of this bondwoman shall not be heir with my son, even with Isaac.
>
> --Genesis 21, KJV

> 24 For I will cast out the nations before thee, and enlarge thy borders: neither shall any man desire thy land, when thou shall go up to appear before the Lord thy God thrice in the year.
>
> --Exodus 34, KJV

> 19 To cast out all thine enemies from before thee, as the Lord hath spoken.
>
> --Deuteronomy 6, KJV

> 7 Then I will cut off Israel out of the land which I have given them; and this house, which I have hallowed for my name, will I cast out of my sight; and Israel shall be a proverb and a byword among all people: . . .
>
> --I Kings 9, KJV

> 15 And I will cast you out of my sight, as I have cast out all your brethren, even the whole seed of Ephraim.
>
> --Jeremiah 7, KJV

When we talk about casting out demons, this can validly mean to cast them out from our presence (spiritual sight), as well as casting them out from indwelling someone. Now let's see how Jesus cast out demons.

HOW JESUS CAST OUT DEMONS

If the Lord wishes to use us to cast out demons, we want to use Jesus as our Example, so let us begin by looking at a few of the instances wherein Jesus cast out demons during His ministry here on earth. In fact, He began casting out demons almost at the very beginning of His ministry. In the very first chapter of the Book of Mark, we read about this:

> 21 And they went into Capernaum; and immediately on the Sabbath He entered the synagogue and began to teach.
> 22 And they were amazed at His teaching; for He was teaching them as one having authority, and not as the scribes.
> 23 And just then there was in their synagogue a man with an unclean spirit; and he cried out,
> 24 saying, "What do we have to do with You, Jesus of Nazareth? Have You come to destroy us? I know who You are--the Holy One of God!"
> 25 And Jesus rebuked him, saying, "Be quiet, and come out of him!"
> 26 And throwing him into convulsions, the unclean spirit cried out with a loud voice, and came out of him.
> 27 And they were all amazed, so that they debated among themselves, saying, "What is this? A new teaching with authority! He commands even the unclean spirits, and they obey Him."
> --Mark 1

In this particular instance, we see that Christ commanded the unclean spirit to "be quiet." When casting out demons, perhaps Christians should more often take this same approach. There are other situations in which Christ commanded the demons to be quiet, such as this one:

> 34 And He healed many who were ill with various diseases, and cast out many demons; and He was not permitting the demons to speak,

because they knew who He was.

--Mark 1

Perhaps the most familiar case of Christ casting out demons is the legion which He commanded to come out of the demoniac at Gerasenes:

26 And they sailed to the country of the Gerasenes, which is opposite Galilee.
27 And when He had come out onto the land, He was met by a certain man from the city who was possessed with demons; and who had not put on any clothing for a long time, and was not living in a house, but in the tombs.
28 And seeing Jesus, he cried out and fell before Him, and said in a loud voice, "What do I have to do with You, Jesus, Son of the Most High God? I beg You, do not torment me."
29 For He had been commanding the unclean spirit to come out of the man. For it had seized him many times; and he was bound with chains and shackles and kept under guard; and yet he would burst his fetters and be driven by the demon into the desert.
30 And Jesus asked him, "What is your name?" And he said "Legion"; for many demons had entered him.
31 And they were entreating Him not to command them to depart into the abyss.
32 Now there was a herd of many swine feeding there on the mountain; and the demons entreated Him to permit them to enter the swine. And He gave them permission.
33 And the demons came out from the man and entered the swine; and the herd rushed down the steep bank into the lake, and were drowned.
34 And when the herdsmen saw what had happened, they ran away and reported it in the city and out in the country.
35 And the people went out to see what had happened; and they came to Jesus, and found the man from whom the demons had gone out, sitting

> **down at the feet of Jesus, clothed and in his right mind; and they became frightened.**
>
> **36 And those who had seen it reported to them how the man who was demon-possessed had been made well.**
>
> --Luke 8

This is the only case that I can find in the Scriptures where Christ asked the name of a demon. Evidently He was not really concerned about their names; He was only concerned about casting them out. Another interesting thing to note, which we will discuss later, is that He cast these demons into living beings, into a herd of swine. This is the only case that tells us where Christ told the demons to go.

In verse 31 we learn another thing about demons: they really do not want to be cast into the abyss. I believe that Christians have authority to cast them into the abyss and can utilize this. We can tell the demons that if they do not depart immediately, they will be cast into the abyss. In my experience, this has caused demons to obey and obey quickly.

One last thought on this passage is that from these verses we know that demons and unclean spirits (or evil spirits) are the same thing. Verse 29 uses the term "unclean spirit" and the term "demon" in an interchangeable way.

Now looking at another passage, in teaching about demons, Christ points out that if they are not cast into an animal or the abyss, the demons simply wander about:

> **43 "Now when the unclean spirit goes out of a man, it passes through waterless places, seeking rest, and does not find it.**
>
> **44 "Then it says, 'I will return to my house from which I came'; and when it comes, it finds it unoccupied, swept, and put in order.**
>
> **45 "Then it goes, and takes along with it seven other spirits more wicked than itself, and they go in and live there; and the last state of that man becomes worse than the first. That is**

> **the way it will also be with this evil generation."**
>
> **--Matthew 12**

This passage above points out that the non-Christian who has demons cast out of him must allow his heart (house) to be occupied by Jesus. Otherwise, the demons can come back and his latter state will be much worse than his former state.

In His ministry, Jesus commanded demons not to return after they were cast out:

> **25 And when Jesus saw that a crowd was rapidly gathering, He rebuked the unclean spirit, saying to it, "You deaf and dumb spirit, I command you, come out of him and do not enter him again."**
>
> **--Mark 9**

Jesus also cast out demons from a long distance. He did not have to be present:

> **25 But after hearing of Him, a woman whose daughter had an unclean spirit, immediately came and fell at His feet.**
>
> **26 Now the woman was a Gentile, of the Syrophoenician race. And she kept asking Him to cast the demon out of her daughter.**
>
> **27 And He was saying to her, "Let the children be satisfied first, for it is not good to take the children's bread and throw it to the dogs."**
>
> **28 But she answered and said to Him, "Yes, Lord, but even the dogs under the table feed on the children's crumbs."**
>
> **29 And He said to her, "Because of this answer go your way; the demon has gone out of your daughter."**
>
> **30 And going back to her home, she found the child lying on the bed, the demon having departed.**
>
> **--Mark 7**

From these examples, and we will use more in the remainder of this chapter, let us see if we can summarize Christ's ministry of casting out demons:

1. We must realize that all the people out of whom Christ cast demons were not Christians. (There were no Christians until Christ's resurrection.)
2. Possibly because they were not Christians, Christ never asked them to confess their sins before He cast out the demons.
3. In most instances, the demon came out immediately, although with the demoniac at Gerasenes, there was a bit of a delay.
4. Christ usually commanded the demons to be quiet and in only one case that we know of did He ask for the name of the demon.
5. Demons can be cast into animals, the abyss or left to wander through dry and waterless places.
6. There is something the non-Christian, who has had demons cast out of him, must do to prevent the demons' return.

WHAT ARE DEMONS?

If we are going to cast out demons, we need to understand a little about them. First we need to realize that the Bible is silent about the origin of demons and, thus, one can only speculate as to how they came to exist. In his book, ARE DEMONS FOR REAL?, Robert Peterson has this to say about the origin of demons:

> Down through the ages, amid much speculation, some absurd theories have been advanced regarding the origin of demons. This has been partly due to the definite reserve of Scripture concerning their genesis, a silence which surely suggests that the important thing is not where the

demons come from, but that they do actually exist, and that a ceaseless warfare must be waged against them. Nevertheless the question is legitimate and one that is often asked.

Dr. Bancroft says, "Demons are an order of spirit beings apparently distinct and separate from angels, and which from the intimations of certain passages of Scripture (Matt. 12:43,44; Mark 5:10-14) seem to be in a disembodied state, having existed in some previous period and place in bodily form." He suggests that the disembodied spirits are from a pre-Adamite race, but this must remain in the realm of theory, for the suggestion has no Scriptural support.

Dr. Chafer advances the theme that demons were probably created as subjects of Satan in his original angelic glory. Then when Satan fell, he drew them after him (John 8:44; II Pet. 2:4; Jude 6). This hypothesis is known as the "fallen angel theory," and it divides the fallen angels into two classes; those that are free and those that are bound. The free are the demons, while the bound are those angels guilty of such enormous wickedness that they are confined to pits of darkness awaiting judgment. (II Pet. 2:4; Jude 6).

The picture becomes more confused when equally able teachers affirm that demons resulted from the union between "sons of God" (fallen angel) and daughters of men. This is "the monstrous offspring of angels and antediluvian women theory." Dr. De Haan is of the opinion that "The sons of God in this passage were none other than fallen angels who caused a supernatural union with the daughters of man, with the resultant birth of these monstrosities." This theory is open to serious doubts that cannot be satisfactorily answered.

These three propositions are the ones most commonly accepted among evangelicals, but the silence of Scripture makes them nothing more than theoretical hypotheses. Others only show how far man can go in absurdity: for example, that demons are the personifications of violent and incurable diseases, or that they are the spirits of the wicked dead as held by the Jewish historian Josephus.

--Moody Press, p. 113-115

As you can see from what Peterson had to say, there is a wide divergence of opinion as to the origin of demons. However, I do believe that it is fairly safe to say that they are indeed different from fallen angels, because fallen angels do not need a body nor seek one, whereas demons evidently need a body in which to dwell and they seek to possess one. Angels, whether fallen or not, have their own bodies that can be materialized whenever necessary. These angel bodies can even eat:

1 Now the two angels came to Sodom in the evening as Lot was sitting in the gate of Sodom. When Lot saw them, he rose to meet them and bowed down with his face to the ground.

2 And he said, "Now behold, my lords, please turn aside into your servant's house, and spend the night, and wash your feet; then you may rise early and go on your way." They said however, "No, but we shall spend the night in the square."

3 Yet he urged them strongly, so they turned aside to him and entered his house; and he prepared a feast for them, and baked unleavened bread, and they ate.

--Genesis 19

On the other hand, demons do not have bodies and are looking for a body to inhabit. To see this we need to reread three verses that we looked at earlier:

43 "Now when the unclean spirit goes out of a man, it passes through waterless places, seeking rest, and does not find it.

44 "Then it says, 'I will return to my house

from which I came'; and when it comes, it finds it unoccupied, swept, and put in order.

45 "Then it goes, and takes along with it seven other spirits more wicked than itself, and they go in and live there; and the last state of that man becomes worse than the first. That is the way it will also be with this evil generation."

--Matthew 12

This passage says that if a demon is cast out of a man, it looks for a new place to inhabit. In this example that Christ gives, the demon cannot find another human being to inhabit and decides to go back and check out the former man who was its "house." When it finds this former residence unoccupied (as would be the case of a non-Christian, who had demons cast out of him and did not receive Christ as his Savior), then it returns to that person, bringing seven other demons with it.

One interesting thing to note here is that there were numerous inanimate objects around in Christ's day that the demons could have inhabited, if demons inhabit inanimate objects. In Christ's example, the demon was **not** looking for an object to indwell, but a living being. I can find no record anyplace in the Scriptures of a demon ever inhabiting an inanimate object.

Some people in deliverance ministries have tied people in knots over inanimate objects and have left many Christians bound up in fear. (We know that creating fear is not of God because His perfect love will cast out fear--I John 4:18.) Let me quote for you one letter I recently received from a lady in California.

I want to thank you so much on your article "Fear Not." Months ago my family got involved in the "Deliverance Ministry." As we became deeper involved, we were told to get rid of the children's dolls and stuffed animals because they gave the demons legal right to gain entrance to our home. I threw out my jewelry, all pictures with people in them, even crosses or stars of David became an object of fear.

I was told not to use the word fantastic because it would mean I had a demon of fantasy. Disneyland and cartoons were out, also any forms of play acting, even Christian puppets were evil. Raggedy Ann and Andy were demonic.

Also I was warned to not purchase any Procter and Gamble products. . . .

I've been prayed over about many fears and it really has helped yet, I am still confused.

Are dolls for children okay? Do they promote fantasy? Is child fantasy always abnormal? Can a demon indwell a body (not spirit) of a Christian?

--Mrs. P.A.

Do you think the fear and confusion, that some well-meaning deliverance ministry created in this woman, was of God? No one should fear objects of any shape, including dolls, rainbows and so forth.

FEAR OF RAINBOWS

What would you think if you walked into someone's home and they had a couple of rainbows hanging on the wall and they were burning incense? (The rainbow has been adopted as the symbol of the New Age Movement.) Many Christians would think that these people were involved in the occult or that they were naive believers in Christ who should get rid of all those occult items. What they may not realize is that these people may be very mature Christians, who are using those items as a part of their worship to God.

Let's take these items one at a time. In the tabernacle was an altar of incense. Incense was God's idea. It was something that He wanted people to use in worshiping him:

> **1 Moreover, you shall make an altar as a place for burning incense; you shall make it of acacia wood. . . .**
>
> **7 And Aaron shall burn fragrant incense on**

it; he shall burn it every morning when he trims the lamps.
8 And when Aaron trims the lamps at twilight, he shall burn incense. There shall be perpetual incense before the Lord throughout your generations.

--Exodus 30

The rainbow was the bow that was around God's throne, which He placed in the sky. It is God's bow and a symbol of His covenant with all flesh and, thus, it is holy:

13 I set My bow in the cloud, and it shall be for a sign of a covenant between Me and the earth.
14 And it shall come about, when I bring a cloud over the earth, that the bow shall be seen in the cloud,
15 and I will remember My covenant, which is between Me and you and every living creature of all flesh; and never again shall the water become a flood to destroy all flesh.
16 When the bow is in the cloud then I will look upon it, to remember the everlasting covenant between God and every living creature of all flesh that is on the earth.
17 And God said to Noah, "This is the sign of the covenant which I have established between Me and all flesh that is on the earth."

--Genesis 9

Some Christian writers today see demons and Satan behind every rainbow and the burning of incense as an evil act, and they advise Christians to avoid all sorts of things, such as wearing a cross around their neck, because these things could act as lures for demons. Unfortunately, I think these well-meaning Christians are often creating unnecessary fear in the body of Christ.

As far as I am concerned, the things that my Father created are good and beautiful and I will use them freely. They are my inheritance. If some demon gets near one of God's symbols, in the name of Jesus Christ, I will chase that demon away. Two of the three presents brought to Jesus Christ at His birth were frankincense and myrrh, which are incense. If someone wants to burn incense to my Father as act of adoration and worship, I believe it is well pleasing to Him. If I wish to have a transparent rainbow on my sliding glass door to remind me of God's goodness, His throne and that He will never break His covenants, then I believe it is well pleasing to Him. Let me repeat: I believe that anything our Father created is good.

If some satanic group starts using the fish as their symbol, should Christians madly run about eliminating all fish symbols from their lives? The answer is obviously "no." We used that symbol first. If some evil Johnny-come-lately group wants to abuse one of the symbols of our Father and our faith, that's their problem. God will eventually deal with them about it. The main thing to remember is that God looks on our hearts. If we are doing any of these things as an act of witnessing, adoration, or worship to Him, it is well pleasing to Him. If we have any reason to suspect that there is a demon attached to any of these things, the solution is not to destroy the rainbow, but to command any demons associated with it, in the name of Jesus Christ, to depart. Ordered in this manner by someone who knows Jesus Christ as his personal Savior, they must obey. Praise the Lord!

If you have been involved in the occult, or have used some of these objects in any way displeasing to God, He probably wants you to get rid of them. The main thing is your heart attitude as to why you have various things around.

In fact, it is almost funny to me. If there were a demon hanging around an object in my house, what would have to go? Certainly not the object; it is the demon that would have to go. Rather than throwing away the object in fear, maybe even burning it in the backyard and leaving the demon to hang around those terrible ashes, the thing to do is to cast the demon out and retain the object, if you believe God has led you to purchase it.

THE BELIEVER AND DEMONS

Up until now, we have talked about demons being able to indwell those who do not believe in Jesus Christ, and I think everyone will probably agree that they can. We have also talked about demons not indwelling inanimate objects. I can find no biblical basis for believing that they can, but on the other hand, the Bible does not say that they cannot. If one chooses to believe that they can do so, that is fine, but certainly we should not live in fear. Unless it is an object you have actually used in the occult, it would be preferable to cast any suspected demon away from the object rather than to cast the inanimate object out.

Now we turn to the subject of demons being "upon" and/or "indwelling" Christians, where there is much disagreement among mature men and women of God. As we begin on this very delicate subject, the first question is whether or not a Christian can "have" a demon. If we are going to look at this properly, we need to define what "to have a demon" means. As far as I can tell from the Scriptures, there are basically four relationships that an individual can have to demons:

1. They can have demons harassing them.
2. They can have demons upon them.
3. They can be indwelt by demons.
4. They can be possessed by demons.

I think about everyone would agree that a Christian cannot be possessed by demons, which means totally controlled by them, certainly not with the Holy Spirit and Jesus Christ living inside him. On the other hand, we would all agree that Christians can certainly be harassed and attacked by Satan and his demons, as was Job, an Old Testament saint and a righteous man. The other two categories are where we run into some difficulty.

Let us first look at what it means to have an evil spirit "upon" an individual. King Saul had an evil spirit "upon" him. This caused him to do bizarre things:

> 10 Now it came about on the next day that an evil spirit from God came mightily upon Saul, and he raved in the midst of the house, while David was playing the harp with his hand, as usual; and a spear was in Saul's hand.
> 11 And Saul hurled the spear for he thought, "I will pin David to the wall." But David escaped from his presence twice.
>
> --1 Samuel 18

In this case, it really didn't matter that the demon was "upon" King Saul and not "in" him; it still caused him to do bizarre things. We read in another passsage that this evil spirit also terrorized King Saul:

> 14 Now the Spirit of the Lord departed from Saul, and an evil spirit from the Lord terrorized him.
> 15 Saul's servants then said to him, "Behold now, an evil spirit from God is terrorizing you.
> 16 "Let our lord now command your servants who are before you. Let them seek a man who is a skillful player on the harp; and it shall come about when the evil spirit from God is on you, that he shall play the harp with his hand, and you will be well." . . .
>
> 23 So it came about whenever the evil spirit from God came to Saul, David would take the harp and play it with his hand; and Saul would be refreshed and be well, and the evil spirit would depart from him.
>
> --1 Samuel 16

Here we see that when a man of God, in this case David, moved at the command of God, the evil spirit departed. It is also interesting to note that the Spirit of the Lord had to depart from King Saul, **before** the evil spirit could terrorize him.

CAN A CHRISTIAN BE INDWELT BY A DEMON?

Let us turn from the subject of a demon being "upon" an individual and examine whether or not a demon can indwell a Christian. We must first realize that the Bible does not directly say anything about this at all, one way or the other, so anything that I or anyone else may say is strictly conjecture. Some will strongly claim that they have cast demons out of Christians (it is possible that the demons have been cast "off" rather than "out," as in the case of David's music causing the evil spirit to leave King Saul). Others state that demons definitely cannot indwell a Christian. Still others believe that a person's spirit, once regenerated in Christ, cannot be indwelt by a demon, yet that person can still be in bondage to demons in the realm of soul and body.

I think we must all realize that we see through a glass darkly, perhaps even more darkly in this case, because Satan and his demonic host are the great deceivers. I feel strongly that we must love each other deeply in the Lord, even if we do not agree on this issue.

As far as my own "opinion," I suspect that demons can indwell Christians in certain situations, but it really doesn't matter if they are harassing from the outside or from the inside. Their function is to try to keep a Christian from doing God's will and to keep him from becoming like Jesus Christ. We want to get rid of these ugly demons, regardless which side of a Christian's skin they are on.

Assuming for a moment that a Christian can be indwelt by a demon, the question comes as how they get in. Again the answer is that the Scriptures do not tell us. I have prayed about this question for about twenty-two years. I have heard many ideas that people have as to how demons enter, everything from the drinking of dirty water, to a Christian having an inferiority complex. To me, these ideas seem a bit far out.

I do not find any scriptural validity for believing that demons can enter just any old way, and my spirit does not witness to it, even though some would fight to the death to claim that these are ways that a demon can enter a Christian. That's between them and God. I love these brothers and praise God for their ministries. However, I do not agree with all of their claims about how demons can enter Christians.

Looking at the Scriptures, we find that there is nothing stated explicitly about how a demon might enter a Christian. The only thing there is by implication. One could conclude that the only possible way for demons to indwell a Christian is through sexual intercourse with someone who has a demon dwelling inside him or her. We know that when we have sexual intercourse, the two people become one flesh:

> **16 Or do you not know that the one who joins himself to a harlot is one body with her? For He says, "THE TWO WILL BECOME ONE FLESH."**
> **17 But the one who joins himself to the Lord is one spirit with Him.**
> **18 Flee immorality. Every other sin that a man commits is outside the body, but the immoral man sins against his own body.**
>
> --1 Corinthians 6

> **8 AND THE TWO SHALL BECOME ONE FLESH; consequently they are no longer two, but one flesh.**
>
> --Mark 10

At the time the two become one flesh (one body), if a demon is indwelling one of the two sexual partners, it is conceivable that it would have free access to move in and take up residence in the other sexual partner. Certainly all non-Christians do not have a demon indwelling them. Yet if a Christian had sex with an unbeliever who did have a demon dwelling inside him, it seems possible that demon could move over and indwell the Christian. The Scriptures do not explicitly state that a Christian can (or cannot) be indwelt by a demon this way. We can only conclude this indirectly, but in praying about this subject, this is what the Lord showed me.

The passage we read from 1 Corinthians 6 warns us that the sin of immorality is a sin "against one's own body." I believe the reason for this could be that it opens the door for demons to come in (as well as for venereal diseases). I am not saying that there are not other ways for a demon to indwell a Christian. All I am saying is that this is the only possible way that I can find in the Bible.

If a Christian feels he has demons dwelling within him and he or she is married, I would encourage both the husband and wife to have the demons cast out of them at the same time, and then to remain faithful to each other. As we read in 1 Corinthians 6:18, immorality is the only sin that is "against your own body," and it is to be avoided at all costs. (Possibly this is why adultery is treated as such a serious offense.) God wants us to get clean and stay clean and free from indwelling demons. Some Christians live in fear that a demon will come dwell inside them. This is not of God. His perfect love will cast out all fear.

Anything beyond what I have just said, concerning how a demon might enter a Christian, is my "opinion" and has no basis in Scripture. It is my opinion that there are likely one or two other ways that a demon could enter a Christian. I do not think it would happen accidentally. They potentially could come in by direct invitation or by deliberate, blatant sin. They possibly could come in at birth, as the baby inherited the sins of his father. But as I said, these ways are only my opinion.

Much of what is considered casting demons "out" of Christians today is possible casting them "off" of Christians, like David did for King Saul. Let me reemphasize that it really does not matter if they are "in" or "upon"; what does matter is that if a Christian is being harassed by demons, they need to be cast away.

A sad thing is that some Christians may be being harassed by demons and not know it. Some sicknesses may be caused by demons and the people involved may not realize it. They need to exercise the gift of "discerning of spirits." That gift lets a Christian know when an evil spirit is present, and whether a demon is causing a sickness, bad behavior, confusion or whatever. If a Christian does not have this gift, he should seek out a mature Christian who does for help in this area. Once the demonic presence is discerned, then the Christian can use the authority that Jesus gave him and bind that demon and order it to leave in the powerful name of Jesus Christ. That demon must obey Jesus; it has no choice.

IS CONFESSION OF SINS NECESSARY?

"Is confession of sins necessary?" is almost a ridiculous question. If a Christian has sinned, he should certainly confess that sin to Father God and be cleansed by the blood of Jesus Christ. This is especially true if there is a sin that a Christian is hanging onto that might prevent a demon from being cast out (or cast off) of him.

If the individual has had any occult involvement, that must be confessed and renounced. The Holy Spirit will show the Christian or, if God is using someone else to cast out the demon, He will show that individual what sins there are and what really needs confessing and renouncing.

I do feel it is unnecessary, and in some cases, perhaps even harmful, for some of these deliverance ministers to require people to renounce long lists of such things as:

1. Every Disney movie they have ever seen
2. Jogging (or aerobic exercises) to Christian music
3. Playing fireman or house when they were children, or any other type of pretending
4. Wearing a cross (or other things) on a chain around their neck

The list could go on and on of the things people are often required to renounce. If a person who really needs deliverance in some area is required to renounce a long list of things and he comes to an item--like Christian aerobics, for example--that he really does not feel there is anything wrong with, then he is forced into a tough dilemma. He can tell the person doing the delivering that he does not feel that he should renounce that, which creates a conflict, or he can renounce it, even though he does not feel there is anything wrong with it. Either choice is not good and could hinder the real deliverance that is needed, by causing the person to be sidetracked.

In Romans 14, we see that what is right for one person may not be right for another. When someone is trying to get a Christian to renounce many things on a list, he could be trying to "play God" in that person's life, to control his behavior and tell him what he should and shouldn't do. Actually, trying to control another person's behavior is a form of witchcraft. People in deliverance ministries must be very careful to avoid this.

In a deliverance situation, it is one thing if the Holy Spirit gives a word of knowledge about a sin or perhaps an object that the individual used in the occult or worshiped at one time. Then, of course, that must be dealt with, but I am not for using long lists of things to confess. I have found that they simply create fear and confusion, and that does not glorify God.

CASTING OUT AND CONTROLLING DEMONS

Jesus Christ has given you, as a believer, authority over demons and the power to control them, to bind them, and to cast them out of people, whether saved or unsaved, and even to cast them out of yourself and your family members. Do not forget that in order to exercise that power and authority to the fullest, it will probably require faith and also prayer and fasting on your part, but that power is available to you!

Let me give you an example. In Mike Warnke's book, SATAN SELLERS, he relates how back before he was a Christian, there was a Christian witnessing to him. He drew back his hand to hit the Christian (it was really the demons inside Mike Warnke that were controlling him). The Christian commanded those demons to stop and bound them right in the middle of the act and Mike could not swing his arm. This is what I mean by control over demons.

A Christian also has the authority and power to cast demons out of his home, if he senses there are any hanging around there. He should pray and ask God if there are any objects in his home (or place of work) that he should get rid of. If the Lord shows him something, then it must go. After that, he should rest in peace.

It is probably a good idea, if one is going to have a Christian meeting in a rented hotel or motel room, to bind any demonic forces that may be lingering around from past episodes there and to dedicate the room to be holy unto God.

The demons must obey Jesus. He has given us His power of attorney and they must obey us when we command them in His name; they have no choice. Praise the Lord! The victory is ours in this spiritual warfare!

I AM THE MATTER WITH ME

Many, many years ago I read a book or an article entitled, "I Am The Matter With Me." It pointed out that as long as we could blame our troubles and faults on our parents, our school, our employer, our childhood, or anything else, then we really would not do anything about correcting these problems or improving ourselves. The book gently and lovingly helped the reader come to an understanding that it was really himself who was the root of most of his faults and difficulties. Once a person acknowledged that, then he would set about to correct those problems.

I would like to give a bit of a balancing word concerning this chapter. Once a Christian swings over from not believing that demons are real or that they should be cast out, to acknowledging that demons do exist and becoming involved in casting them out, I have seen so many Christians go overboard and blame everything, from a little headache to a picture falling off of its hook, on demons. That isn't so serious, although I doubt that all of those things are caused by demons. However, what is serious is that they also tend to blame many of their sins and fleshly indulgences on demons and, thus, they really do not do anything about disciplining themselves and exercising self-control. Self-control is important.

Galatians tells us the different aspects of the fruit of the Holy Spirit--that is, what is the "fruit" or result of being filled with and controlled by the Holy Spirit:

> **22 But the fruit of the Spirit is love, joy, peace, patience, kindness, goodness, faithfulness,**
> **23 gentleness, self-control; against such things there is no law.**
>
> **--Galatians 5**

The last in this list is "self-control." That is the one that Christians most often neglect to talk about. If you get into a group of Christians who are spiritually sloppy and start talking about self-discipline, it is like arousing a bunch of old wet hens. They do not want to be disciplined. They like to blame their fleshly sins and shortcomings on something external, and they will accuse you of being legalistic. They are wishing for some "instant" and easy way to overcome the flesh.

What these Christians need to realize is that we are in a battle against our flesh. Our "old man" is dead. That old man is the man who was trying to get to God through the law. However, our flesh is very much alive and continually sends us messages, desires and demands. In writing to Christians (brethren), Paul had the following to say on this subject:

> **12 So then, brethren, we are under obligation, not to the flesh, to live according to the flesh--**
> **13 for if you are living according to the flesh,**

you must die; but if by the Spirit you are putting to death the deeds of the body, you will live.
--Romans 8

14 but put on the Lord Jesus Christ, and make no provision for the flesh in regard to its lusts.
--Romans 13

16 But I say, walk by the Spirit, and you will not carry out the desire of the flesh.
--Galatians 5

27 but I buffet my body and make it my slave, lest possibly, after I have preached to others, I myself should be disqualified.
--1 Corinthians 9

As we have observed in other chapters in this book, God expects us to cleanse ourselves and to purify ourselves. He expects us to sanctify ourselves and to make ourselves holy, just as Jesus did. If there is a habit that is particularly hard to break, we can ask God if there is a demon involved or if it is our own flesh. He will show us. If there is a demon involved, we need to exercise our authority in Christ over it and cast it out. If it is our own fleshly appetites, then we need to exercise self-control. Either way, something needs to be exercised, either our authority in Christ over the demon or our self-control over the flesh. God will show you which, if you ask Him and are willing to discipline yourself and control yourself, if He shows you that it is your own flesh.

THE TOOTHLESS LION

There is a major spiritual war coming as this age ends. It is not within the scope of this book to deal with that subject. I dealt with it in the in book YOU CAN OVERCOME. However, recently David Wilkerson sent me a manuscript of an article he was writing entitled THE TOOTHLESS LION. I feel the Lord wants me to pass onto you a portion of what he had to say:

There are two lions mentioned in God's Holy Word. One is the Lion of the tribe of Judah; the other is the roaring lion that goes about seeking to destroy.

John, the revelator, saw Christ as the Lion that has prevailed. "And one of the elders said unto me, Weep not: behold, the Lion of the tribe of Juda, the Root of David, hath prevailed . . ." (Rev. 5:5).

Peter recognized Satan as an adversary lion seeking to devour God's people. "Be sober, be vigilant; because your adversary the devil, as a roaring lion, walketh about, seeking whom he may devour: Whom resist steadfast in the faith . . ." (1 Peter 5:8,9).

The Purpose of this Message is Threefold:

1. To show that the Lion of Judah has prevailed against the roaring lion, rendering him toothless against the overcomer.
2. To show that it is possible for disobedient children of God to give the lion back his teeth and be devoured by him.
3. To show there is a place in God where the roaring lion dares not trespass.

Before going any further, let me explain what I mean by "toothless." This is a modern idiom suggesting "no authority." When a law has no teeth, we mean it has no authority. It is not backed by enough power or authority to enforce it. It may sound authoritative; it may seem ominous and threatening. But if it cannot be enforced, it has no teeth. It is useless, and no one need fear it. . . .

Satan must not be ignored, but neither should he be given more attention than is warranted by the Scriptures. The overcomer who has been conformed to the death of Christ and who lives infused with His resurrection power, can stand on God's promise that he will never have to fear the teeth of Satan.

I declare to you that the true overcomer can stand before the power of hell, the principalities and powers of darkness, and shout--"Because I am dead to this world and sin, because I have been translated from the kingdom of darkness into the kingdom of light--the roaring lion can roar all he wants to. As far as I am concerned, he has no teeth. He comes and touches me not . . . he has no authority in my life!"

Not so for the ungodly and the disobedient. Satan and his demon whelps come against them with ravenous appetite and sharp teeth. When the fifth angel of John's revelation opened the bottomless pit, Satan's hordes were released and given power over all who did not have the seal of God in their foreheads. "Their faces were as the faces of men . . . and their teeth were as the teeth of lions . . ." (Rev. 9:1-8). This suggests they were given authority by Abaddon, the king of the bottomless pit (Rev. 9:11). They had teeth. They would not be ineffective against those who were not sealed. They would hurt; they would have power. . . .

God has spoken to us in clearer terms than to this prophet out of Judah. Could the Lord be any more specific than this: "Be not unequally yoked together with unbelievers . . . come out from among them and be ye separate . . . touch not the unclean thing . . ." (2 Corinthians 6:14-18).

Like the prophet, multitudes of God's people are not fleeing from the cursed place. They socialize with the wicked; they eat and drink with the ungodly; they are deceived by the lies of false prophets; they have never separated themselves from the unclean, the workers of iniquity. No wonder there are so many dead carcasses lying by the wayside! So many shipwrecked preachers. Men and women of God commit adultery, they fornicate, they flaunt their disobedience. Then they wonder why such darkness and despair flood their souls.

Can the devil touch a man of God? Does his lion have teeth? If that man goes on in rebellion and disobedience, yes! There will be a lion to meet him on the way. . . .

We are not talking now about the Christian who is waging a battle against a sin he hates. This is not the tenderhearted believer who falls into temptation. It is not the one who cries out to be delivered from the body of death. We are talking about the willful transgressor. The hardhearted Christian who has seared his conscience and refuses to deal with sin, who goes on year after year indulging--grieving the Holy Spirit. He is the one who wants God and his sin.

Can such a Christan be overcome by the roaring lion? Yes! But he is still not without hope of resurrection if he will return to the Lord and tremble in His presence.

"Nevertheless, I will not make a full end with you . . . if you will fear me . . . and tremble at my presence . . ." (Jer. 5:18-22).

I say to the Christian who has become an habitual transgressor: You are on Satan's territory. He lurks even now, ready to move in on his prey. . . .

Now let us move to my primary premise: **The Lion of Judah has prevailed against the roaring lion, rendering him ineffective against the overcomer. . . .**

Both Daniel in the Old Testament, and Paul in the New, had to deal with the roaring lion. Theirs is the story of a toothless enemy, unable to touch or break their spirits.

Consider Daniel's Encounter with the Lion

The lion condemned Daniel, then put him in his own den to destory him, but could not! Who was this King Darius who sentenced Daniel to the lion's den? He was a heathen ruler, a tool of Satan. "As a roaring lion, and a ranging bear--so is a wicked ruler" (Prov. 28:15). Again, in Zephaniah, "Her princes within her are roaring lions" (3:3).

Who was King Nebuchadnezzar but a tool of the roaring lion who cast the Hebrew children into the fire? Daniel was not only cast into the lion's den, but the den was locked and sealed. There was no escape, no way out!

A holy, overcoming man of God was maneuvered by Satan into a face-to-face confrontation. Would the lion pounce on him, tear him apart, devour him? Or, did Daniel know something God had told him about the lions? Did God reveal to him that they were toothless--that he could not be touched--that he was as safe in the presence of satanic power as if he were in heaven?

"Then the king arose very early in the morning, and went in haste unto the den of lions . . ." (Dan. 6:19). King Darius asked the question I want to ask every Christian, a question that must be answered and settled once and for all, beyond doubt: Can the roaring lion hurt, in any way, a holy child of God?

Darius ". . . cried with a pitiful voice unto Daniel, O Daniel, servant of the living God, is thy God, whom thou servest continually, able to deliver thee from the mouth of the lion?" (Dan. 6:20). You do not comprehend the victory of the Cross unless you can answer, with Daniel, "My God sent his angel, and hath shut the lion's mouth, that he has not hurt me: forasmuch as before him innocency was found in me . . ." (6:22).

A Christian who is clear before God, innocent in heart--serving the Lord continually as did Daniel--cannot be hurt by the roaring lion, nor by his whelps. This must be our testimony before a wicked world. We serve a God who can shut the mouth of the roaring lion, make him toothless before His holy people, and deliver them as He delivered Daniel, "from the paw of the lion." (1 Sam 17:37). . . .

Can Satan maneuver an overcomer into a confrontation--throw him in a lion's den or a fiery furnace? Yes! Can the lion prevail in that confrontation? No! We are more than conquerors through Christ--over lions!

Consider Paul's Witness to the Overcomer's Victory over the Roaring Lion

The roaring lion was able to maneuver Paul into a prison in Rome, but he could not possess him or in any way touch his inner man. Paul calls himself the prisoner of the Lord Jesus Christ. And though all men forsook him, he rejoiced in knowing the lion could not hurt him, nor hinder the gospel.

"Notwithstanding the Lord stood with me, and strengthened me; that by me the preaching might be fully known . . . And I was delivered out of the mouth of the lion. And the Lord shall deliver me from every evil work, and will preserve me unto his heavenly kingdom: to whom be glory for ever and ever . . ." (2 Tim. 4:17,18).

The roaring lion was of no effect against this dedicated man of God! How many times this man looked down the mouth of the lion, and how many times the lion hungered to devour him. Yet not once did he fear this enemy! He saw the Lord standing by him, with majestic strength. He had his eyes on the Mighty Lion--the Lion of the tribe of Judah--and he was fearless.

He could say with all confidence, "I was shipwrecked, beaten, stoned, robbed, forsaken, and all alone--but never once did the lion bite! I was delivered from his power!"

I stand here in my time, and with David and Paul I can boldly say--"My Lord stands by me. I am under the protection of the Lion of Judah.

God has sent His Son and shut the roaring lion's mouth, and He will keep on preserving me from all evil powers until the day of His coming."

David Wilkerson

I praise God for a man like Dave Wilkerson and the insights that God gives to him. Weren't these thoughts about the victory of overcomers over Satan helpful and inspiring? Praise the Lord! I agree with Dave that **obedience** to the Lord is a key element in our warfare against the evil one.

SUMMARY AND CONCLUSION

Let's look back at the last two chapters on both healing and casting out of demons. We want to be as much like Jesus in these ministries as we possibly can be. This requires the supernatural power of the Holy Spirit. We cannot do these things alone. Both of these ministries require a price, a sacrifice: that of faith, prayer, and fasting. If you are not willing to pay that price, as Jesus was willing to do, then you will not be used mightily in these areas.

However, I believe that every Christian has the potential within him to be able to be used of God, both to heal diseases and to cast out demons. As you begin to exercise these gifts, God will multiply the opportunities that you have to use them. It all should be done with a heart of love and compassion for people who are hurting and suffering. We need to love these people with the love of Christ, which means being willing to lay down our very lives for them, being willing to experience inconvenience, and even loss, in order to help someone be healed or be set free from demons.

It is my "opinion" that Christians can be indwelt by demons and that they can come in via the route of sexual intercourse with someone who has a demon. If a couple believes they have demons, the husband and wife should simultaneously have any demons cast out of them and then be free from the fear of demons returning to indwell them.

We certainly should not be in fear of demons because of an object that God has told us to buy. However, we need to be careful, because I doubt very seriously that God would ever lead anyone to buy something occult, like a ouija board. However, if God leads you to buy a doll for your little girl, a baseball cap for your little boy, or a beautiful rainbow to put on your sliding glass door, there is no way that I see in the Scriptures that demons inhabit these items, nor are they an invitation for demons to harass you.

In the event that a demon comes around, you have the authority from Christ to chase it away, and it must obey you, as you move in God's will, in the power of the Holy Spirit, and in the name of Jesus Christ. The victory is ours in Christ. Without any doubt, you can believe that the victory will be yours!

Overcoming Christians should have no fear of demons or even Satan himself. Conversely, they fear us and the power that we have over them in Jesus Christ. As Dave Wilkerson so beautifully put it, to overcoming Christians, Satan is a toothless lion and demons must obey us when we come in the name of Jesus Christ and are living in obedience to God.

Now that we have overcome fear of Satan, demons and various inanimate objects, and we realize the power and authority that we have in Christ, let us move from the defense to the offense.

14
YOU WILL ATTACK AND WIN

You may raise your eyebrows at the title of this chapter. We Christians tend to think that "attacking" someone or something is not "Christlike." Christians today tend to be such a passive lot. However, as we look fresh at the life of Christ, we find that He "attacked" many things, and He taught His disciples to do likewise.

Of the many examples of this, perhaps the most dramatic is His cleansing of the temple:

> **13 And the Passover of the Jews was at hand, and Jesus went up to Jerusalem.**
> **14 And He found in the temple those who were selling oxen and sheep and doves, and the moneychangers seated.**
> **15 And He made a scourge of cords, and drove them all out of the temple, with the sheep and the oxen; and He poured out the coins of the moneychangers, and overturned their tables;**
> **16 and to those who were selling the doves He said, "Take these things away; stop making My Father's house a house of merchandise."**
> --John 2

Verse 15 says that Jesus made a whip out of cords, evidently braiding them together, and He **drove** the sheep, the oxen, and those who were selling them out of the temple, and He **turned over** the moneychangers' tables, so that the coins went all over. Would you say that He "attacked" those who were doing unclean, unholy things in the temple? I definitely think He attacked them. Mark amplifies on this:

> **15 And they came to Jerusalem. And He entered the temple and began to cast out those who were buying and selling in the temple, and overturned the tables of the moneychangers and the seats of those who were selling doves;**
> **16 and He would not permit anyone to carry goods through the temple.**
> **17 And He began to teach and say to them, "Is it not written, 'MY HOUSE SHALL BE CALLED A HOUSE OF PRAYER FOR ALL THE NATIONS'? But you have made it a ROBBERS' DEN."**
>
> **--Mark 11**

Verse 16 says that He would not even permit anyone to carry goods through the temple. When the Spirit of God told Him to, Jesus did not hesitate to aggressively "attack," and the victory was His!

Jesus also taught His disciples to attack. He did not say that if the gates of hell came after them, they were to stand and resist. What I believe He really said was that when they attacked the gates of hell, they would not be able to stand up against their attack:

> **18 And I say also unto thee, That thou art Peter, and upon this rock I will build my church; and the gates of hell shall not prevail against it.**
>
> **--Matthew 16, KJV**

In the AMPLIFIED BIBLE, the last part of this verse about the church reads, "the gates of Hades shall not overpower it--or be strong to its detriment, or **hold out against it.**" Since we, too, are disciples of Christ our Lord and part of "the church," this also applies to us! The gates of hell will not be able to "hold out against" us, as we advance in the name of Christ and actively **possess** our spiritual "promised land."

In giving the great commission, Jesus did not tell the disciples to stay there in Jerusalem and eventually all the world would come to them and gradually hear the gospel. Rather, He told them to **go out** to the nations and preach the gospel. They were to move out and to attack in those areas where Satan reigned:

> **18 And Jesus came up and spoke to them, saying, "All authority has been given to Me in heaven and on earth.**
> **19 "Go therefore and make disciples of all the nations, baptizing them in the name of the Father and the Son and the Holy Spirit,**
> **20 teaching them to observe all that I commanded you; and lo, I am with you always, even to the end of the age."**
>
> **--Matthew 28**

I praise God that all the disciples of the first century were faithful to carry out that command, and that so many men and women of God have been faithful to carry out this great commission, down through the ages. You could say that Paul "attacked" the area around the Mediterranean Sea. Hudson Taylor went out and attacked China. Billy Graham and other men of God attack pagan cities and even pagan countries, as they hold their crusades there. When we attack or take the offensive, under the guidance of God, the victory will most assuredly be ours and the glory will go to Christ!

ATTACKERS FROM THE OLD TESTAMENT

The Old Testament is full of examples of men and women of God who, under the direction of Almighty God, attacked the enemy, both physically and spiritually. One beautiful example of this is the episode with David and Goliath. David actually **ran toward** Goliath, he was so eager to attack:

> **45 Then David said to the Philistine, "You come to me with a sword, a spear, and a javelin,**

but I come to you in the name of the LORD of hosts, the God of the armies of Israel, whom you have taunted.

46 "This day the LORD will deliver you up into my hands, and I will strike you down and remove your head from you. And I will give the dead bodies of the army of the Philistines this day to the birds of the sky and the wild beasts of the earth, that all the earth may know that there is a God in Israel,

47 and that all this assembly may know that the LORD does not deliver by sword or by spear; for the battle is the LORD'S and He will give you into our hands."

48 Then it happened when the Philistine rose and came and drew near to meet David, that David ran quickly toward the battle line to meet the Philistine.

49 And David put his hand into his bag and took from it a stone and slung it, and struck the Philistine on his forehead. And the stone sank into his forehead, so that he fell on his face to the ground.

50 Thus David prevailed over the Philistine with a sling and a stone, and he struck the Philistine and killed him; but there was no sword in David's hand.

51 Then David ran and stood over the Philistine and took his sword and drew it out of its sheath and killed him, and cut off his head with it. When the Philistines saw that their champion was dead, they fled.

--1 Samuel 17

Here we see that David attacked the enemy, under the guidance of Almighty God and in the name of the Lord, with confidence and without fear. I am sure you will agree that he did attack and God gave him the victory! He did not wait for Goliath to come after him and then hope and pray that God would defend him. He went out on the offense and won. Praise the Lord! Let's take two other examples from David, which develop this pattern:

> 8 When there was war again, David went out and fought with the Philistines, and defeated them with great slaughter, so that they fled before him.
>
> --1 Samuel 19

When the Philistines declared war against Israel, David did not sit back and wait for them to come to him. The Scriptures say that "David went out and fought." He did the attacking, under God's guidance and the victory was overwhelming, to the glory of God! A similar thing happened a little bit later:

> 4 Then David inquired of the LORD once more. And the LORD answered him and said, "Arise, go down to Keilah, for I will give the Philistines into your hand."
>
> 5 So David and his men went to Keilah and fought with the Philistines; and he led away their livestock and struck them with a great slaughter. Thus David delivered the inhabitants of Keilah.
>
> --1 Samuel 23

One of the keys to David's beautiful heart (God called him, "a man after My own heart, who will do all My will"--Acts 13:22), was that he always "inquired of the Lord." He repeatedly sought God's guidance and direction, and God directed him. In the preceding verses, we see God telling him clearly to go down and attack the Philistines. God also told him that there would be victory in it, and there was. Isn't that exciting?

We could look at many other examples in the Old Testament, but for the sake of space we will take just a few more. First let me ask you this: do you think Joshua and the children of Israel "attacked" Jericho? The answer is obviously, "yes." The inhabitants of Jericho were huddled up in their city, trying to defend themselves against Joshua's attack:

> 1 Now Jericho was tightly shut because of the sons of Israel; no one went out and no one

came in.

2 And the LORD said to Joshua, "See, I have given Jericho into your hand, with its king and the valiant warriors.

3 "And you shall march around the city, all the men of war circling the city once. You shall do so for six days.

4 "Also seven priests shall carry seven trumpets of rams' horns before the ark; then on the seventh day you shall march around the city seven times, and the priests shall blow the trumpets.

5 "And it shall be that when they make a long blast with the ram's horn, and when you hear the sound of the trumpet, all the people shall shout with a great shout; and the wall of the city will fall down flat, and the people will go up every man straight ahead." . . .

21 And they utterly destroyed everything in the city, both man and woman, young and old, and ox and sheep and donkey, with the edge of the sword.

--Joshua 6

Another example out of the life of Joshua occurs not too long after the conquest of Jericho:

6 Then the men of Gibeon sent word to Joshua to the camp at Gilgal, saying, "Do not abandon your servants; come up to us quickly and save us and help us, for all the kings of the Amorites that live in the hill country have asembled against us."

7 So Joshua went up from Gilgal, he and all the people of war with him and all the valiant warriors.

8 And the LORD said to Joshua, "Do not fear them, for I have given them into your hands; not one of them shall stand before you."

9 So Joshua came upon them suddenly by marching all night from Gilgal.

10 And the LORD confounded them before Israel, and He slew them with a great slaughter

at Gibeon, and pursued them by the way of the ascent of Beth-Horon, and struck them as far as Azekah and Makkedah.

11 And it came about as they fled from before Israel, while they were at the descent of Beth-horon, that the LORD threw large stones from heaven on them as far as Azekah, and they died; there were more who died from the hailstones than those whom the sons of Israel killed with the sword.

--Joshua 10

We will take just one more example out of Joshua's life:

5 So all of these kings having agreed to meet, came and encamped together at the waters of Merom, to fight against Israel.

6 Then the LORD said to Joshua, "Do not be afraid because of them, for tomorrow at this time I will deliver all of them slain before Israel; you shall hamstring their horses and burn their chariots with fire."

7 So Joshua and all the people of war with him came upon them suddenly by the waters of Merom, and attacked them.

8 And the LORD delivered them into the hand of Israel, so that they defeated them, and pursued them as far as Great Sidon and Misrephoth-maim and the valley of Mizpeh to the east; and they struck them until no survivor was left to them.

9 And Joshua did to them as the LORD had told him; he hamstrung their horses, and burned their chariots with fire.

--Joshua 11

In the same manner as Joshua and David, as well as Paul and the other disciples, we must be willing and ready to attack under the Lord's orders and direction. We must not draw back or hang back defensively, but actually advance against the enemy in an offensive posture. If we are moving under God's control, we can always know that the end result will be victory to His glory.

ATTACKING IN THE NEW TESTAMENT

In the Old Testament, the promised land was occupied by people who were living there and had built homes and cities and farms. God led the children of Israel to attack these people, to kill them and to take over their homes, farms and cities, and to live there.

In a spiritual sense, Christ has asked us to do the same thing in the New Testament, except we are to go into all the world conquering in His name, fighting our battles in the spiritual realm. I believe that the white horse in Revelation 6 is a beautiful picture of our going out to conquer for Christ:

> **1 And I saw when the Lamb broke one of the seven seals, and I heard one of the four living creatures saying as with a voice of thunder, "Come."**
>
> **2 And I looked, and behold, a white horse, and he who sat on it had a bow; and a crown was given to him; and he went out conquering, and to conquer.**
>
> **--Revelation 6**

Others may have differing interpretations of what this white horse is in the seven seals. (We know that it is not Jesus. He comes on a white horse later, in Revelation 19. We know it is not the beast--the antichrist--because evil is never depicted as white.) I believe that this white horse in Revelation 6 represents the gospel going forth to all nations. In other words, Christians will go out as sons of the King (wearing a crown) and will conquer in the name of Christ, just as the Israelites conquered the promised land in the Old Testament.

When you read about the life of Paul, you read about a man who repeatedly went out and attacked the strongholds of Satan, conquering in the name of Christ.

From the moment that he was sent out from Antioch (Acts 13), through the remainder of the Book of Acts, his life is filled with journeys into pagan lands to present Christ. Here is one example of this:

> 6 And they passed through the Phrygian and Galatian region, having been forbidden by the Holy Spirit to speak the word in Asia;
> 7 and when they had come to Mysia, they were trying to go into Bithynia, and the Spirit of Jesus did not permit them;
> 8 and passing by Mysia, they came down to Troas.
> 9 And a vision appeared to Paul in the night: a certain man of Macedonia was standing and appealing to him, and saying, "Come over to Macedonia and help us."
> 10 And when he had seen the vision, immediately we sought to go into Macedonia, concluding that God had called us to preach the gospel to them.
>
> --Acts 16

Here we see that the Lord led Paul and his companions to go over into Europe (Macedonia is in Greece) to present the gospel there. After they got to Macedonia, they ran into a girl who had a demon. Then Paul conquers Satan's stronghold in that girl:

> 16 And it happened that as we were going to the place of prayer, a certain slave-girl having a spirit of divination met us, who was bringing her masters much profit by fortunetelling.
> 17 Following after Paul and us, she kept crying out, saying, "These men are bond-servants of the Most High God, who are proclaiming to you the way of salvation."
> 18 And she continued doing this for many days. But Paul was greatly annoyed, and turned and said to the spirit, "I command you in the name of Jesus Christ to come out of her!" And it came out at that very moment.

> 19 But when her masters saw that their hope of profit was gone, they seized Paul and Silas and dragged them into the market place before the authorities, . . .
>
> --Acts 16

Because he was boldly proclaiming Christ in Philippi, we know that later Paul was thrown into prison, where he rejoiced in the Lord. While he and Silas were praising the Lord about midnight, God used an earthquake to shake the prison and set him free. As a result of all this, the Philippian jailor received Christ. Even while he was in jail, Paul was still conquering in the name of Christ and the gates of hell could not prevail against him!

You are familiar with the many other places where the Holy Spirit led Paul to attack the strongholds of Satan. One that comes to mind was in Ephesus, where all the craftsmen reacted to Paul's attack:

> 24 For a certain man named Demetrius, a silversmith, who made silver shrines of Artemis, was bringing no little business to the craftsmen;
> 25 these he gathered together with the workmen of similar trades, and said, "Men, you know that our prosperity depends upon this business.
> 26 "And you see and hear that not only in Ephesus, but in almost all of Asia, this Paul has persuaded and turned away a considerable number of people, saying that gods made with hands are no gods at all.
> 27 "And not only is there danger that this trade of ours fall into disrepute, but also that the temple of the great goddess Artemis be regarded as worthless and that she whom all of Asia and the world worship should even be dethroned from her magnificence."
> 28 And when they heard this and were filled with rage, they began crying out, saying, "Great is Artemis of the Ephesians!"
>
> --Acts 19

Evidently, by his aggressive preaching, Paul was turning many people away from worshiping these idols, by which these men made their living. He was not quietly and unobtrusively sharing about Jesus in out-of-the-way places. He was boldly proclaiming the truth without reservation, which threatened to disrupt the very trade and livelihood of these craftsmen who fashioned man-made idols.

In writing to Timothy, Paul tells him to fight (to attack):

> **12 Fight the good fight of faith; take hold of the eternal life to which you were called, and you made the good confession in the presence of many witnesses.**
>
> **--1 Timothy 6**

> **7 I have fought the good fight, I have finished the course, I have kept the faith; . . .**
>
> **--2 Timothy 4**

In this last verse, Paul tells Timothy that he had indeed fought that good fight. Evidently, it was not just a defensive fight or battle; it was an offensive one. Paul went out and attacked the strongholds of Satan and won.

THE OVERCOMING CHRISTIAN IS AGGRESSIVE

Perhaps you have reacted to the word "attack" as being a bit too strong, although I'm not sure it is. I feel the Lord had me use it deliberately to help move many Christians from the "comfortable" position where they are. By and large, Christians today are such a comfortable, passive lot that they have really lost all aggressiveness. Even America has really become a nonaggressive nation. (I am **not** advocating mindless aggression, which is as bad as being superpassive.)

In the meantime, Communism, the Muslims and other forces of Satan have become very aggressive. Let me ask you a question. If one football team always played offense, while the other team only played defense, which one do you think would win? Obviously the team that played offense, the aggressive team. Being **victorious** in the Christian life requires that a Christian be **aggressive** and **take the offense.**

We Christians sometimes complain that Christian ministries are always appealing for funds. We really should praise God that they are doing this, because that means that they want to aggressively go out and reach more people for Jesus Christ. I praise God for such men as Billy Graham, Jimmy Swaggart, Pat Robertson, Jim Bakker, Demos Shakarian and James Robison, who take their crusades to other countries and aggressively move into areas where Satan is strong, in order to present the gospel of Jesus Christ to people who need to hear it. The very thrust of our missionary efforts is aggression. When a Christian will go into a country or a community, where there is perhaps not even a single Christian, and will aggressively begin to witness, he can win many for Jesus Christ and further God's kingdom.

This is why Christianity in the first century spread so rapidly. Every single one of the disciples was aggressive in his obedience to Christ's command to go into all the world and preach the gospel to every single creature. If that command was burned on our hearts with the fire of God like it was on theirs, we would be just as aggressive in trying to win others to Christ, such as our fellow workers and the people in our neighborhood.

We need to aggressively pursue the deeper things of God. We need to aggressively pursue having a closer relationship with God, Jesus and the Holy Spirit. We need to aggressively pursue becoming more like Jesus Christ. I pray that God would build a fire in our hearts, move us from our "comfortable" positions, and send us out with energy, power, excitement and eagerness in our quest to become like Jesus Christ.

The Bible is certainly not a passive book. It is full of exhortations to actively pursue God and His will in our lives. If you would like to do an exciting study along these lines, begin to look for Scriptures with "action-type" verbs, given in **command** form. Here are just a few examples to give you the idea:

- Put on love (Col. 3:14)
- Put on a heart of compassion (Col. 3:12)
- Put on the Lord Jesus Christ; make no provision for the flesh (Rom. 13:14)
- Lay aside the old self and put on the new (Eph. 4:22-24)
- Put on the full armor of God (Eph. 6:11)
- Cleanse yourselves from defilement; perfect holiness (2 Cor. 7:1)
- Grow up in all aspects into Him (Eph. 4:14,15)
- Be made complete; rejoice; live in peace (2 Cor. 13:11)
- Be imitators of God (Eph. 5:1-4)
- Do nothing from selfishness (Phil 2:3)
- Supply moral excellence, self-control, godliness (1 Pet. 1:14-16)
- Walk by the Spirit (Gal. 5:16)
- Pursue righteousness (1 Tim. 6:11-14)
- Suffer hardship as a good soldier (2 Tim. 2:3,4)
- Do not be conformed to this world (Rom. 12:2)
- Abhor what is evil; cling to what is good (Rom. 12:9)
- Overcome evil with good (Rom. 12:21)

This is just a sampling of things that we are told to **actively pursue.** As you start looking for them when you read the Scriptures, God will unfold to you the vision of the overcoming army that He wants Christians to be.

OFFENSIVE WEAPONS

An entire book could easily be written on the offensive weapons in our arsenal as Christians. We have touched on some of them in previous chapters. We know that prayer and fasting can bring victories in the spiritual realm. We know that by reading and meditating on the Scriptures, we can gird up our minds and hearts to withstand the attacks of the enemy.

The ministries of healing and deliverance are offensive weapons that can break down strongholds of Satan. This passage from Revelation gives us further insight into how to overcome the evil one:

> **10 And I heard a loud voice in heaven, saying,**
> **"Now the salvation, and the power, and the kingdom of our God and the authority of His Christ have come, for the accuser of our brethren has been thrown down, who accuses them before our God day and night.**
> **11 "And they overcame him because of the blood of the Lamb and because of the word of their testimony, and they did not love their life even to death. . . ."**
>
> --Revelation 12

We have already seen that boldly proclaiming the gospel is a form of "attacking" (1 Corinthians 1:21).

Praise is a very strong offensive weapon, which we have not delved into at all. Satan seems to be totally frustrated by Christians who will praise God in all things. If His praise fills our "temple," there is no room in us for fear or defeat. The psalmist tells us the following:

> **2 Out of the mouth of babes and sucklings hast thou ordained strength because of thine enemies, that thou mightest still the enemy and the avenger.**
>
> --Psalm 8, KJV

There is real power in praise, for the Scriptures also tell us that God inhabits the praises of His people (Psalm 22:3). The next time you find yourself feeling defeated, try praising God in the midst of your troubles and see if He does not bring you through it in victory!

THE VICTORY WILL BE OURS

As we move out and, when God tells us to, attack the strongholds of Satan, and aggressively pursue becoming like Jesus Christ and seek a deeper relationship with Father God, we know that the victory will be ours. The Bible promises this to us.

Satan has many strongholds today. These may be strongholds of evil in your community or even in another country. There may be strongholds even within your own church or in your personal life. As we attack these strongholds, they will be pulled down:

> **3 For though we walk in the flesh, we do not war after the flesh:**
> **4 (For the weapons of our warfare are not carnal, but mighty through God to the pulling down of strongholds) . . .**
>
> --2 Corinthians 10, KJV

> **3 For though we walk in the flesh, we do not war according to the flesh,**
> **4 for the weapons of our warfare are not of the flesh, but divinely powerful for the destruction of fortresses.**
>
> --2 Corinthians 10, NAS

The preceding verses, out of two different translations, point out that we are at war. As part of this warfare, we are to destroy and pull down Satan's strongholds. We are not going to do that unless we aggressively come against them. But as we do, we know that the victory will be ours, because Jesus is greater than Satan. We know that Satan is the one who is in the world and Jesus is in us:

> **31 What then shall we say to these things? If God is for us, who is against us?**
> **32 He who did not spare His own Son, but delivered Him up for us all, how will He not also with Him freely give us all things?**
> **33 Who will bring a charge against God's**

elect? God is the one who justifies;
34 Who is the one who condemns? Christ
Jesus is He who died, yes, rather who was
raised, who is at the right hand of God, who also
intercedes for us.
35 Who shall separate us from the love of
Christ? Shall tribulation, or distress, or persecution, or famine, or nakedness, or peril, or
sword?
36 Just as it is written,
"FOR THY SAKE WE ARE BEING PUT TO
DEATH ALL DAY LONG;
WE WERE CONSIDERED AS SHEEP TO BE
SLAUGHTERED."
37 But in all these things we overwhelmingly
conquer through Him who loved us.
38 For I am convinced that neither death, nor
life, nor angels, nor principalities, nor things
present, nor things to come, nor powers,
39 nor height, nor depth, nor any other
created thing, shall be able to separate us from
the love of God, which is in Christ Jesus our
Lord.

--Romans 8

Look especially at verses 35 and 36. There will be tribulation, persecution, famine and other perils that we will face, perhaps even death. However, according to verse 37, even in the midst of all these things, it does not say that we "barely conquer;" it says that we **overwhelmingly** conquer through Jesus Christ.

Praise the Lord! The victory does not rely on our own strength or power. The victory is through the strength and power of Jesus Christ:

56 The sting of death is sin, and the power of
sin is the law;
57 but thanks be to God, who gives us the
victory through our Lord Jesus Christ.
58 Therefore, my beloved brethren, be steadfast, immovable, always abounding in the work of

the Lord, knowing that your toil is not in vain in the Lord.

--1 Corinthians 15

One of my favorite Psalms talks about the victory that the Lord has won. It is not our right arm that is going to bring victory. It is the right arm of God Almighty:

1 O sing to the LORD a new song,
For He has done wonderful things,
His right hand and His holy arm have gained the victory for Him.
2 The LORD has made known His salvation;
He has revealed His righteousness in the sight of the nations.
3 He has remembered His lovingkindness and His faithfulness to the house of Israel;
All the ends of the earth have seen the salvation of our God.
4 Shout joyfully to the LORD, all the earth;
Break forth and sing for joy and sing praises.
5 Sing praises to the LORD with the lyre;
With the lyre and the sound of melody.
6 With trumpets and the sound of the horn
Shout joyfully before the King, the LORD.
7 Let the sea roar and all it contains,
The world and those who dwell in it.
8 Let the rivers clap their hands;
Let the mountains sing together for joy
9 Before the LORD; for He is coming to judge the earth;
He will judge the world with righteousness,
And the peoples with equity.

--Psalm 98

SUMMARY AND CONCLUSION

In this chapter, we have looked at the fact that most Christians are so passive that they have lost their aggressiveness. When they see evil and sin in their community, they do not aggressively attack it. When they see an opportunity to win someone to Jesus Christ, perhaps someone in their neighborhood whom they have never met, they sit back and watch television, rather than aggressively making attempts to meet that person and to share with him the exciting news of Jesus Christ.

The biblical pattern has been to "attack." David ran toward Goliath and attacked him, as he did other armies that came against God's chosen people. In conquering the promised land and ridding it of the pagans that lived there, Joshua certainly attacked the cities and inhabitants. Other men of old, such as Gideon, went out under God's orders and attacked the enemy.

In the New Testament, we see Paul and others of the apostles going into territories where Satan had strongholds and attacking these strongholds, pulling them down in the name of Christ and winning large numbers to a saving knowledge of Jesus Christ. All of this was done under God's guidance and control.

In our lives today, Satan has strongholds in our communities, in the countries around the world, and perhaps even within our church or in our own personal lives. We need not have any fear of Satan and his forces. Instead, we need to aggressively come against those strongholds, and the victory will be ours in the power of Jesus Christ. We know that greater is He Who is in us, than he who is in the world (1 John 4:4). Jesus is more powerful than Satan and the victory will be His! We will overwhelmingly conquer in the name of Christ, as He leads, guides and controls us!

However, even though the victory will be ours, as we aggressively pursue all that God charges us to do, there is a price to pay. Jesus paid that price and, if we are going to be like Jesus, we too will need to pay that price. Just what is that price? Let us now explore that question.

15
THERE IS A PRICE TO PAY

What a wonderful adventure it has been to explore what is really required to become like Jesus! It will be so marvelous to be holy and pure like Him. How great it would be to have a prayer life and to know the Scriptures as He did. How wonderful it would be to walk in supernatural power like that which He exercised, not for His own good but for the good of others. How marvelous to be obedient to the will of God, like He was, and to do good works, like He did.

We need to realize, however, that all of these powerful, marvelous things did not come freely and easily for Jesus. There was a deep price to pay. Jesus had to suffer and to be persecuted, as part of the price that He paid. He had to become a humble servant, which is really a form of suffering. He was willing to pay the price in order that He might be all that God wanted Him to be. If we want to be all that God wants us to be, then we too must be willing to pay the price, to follow Jesus' example of sacrificial love.

Peter Marshall Jr. once commented to me that the big weakness of Christianity in America today is that there is no theology of suffering. Everyone is preaching a gospel of complete health and prosperity, almost to the point that if anyone is suffering, he must be out of the will of God. Nothing could be further from the truth. If you look at Christians in the first centuries, they suffered a great deal. They were chased from their homes; they were torn to bits by ferocious lions in arenas while people cheered; they were burnt to death as human torches, covered by tar and set afire. And yet, through their suffering and persecution came the victory and the power that spread Christianity to the world.

Even in many countries today, such as the U.S.S.R., Red China, many of the communist countries, and many of the Arabic countries, Christians are suffering because of their faith in Christ and because of their desire to become like Him. If we are going to follow Jesus as our Example, and He suffered, then we too should expect to suffer.

JESUS SUFFERED VERY MUCH

We all realize that Jesus Christ suffered greatly at the time of the cross: He was beaten, He wore a crown of thorns and His final execution on the cross was a very painful way to die, not to mention that He bore the sins of the world. But Jesus' suffering was not limited to His death. He suffered much more than that, and the Scriptures tell about it in many places:

> **12 but I say to you, that Elijah already came, and they did not recognize him, but did to him whatever they wished. So also the Son of Man is going to suffer at their hands."**
> **13 Then the disciples understood that He had spoken to them about John the Baptist.**
>
> --Matthew 17

In verse 12, we see that Jesus knew He was going to suffer at the hands of the leaders, in a similar way to that which John the Baptist had suffered. A parallel passage is found in Mark but, in addition to suffering physically, Jesus said that He was going to be treated with contempt:

> **11 And they asked Him, saying, "Why is it that the scribes say that Elijah must come first?"**
> **12 And He said to them, "Elijah does first come and restore all things. And yet how is it written of the Son of Man that He should suffer**

> many things and be treated with contempt?
> 13 "But I say to you, that Elijah has indeed come, and they did to him whatever they wished, just as it is written of him."
>
> --Mark 9

In the following passage, Jesus spoke of His powerful return at the Second Coming, but then He talked about what He would experience first on the earth. He said that not only was He going to suffer, but He was going to be rejected:

> 24 "For just as the lightning, when it flashes out of one part of the sky, shines to the other part of the sky, so will the Son of Man be in His day.
> 25 "But first He must suffer many things and be rejected by this generation. . . ."
>
> --Luke 17

Jesus knew that His final suffering was going to be on the cross and He yearned to have one final time of fellowship, love and comfort with the disciples before He suffered on the cross:

> 15 And He said to them, "I have earnestly desired to eat this Passover with you before I suffer; . . ."
>
> --Luke 22

> 2 "You know that after two days the Passover is coming, and the Son of Man is to be delivered up for crucifixion."
>
> --Matthew 26

There are numerous places where Jesus said that He must suffer and be killed and on the third day rise again:

> 21 From that time Jesus Christ began to show His disciples that He must go to Jerusalem, and suffer many things from the elders and chief

priests and scribes, and be killed, and be raised up on the third day.

--Matthew 16

31 And He began to teach them that the Son of Man must suffer many things and be rejected by the elders and the chief priests and the scribes, and be killed, and after three days rise again.

--Mark 8

46 and He said to them, "Thus it is written, that the Christ should suffer and rise again from the dead the third day; . . ."

--Luke 24

In looking further at the suffering of Jesus Christ, we know that the religious leaders confronted Him continuously throughout His ministry. He was criticized for eating with sinners (Luke 5:30,31) and for healing on the Sabbath (Luke 6:6-11). On one occasion, those in the synagogue sought to throw Him over a cliff because of the things that He taught (Luke 4:28-30). Other times, some Jews sought to stone Him (John 8:59, 10:31). The Pharisees counseled about how they might destroy Him (Matthew 12:14). In short, Jesus suffered greatly throughout His life and ministry.

So in this brief look at the suffering of Jesus, we see that He experienced:

1. Contempt of people
2. Anger of people
3. Rejection by people
4. Hostility of people
5. People attempting to kill Him
6. People spitting on Him and hitting Him (Mark 14:65)
7. Being whipped with a horrible whip (Mark 15:15)
8. Having the top of His head punctured pain-

fully by a crown of thorns (Matthew 27:28-30)

9. In a weakened condition, being forced to carry His own cross (John 19:17)
10. Having His wrists and feet nailed to the cross
11. Being lifted on a cross to die a very agonizing death

It is difficult to separate where suffering ends and persecution begins, because they are interrelated. We know that Jesus was hated and also persecuted:

> **18 "If the world hates you, you know that it has hated Me before it hated you.**
> **19 "If you were of the world, the world would love its own; but because you are not of the world, but I chose you out of the world, therefore the world hates you.**
> **20 "Remember the word that I said to you, 'A slave is not greater than his master.' If they persecuted Me, they will also persecute you; if they kept My word, they will keep yours also. . . ."**
>
> --John 15

Here Jesus says that we will never be greater than Him (a slave is not greater than his master), but--as we have already seen in this book--He strongly encourages us to become like Him. According to this passage, if they hated and persecuted Him, they will also hate and persecute us. We need to let that thoroughly soak in: if we are going to become like Jesus Christ, we will be hated and persecuted.

This is not my idea, this is what Jesus plainly said. Go back and read the verses for yourself. He said, "If they persecuted Me, they **will** also persecute you" (author's emphasis). If you become like Jesus Christ you will be persecuted.

Jesus was not persecuted for what He did. He was persecuted for what He **said**. He was killed because of the truth. As you and I speak the whole truth of God, we too will experience hatred and persecution.

We are not greater than our Master (Jesus) and we will experience persecution, as He did, but the Bible also gives us this encouragement:

> **12 If we endure, we shall also reign with Him; . . .**
>
> --2 Timothy 2

The suffering and the persecution will be worth it, for the joy, power, glory and peace that lie ahead of us. However, suffering will come and this suffering will not only be emotional, but physical. It will come from Satan and the human beings that he and his demons influence and control. Persecution and suffering will come, but we can overcome them and victoriously go through what lies ahead. In the end the victory will be ours! Praise His holy Name!

SUFFERING IS NECESSARY

They say there is no royal road to learning. Everyone who wants to learn must read, study and analyze. There is no magic pill that someone can take to instantly become "knowledgeable."

Similarly, suffering is also necessary, as there are many things that we learn through suffering that we cannot learn any other way. We like to think that Jesus was instantly obedient to God. Not so. He had to learn to be obedient. How did He learn obedience?

> **8 Although He was a Son, He learned obedience from the things which He suffered.**
>
> --Hebrews 5

Another fantastic result of suffering is shown in the letter by Peter:

> **10 And after you have suffered for a little while, the God of all grace, who called you to His eternal glory in Christ, will Himself perfect,**

> confirm, strengthen and establish you.
>
> --1 Peter 5

Did you get what that verse really said? It said that after we have suffered (suffering is necessary), then God Himself will perfect us, confirm us, strengthen us (I believe with His supernatural power) and establish us (most likely in Christ's overcomer army). Praise the Lord!

What Peter has to say about suffering in the following verses might be a little harder to comprehend, but is well worth it if you will allow the Holy Spirit to speak the depth of His truth to you:

> 1 Therefore, since Christ has suffered in the flesh, arm yourselves also with the same purpose, because he who has suffered in the flesh has ceased from sin,
>
> 2 so as to live the rest of the time in the flesh no longer for the lusts of men, but for the will of God. . . .
>
> 12 Beloved, do not be surprised at the fiery ordeal among you, which comes upon you for your testing, as though some strange thing were happening to you;
>
> 13 but to the degree that you share the sufferings of Christ, keep on rejoicing; so that also at the revelation of His glory, you may rejoice with exultation.
>
> 14 If you are reviled for the name of Christ, you are blessed, because the Spirit of glory and of God rests upon you.
>
> 15 By no means let any of you suffer as a murderer, or thief, or evildoer, or a troublesome meddler;
>
> 16 but if anyone suffers as a Christian, let him not feel ashamed, but in that name let him glorify God.
>
> 17 For it is time for judgment to begin with the household of God; and if it begins with us first, what will be the outcome for those who do not obey the gospel of God?

> 18 AND IF IT IS WITH DIFFICULTY THAT THE RIGHTEOUS IS SAVED, WHAT WILL BECOME OF THE GODLESS MAN AND THE SINNER?
>
> 19 Therefore, let those also who suffer according to the will of God entrust their souls to a faithful Creator in doing what is right.
>
> --1 Peter 4

You may wish to reread those verses and let God speak to you through them, before we proceed.

It is a comfort to know that Peter, Paul and the other apostles suffered. We are certainly no more privileged than they were. As they suffered, so can we expect to suffer:

> 9 For, I think, God has exhibited us apostles last of all, as men condemned to death; because we have become a spectacle to the world, both to angels and to men.
>
> 10 We are fools for Christ's sake, but you are prudent in Christ; we are weak, but you are strong; you are distinguished, but we are without honor.
>
> 11 To this present hour we are both hungry and thirsty, and are poorly clothed, and are roughly treated, and are homeless;
>
> 12 and we toil, working with our own hands; when we are reviled, we bless; when we are persecuted, we endure;
>
> 13 when we are slandered, we try to conciliate; we have become as the scum of the world, the dregs of all things, even until now.
>
> --1 Corinthians 4

Now let us turn to another subject. Would you like to enter the kingdom of God? You might be thinking: "Of course I would. Don't be silly." Then be prepared for tribulation:

> 21 And after they had preached the gospel to that city and had made many disciples, they returned to Lystra and Iconium and to Antioch,

> 22 strengthening the souls of the disciples, encouraging them to continue in the faith, and saying, "Through many tribulations we must enter the kingdom of God."
>
> --Acts 14

GOD'S PEOPLE HAVE SUFFERED THROUGH THE CENTURIES

It may be hard for us to understand how a loving God either allows His people to suffer or wants them to suffer, in order to purify them, to test them, and to know what is in their hearts. But that is exactly what has happened through the centuries.

One classic example is that of Job. We know that Job was an upright man, blameless, fearing God and turning away from evil (Job 1:1). We must ask ourselves whether it was God's will for Job to experience the loss of all of his possessions and his family, to suffer humiliation and even to have excruciatingly painful sores over his body. That is a very critical question. Some would glibly say that it was within the "permissive will" of God but not within the "perfect will" of God. I really do not find those two concepts in the Bible. Perhaps they are just man-made concepts that confuse things for us. Either something that you do is in the will of God or it is not.

Let's assume for a minute that it was God's will for Job to suffer and to be tried. We know that the end result was glory for the Lord:

> 1 Then Job answered the LORD, and said,
> 2 "I know that Thou canst do all things,
> And that no purpose of Thine can be
> thwarted. . . ."
>
> 10 And the LORD restored the fortunes of Job when he prayed for his friends, and the LORD increased all that Job had twofold.
> 11 Then all his brothers, and all his sisters, and all who had known him before, came to him, and they ate bread with him in his house; and they consoled him and comforted him for all the

evil that the LORD had brought on him. And each one gave him one piece of money, and each a ring of gold.

12 And the LORD blessed the latter days of Job more than his beginning, and he had 14,000 sheep, and 6,000 camels, and 1,000 yoke of oxen, and 1,000 female donkeys.

--Job 42

Not all of God's people, particularly those who went all the way for God, fared as well as Job. We know that some of them suffered incredible things and persecution. In Chapter 11, the writer of the book of Hebrews talked about the tremendous men and women of faith in the Old Testament, among them Abraham, Sarah, Isaac, Jacob, Moses, Joseph and Rahab. At the end of the chapter, he has this to say:

32 And what more shall I say? For time will fail me if I tell of Gideon, Barak, Samson, Jephthah, of David and Samuel and the prophets,

33 who by faith conquered kingdoms, performed acts of righteousness, obtained promises, shut the mouths of lions,

34 quenched the power of fire, escaped the edge of the sword, from weakness were made strong, became mighty in war, put foreign armies to flight.

35 Women received back their dead by resurrection; and others were tortured, not accepting their release, in order that they might obtain a better resurrection;

36 and others experienced mockings and scourgings, yes, also chains and imprisonment.

37 They were stoned, they were sawn in two, they were tempted, they were put to death with the sword; they went about in sheepskins, in goatskins, being destitute, afflicted, ill-treated

38 (men of whom the world was not worthy), wandering in deserts and mountains and caves and holes in the ground.

39 And all these, having gained approval

> through their faith, did not receive what was promised,
>
> 40 because God had provided something better for us, so that apart from us they should not be made perfect.
>
> --Hebrews 11

Here we see that tremendous men of faith who followed God and obeyed Him to the death were frequently delivered in miraculous ways. On the other hand, others were actually imprisoned, mistreated, afflicted and killed, some in very horrible ways. Was their suffering part of the will of God? Yes, indeed it was and--praise God--they will eventually receive the promise!

In His story about the vineyard, Jesus talks about what happened to so many of the Old Testament prophets:

> 33 "Listen to another parable. There was a landowner who PLANTED A VINEYARD AND PUT A WALL AROUND IT AND DUG A WINE PRESS IN IT, AND BUILT A TOWER, and rented it out to vine-growers, and went on a journey.
>
> 34 "And when the harvest time approached, he sent his slaves to the vine-growers to receive his produce.
>
> 35 "And the vine-growers took his slaves and beat one, and killed another, and stoned a third.
>
> 36 "Again he sent another group of slaves larger than the first; and they did the same thing to them.
>
> 37 "But afterward he sent his son to them, saying, 'They will respect my son.'
>
> 38 "But when the vine-growers saw the son, they said among themselves, 'This is the heir; come, let us kill him, and seize his inheritance.'
>
> 39 "And they took him, and threw him out of the vineyard, and killed him.
>
> 40 "Therefore when the owner of the vineyard comes, what will he do to those vine-growers?"
>
> 41 They said to Him, "He will bring those

wretches to a wretched end, and will rent out the vineyard to other vine-growers, who will pay him the proceeds at the proper seasons."

42 Jesus said to them, "Did you never read in the Scriptures,

'THE STONE WHICH THE BUILDERS
REJECTED
THIS BECAME THE CHIEF CORNER
stone;
THIS CAME ABOUT FROM THE LORD,
AND IT IS MARVELOUS IN OUR EYES'?

43 "Therefore I say to you, the kingdom of God will be taken away from you, and be given to a nation producing the fruit of it.

44 "And he who falls on this stone will be broken to pieces; but on whomever it falls, it will scatter him like dust."

45 And when the chief priests and the Pharisees heard His parables, they understood that He was speaking about them.

--Matthew 21

In this parable, the vineyard is Israel and the servants that were sent were God's prophets of the Old Testament. Each one of them suffered. Some were beaten, some were stoned, and others were killed. Eventually, God took the vineyard (Israel) away from the evil people (the Hebrews who killed the prophets) and gave it to someone else (the church who is now Israel). There is absolutely no doubt about what Jesus meant by this parable, because verse 45 says that the Pharisees understood that He was talking about them (as the occupants of the vineyard at that time.)

In reviewing the Old Testament, we know that there were numerous incidents wherein prophets suffered. Repeatedly they suffered rejection by men because of their dedication to God and their "unpopular" prophecies. At times they very likely went hungry. Elijah had to flee for his life to escape Jezebel's wrath (1 Kings 19:2-4). Jeremiah lamented his many trials and even his very birth (Jeremiah 20:7,14-18). Jonah begged that God would let him die

(Jonah 4:8). Doubtless, many of the prophets lived very lonely lives. It appears that if one is going to be a real man or woman of God, persecution and suffering will come.

IF WE BECOME LIKE JESUS, SUFFERING AND PERSECUTION WILL COME

If we are going to become like Jesus Christ and truly be men and women of God, in the fullest sense, then we are actually promised that we will suffer and be persecuted:

> **20 "Remember the word that I said to you, 'A slave is not greater than his master.' If they persecuted Me, they will also persecute you; if they kept My word, they will keep yours also. . . ."**
>
> --John 15

We looked at this verse earlier, but we need to be reminded afresh that if Christ was persecuted (and He was), we will indeed be persecuted, if we become like Him. If we are a mushy, milk-toast Christian, who stands for little, there will not be persecution. But if we actually follow in Christ's steps and try to become like Him, there will be persecution. We can count on it.

Do you desire to live a godly life? I certainly hope so. I do. It is a wonderful goal to have. However, do you realize that there is a promised result, if you live a godly life:

> **12 And indeed, all who desire to live godly in Christ Jesus will be persecuted.**
>
> --2 Timothy 3

If you are not being persecuted, guess what? If you are a Christian who really does not stand against the moral evils and corruption in your community, then you will not be persecuted. If you tolerate all of the immorality, and simply "smile it off" when those around you curse your God, then you won't be persecuted. However, the Bible says that if you are really going to live a godly life in Christ Jesus, you will be persecuted.

So the final question is, are you being persecuted? If not, why not? Right now the persecution may be rejection and verbal abuse. Before the end of this age comes, as we will see later in this chapter, that persecution will become physical.

Turning to a new thought, would you like to be glorified with Jesus Christ? I certainly would. Isn't it going to be wonderful to be glorified with Him? However, did you realize that there is a condition that we have to meet in order to be glorified with Him?

> **16 The Spirit Himself bears witness with our spirit that we are children of God,**
> **17 and if children, heirs also, heirs of God and fellow heirs with Christ, if indeed we suffer with Him in order that we may also be glorified with Him.**
>
> --Romans 8

Did you read the last part of verse 17? It says, "if indeed we suffer with Him in order that we may be glorified with Him." Suffering with Christ, as we seek to become like Him, is a **prerequisite** to being glorified with Him.

There are many Scriptures which point out that we are indeed to share in the sufferings of Christ. That is not in the figurative sense; that is in an actual sense. We will suffer, if we stand against evil and if we live pure, godly lives and become like Jesus Christ. The Bible tells us this as a fact:

> **5 For just as the sufferings of Christ are ours in abundance, so also our comfort is abundant through Christ.**
>
> --2 Corinthians 1

> **29 For to you it has been granted for Christ's sake, not only to believe in Him, but also to**

suffer for His sake, . . .

--Philippians 1

24 Then Jesus said to His disciples, "If anyone wishes to come after Me, let him deny himself, and take up his cross and follow Me. . . ."

--Matthew 16

12 If we suffer, we shall also reign with him: if we deny him, he also will deny us: . . .

--2 Timothy 2, KJV

8 we are afflicted in every way, but not crushed; perplexed, but not despairing;
9 persecuted, but not forsaken; struck down, but not destroyed;
10 always carrying about in the body the dying of Jesus, that the life of Jesus also may be manifested in our body.
11 For we who live are constantly being delivered over to death for Jesus' sake, that the life of Jesus also may be manifested in our mortal flesh.

--2 Corinthians 4

Would you like to share in the power of the resurrection of Jesus? I certainly would like to have that power operating in my life. But again there is a price to pay for it:

8 More than that, I count all things to be loss in view of the surpassing value of knowing Christ Jesus my Lord, for whom I have suffered the loss of all things, and count them but rubbish in order that I may gain Christ,
9 and may be found in Him, not having a righteousness of my own derived from the Law, but that which is through faith in Christ, the righteousness which comes from God on the basis of faith,
10 that I may know Him, and the power of His resurrection and the fellowship of His sufferings,

> **being conformed to His death;**
> **11 in order that I may attain to the resurrection from the dead.**
>
> **--Philippians 3**

Like Paul, we need to be willing to suffer the loss of all things. We are going to be without anything that we own, if we count all things as loss that we might gain Christ. Everything we do have will belong to Him to do with as He wills. In verse 10, Paul connects knowing Him with knowing the power of His resurrection and the fellowship of His sufferings, even unto death. The fellowship of His sufferings is not something to be dreaded; rather, we can rejoice if He counts us worthy to suffer for Him:

> **41 So they went on their way from the presence of the Council, rejoicing that they had been considered worthy to suffer shame for His name.**
>
> **--Acts 5**

However you want to look at it, we know that Jesus told us we would be persecuted and we would suffer. We should rejoice in it, for it is going to work wonderful things in our lives and help to make us like Jesus Christ.

PHYSICAL PERSECUTION IS COMING

The Christians in the English-speaking world must be deaf and blind! In his book, TILL ARMAGEDDON, Billy Graham talked about getting ready to suffer right up to the battle of Armageddon, which is at the end of the great tribulation. In his book, THE VISION, David Wilkerson foretold that persecution was coming to Christians in America. James Robison, myself and many others are warning the Christians in America to get ready for persecution and yet, by and large, they are doing nothing about it. If Christians will not listen to any of us, certainly they should listen to Jesus:

> 29 Jesus said, "Truly I say to you, there is no one who has left house or brothers or sisters or mother or father or children or farms, for My sake and for the gospel's sake,
> 30 but that he shall receive a hundred times as much now in the present age, houses and brothers and sisters and mothers and children and farms, along with persecutions; and in the age to come, eternal life.
>
> --Mark 10

In addition to many of the blessings that Christ promises, He also promises persecution. But the final thing He promises in this passage is eternal life with Him! Hallelujah!

In the famed Sermon on the Mount, Christ also talked about persecution:

> 10 "Blessed are those who have been persecuted for the sake of righteousness, for theirs is the kingdom of heaven.
> 11 "Blessed are you when men cast insults at you, and persecute you, and say all kinds of evil against you falsely, on account of Me.
> 12 "Rejoice, and be glad, for your reward in heaven is great, for so they persecuted the prophets who were before you. . . ."
>
> --Matthew 5

I would encourage you to memorize those three short verses. They would be a comfort when persecution comes, and it will come. If you really become like Jesus Christ, stand up for God and righteousness, and stand against evil and Satan, you are going to be persecuted and people are going to cast insults at you and accuse you of false things. You can be encouraged by knowing that the prophets who came before you were persecuted in the same way. But if you stay true to God, your reward in heaven is going to be very great. Isn't that comforting? Praise His name!

One of these days I hope the Lord leads me to write a book on "PREPARATION FOR PERSECUTION." It is one subject that Christians vitally need today, and one which no one is addressing. In discussing the end of this age in Matthew 24, Christ clearly said that persecution was coming:

> **3 And as He was sitting on the Mount of Olives, the disciples came to Him privately, saying, "Tell us, when will these things be, and what will be the sign of Your coming, and of the end of the age?"**
> **4 And Jesus answered and said to them, "See to it that no one misleads you. . . .**
>
> **9 "Then they will deliver you to tribulation, and will kill you, and you will be hated by all nations on account of My name.**
> **10 "And at that time many will fall away and will deliver up one another and hate one another.**
> **11 "And many false prophets will arise, and will mislead many. . . .**
>
> **14 "And this gospel of the kingdom shall be preached in the whole world for a witness to all the nations, and then the end shall come. . . .**
>
> **21 for then there will be a great tribulation, such as has not occurred since the beginning of the world until now, nor ever shall.**
>
> **--Matthew 24**

Please forgive me for leaving out some of the verses. I do so for the sake of space. I hope you will go back and read the entire passage. (I have dealt with this passage in much more detail in previous books.) I wanted to include enough here so that you could see that Christ was describing what the end of our age is going to be like. The great tribulation begins down in verse 21. There are some disastrous things that are going to occur prior to the tribulation.

Even if you believe the rapture is going to happen before the tribulation, you are still going to experience all the things outlined in verses 4-20. (Of course, I believe Christians will go through the entire tribulation, but if I can help people get ready for this time of birth pangs that precedes the great tribulation, they will be in better shape to go through the tribulation, just in case they are wrong in their rapture theory.)

The main thing I want to point out here, starting with verse 9, is the degree of the persecution that we are talking about. It says that "they will deliver you to tribulation, and will kill you." We are not just talking about insults or rejection or anything so mild. We are talking about people actually dying and being martyred for Jesus Christ.

We know that at the end of this age, many Christians are going to be martyred. In the Book of Revelation, those martyrs cry out from under the altar of God:

> 9 And when He broke the fifth seal, I saw underneath the altar the souls of those who had been slain because of the word of God, and because of the testimony which they had maintained;
> 10 and they cried out with a loud voice, saying, "How long, O Lord, holy and true, wilt Thou refrain from judging and avenging our blood on those who dwell on the earth?"
>
> --Revelation 6

Again this shows that we are not talking just about verbal and mental persecution. Physical martyrdom will also be a part of the intense persecution at the end of the age.

What should you do when people persecute you? The Bible has some very good helps there. Jesus Himself gave us one of the best:

> 44 "But I say to you, love your enemies, and pray for those who persecute you
> 45 in order that you may be sons of your Father who is in heaven; for He causes His sun to rise on the evil and the good, and sends rain on the righteous and the unrighteous.

> 46 "For if you love those who love you, what reward have you? Do not even the tax-gatherers do the same?
> 47 "And if you greet your brothers only, what do you do more than others? Do not even the Gentiles do the same?
> 48 "Therefore you are to be perfect, as your heavenly Father is perfect. . . ."
>
> --Matthew 5

Jesus says here that we are to love our enemies and we are to pray for those who persecute us. Even if you are in a prison and being beaten by a sadistic jailor, the Bible says you are to love him and to pray for him. Never forget those two things; you are to love your enemies and to pray for them. If you do this, verse 48 tells us the end result: you will wind up perfect as your Father in heaven is perfect.

Paul had more to say about this subject in his letter to the Romans:

> 14 Bless those who persecute you; bless and curse not.
> 15 Rejoice with those who rejoice, and weep with those who weep.
> 16 Be of the same mind toward one another; do not be haughty in mind, but associate with the lowly. Do not be wise in your own estimation.
> 17 Never pay back evil for evil to anyone. Respect what is right in the sight of all men.
> 18 If possible, so far as it depends on you, be at peace with all men.
> 19 Never take your own revenge, beloved, but leave room for the wrath of God, for it is written, "VENGEANCE IS MINE, I WILL REPAY," says the Lord.
> 20 "BUT IF YOUR ENEMY IS HUNGRY, FEED HIM, AND IF HE IS THIRSTY, GIVE HIM A DRINK: FOR IN SO DOING YOU WILL HEAP BURNING COALS UPON HIS HEAD."
> 21 Do not be overcome by evil, but overcome evil with good.
>
> --Romans 12

These verses say that we are to bless those who persecute us and not to curse them. This might be fairly easy if someone were to do something physically harmful to us, but if he were to harm our children or someone we loved, we would want to curse him rather than bless him. Yet the Bible says that we are to bless that individual. Verse 19 tells us that we are never to take our own revenge in situations like that. Verse 20 goes even further. If the enemy who is persecuting us is hungry, we are to cook him a meal and feed him. If he is thirsty, we are to serve him something to drink and even to wash his cup. We will overcome evil, not by striking back, but with good, and ultimately the victory will be ours.

There will be certain situations in which the Lord will tell us to "move on," if we are being persecuted. These are the same instructions that He gave to His followers in the first century:

> 23 "But whenever they persecute you in this city, flee to the next; for truly I say to you, you shall not finish going through the cities of Israel, until the Son of Man comes.
> 24 "A disciple is not above his teacher, nor a slave above his master.
> 25 "It is enough for the disciple that he become as his teacher, and the slave as his master. If they have called the head of the house Beelzebul, how much more the members of his household!
> 26 "Therefore do not fear them, for there is nothing covered that will not be revealed, and hidden that will not be known.
> 27 "What I tell you in the darkness, speak in the light; and what you hear whispered in your ear, proclaim upon the housetops.
> 28 "And do not fear those who kill the body, but are unable to kill the soul; but rather fear Him who is able to destroy both soul and body in hell. . . ."
>
> --Matthew 10

According to this passage, if the persecution gets too intense in the city where you are, move on. I believe that when this persecution begins, the Lord's return will not be too far away. Verse 25 says that if they called Jesus Christ "Satan" (Beelzebul--a derogatory term meaning the prince of moral impurity), they are going to call us--who are members of His household--that and even worse. Verse 28 gives us another real key: we should never fear anyone who can kill the body; we only need to fear those who can kill the soul. "Killing the soul" would involve denying Jesus Christ. If it ever comes a choice between physically dying or denying Jesus Christ, the choice should be easy and instantaneous. I would far rather die than deny my precious Savior.

SUMMARY AND CONCLUSION

We have just barely touched on a vast subject in this chapter. One of the cries of the Christian leaders in China to Corrie Ten Boom, when she visited there years ago, was that the Christians in China were not prepared to suffer. They pleaded with her to go to America and help the Christians here get ready to suffer. Unfortunately, most Christians in America are still not prepared to suffer.

Suffering and persecution are coming to Christians all over the world, including Christians in America. Most Christians unfortunately are so "soft and flabby," from being fed a menu of pabulum, that they are totally unprepared for any type of suffering. By "pabulum," I mean teachings that everything is going to be wonderful, for example, and that they will be raptured out before any trouble comes. Yet there are some real men of God in America today who are warning Christians to get ready for persecution, which I believe is coming.

Jesus said that we would indeed suffer and be persecuted for His name's sake. In fact, if we are going to live a life that is like that of Christ, and if we are going to pursue godliness, speak the whole truth and stand against evil, false doctrine, and weaknesses and falsity in the church, then we will be persecuted. Eventually, as the government becomes progressively more anti-Christian, we know that that persecution will take on a physical dimension and ultimately will lead to the martyrdom of many Christians.

My burning desire for you is that when suffering and persecution come, you will still be able to rejoice. Then you will be able to love those who persecute you, to pray for them, to bless them and to feed them. This is what Jesus did and--I keep coming back to the same premise--if we are going to become like Jesus Christ, this is what we will do also.

Jesus is our Master, and we are His followers (disciples). How wonderful it is to be taught by Him. Oh, that we could become like the Master.

16
A DISCIPLE BECOMES LIKE HIS MASTER

In earlier chapters we looked at the supernatural power that God gives us over diseases, demons and nature, and how He expects us not to sit back passively but to go out and aggressively come against the evil of the world and to overcome it. In the last chapter, we saw that there is a price to pay in order to be all that God desires us to be, as we become like Jesus Christ.

In some ways, whether we realize it or not, we are really talking about "discipleship." However, we are not talking about the kind of discipleship that is frequently discussed in Christendom today, wherein one is a disciple of another human being; rather, we are discussing becoming a disciple of Jesus Christ directly. Christ still has disciples in the world today, just as He did in the first century.

Let me describe the relationship of a disciple to his master during the New Testament era. Someone would find a wise man or an individual whom he greatly admired and would request that that great "master" allow him to be his disciple. Plato had disciples, Aristotle had disciples, as did many of the other great men of antiquity. When a person became a disciple, he was willing to give up absolutely everything in order to spend his full time with the master, in effect sitting at his feet, learning all that the master had to teach, that he might have knowledge like the master, think like the master and behave like the master. If a person was not willing to devote full time to this, chances are that he would not become a disciple.

We certainly see this singleness of purpose when Christ called His disciples. Basically they had the choice of leaving everything, following Him and spending full time with Him, or not becoming His disciples at all. But remember, the significant thing is that the disciple would try with all of his heart to become like his master.

DISCIPLES OF JESUS CHRIST TODAY

If you were to walk up to the average Christian and ask him if he was a disciple of Christ, he would likely answer, "Yes." However, do you realize that Jesus Himself placed some very stringent conditions upon being His disciple? I trust that you and I really want to be Jesus' disciples and to experience the end result of becoming like our Master and Teacher.

To help us evalute whether or not we are His disciples right now, let us look at the requirements that Jesus Himself laid down for being His disciple. He explicitly said that we **cannot** be His disciple unless we do the following things.

1. Love Him More Than Our Relatives And Even Our Own Lives

> **25 Now great multitudes were going along with Him; and He turned and said to them,**
> **26 "If anyone comes to Me, and does not hate his own father and mother and wife and children and brothers and sisters, yes, and even his own life, he cannot be My disciple.**
> **27 "Whoever does not carry his own cross and come after Me cannot be My disciple. . . ."**
> --Luke 14

In these verses, we see there is a great multitude following Jesus. I believe these would be equivalent to the great multitude of Christians who are generally following Jesus today. However, He turned around and said to them that if any out of that great multitude really wanted to be His disciple, then he had to hate his father, mother, brothers, sisters and even his own spouse and children (in the Bible "hate" means "to love less"). Jesus knew that there were some people who would love their spouse more than Him and, therefore, could not be His disciple. He knew that there were some fathers and mothers who would love their children more than Him and, therefore, could not be His disciples. The same is true of some Christian parents today: if their children were killed, life would lose meaning for them. Obviously, they are not Christ's disciples, according to the definition Christ gave us in Luke 14.

Later, we will have more to say about carrying your own cross and coming after Jesus, for that, too, is a requirement in order to be a disciple of Jesus Christ. These are not my words; these are the requirements that Jesus Himself laid down.

2. Deny Ourselves And Be Willing To Die

> **34 And He summoned the multitude with His disciples, and said to them, "If anyone wishes to come after Me, let him deny himself, and take up his cross, and follow Me.**
> **35 "For whoever wishes to save his life shall lose it; but whoever loses his life for My sake and the gospel's shall save it. . . ."**
>
> **--Mark 8**

Another thing that Jesus said was necessary in order to be His disciple was that we had to be ready to deny ourselves. If there is one significant thing that is characteristic of most Christians, at least in this country, it is that they indulge themselves. If a Christian sees something he wants, by and large, he buys it. If he sees a position or a ministry that he desires, he goes after it. It is rare to meet a Christian who really knows what it is to deny himself.

There was a lady who was widowed and put three sons through college by taking in washing, scrubbing floors for people and living in virtual poverty. Someone once told her that she would give up everything, if she could have three boys like that lady had. Her reply was, "I did." That is the kind of "denying oneself" that Jesus is talking about.

In addition, Jesus says that we must take up our cross and follow Him. In those days, the cross was an instrument of torture and execution. If Jesus were saying this today, He would likely say, "Take up your electric chair and follow Me." Those who were considering becoming His disciples understood what He meant. If they were going to be His disciples, they had to be willing even to be tortured and executed for the sake of Jesus Christ.

3. Give Up All Of Our Possessions

> **22 And when Jesus heard this, He said to him, "One thing you still lack; sell all that you possess, and distribute it to the poor, and you shall have treasure in heaven; and come, follow Me."**
>
> **--Luke 18**

Christ taught the multitudes following Him that they could not be His disciples unless they were willing to give up all of their possessions. The rich young ruler was certainly an example of this. He wanted to follow Christ, but he was not willing to give up his possessions (Luke 18:18-24). When we make a commitment to be a bondslave of God, we give all of our possessions to the Lord. (I discuss this in much more detail in the book, YOU CAN OVERCOME.) He may tell us to sell them all and give the money to the poor. He may allow us to retain some or even all of our possessions for our use, until a later time when He may tell us to sell them. The main thing is that in one's heart the ownership is transferred to the Lord. All possessions and material wealth no longer belong to the individual.

For example, a Christian may own a house and a car. When he takes a vow to become a disciple of Christ and gives up all of his possessions to the Lord, the Lord may allow him to drive that car and to live in that house for a day, for a month or for thirty years. However, at a moment's notice, the Lord may say, "Sell it" and that Christian--if he is indeed a disciple--will instantly be ready and willing to dispose of the thing that the Lord told him to sell. At the end of this age, many Christians' possessions are going to be a weight that drags them back and lures them into being part of the world.

4. Abide In His Word And Truth

> **31 Jesus therefore was saying to those Jews who had believed Him, "If you abide in My word, then you are truly disciples of Mine;**
> **32 and you shall know the truth, and the truth shall make you free."**
>
> **--John 8**

Here Jesus was talking to those who had believed in Him, yet He was saying that something else was necessary if they truly wanted to be His disciples. They had to abide--to really live--in His word. I think a good example of living in His word is found in the Psalms:

> **2 But his delight is in the law of the LORD,**
> **And in His law he meditates day and night.**
> **3 And he will be like a tree firmly planted by streams of water,**
> **Which yields its fruit in its season,**
> **And its leaf does not wither;**
> **And in whatever he does, he prospers.**
>
> **--Psalm 1**

A righteous man meditates in God's word day and night. In the verses we read from John 8, Jesus told us that, as we abide in His word, we will know the truth. Most people have no idea how important truth really is. Remember, truth is the thing that will cause us to suffer and be persecuted. But knowing the truth, as we abide in His word, is the thing that will set us free. We may be in jail, we may be in a prison, but if we abide in His word and in His truth, we will indeed be free! Yet, as we evaluate ourselves to see whether or not we are His disciples, we have to honestly ask ourselves if we truly "abide" in His word.

5. Love Our Brothers And Sisters In Christ

> **35 "By this all men will know that you are My disciples, if you have love for one another."**
>
> **--John 13**

If you are going to be a disciple of Jesus Christ, then you are going to love all other disciples. There may be some disciples with whom you do not agree theologically. There may be others who are physically or socially obnoxious to you. There will be those of various sizes, shapes and races, perhaps not all equally attractive to you. There will be those of different educational levels to you. However, the Lord says that we are to really love all of these people, if we are to be His disciples.

If you really love someone, you are happy to see him. Is there any Christian or Christian leader whom you would not be delighted to see and spend an hour with? Do you love the "unlovely," as well as those who are easy to love?

6. Bear Much Fruit

> **8 "By this is My Father glorified, that you bear much fruit, and so prove to be My disciples. . . ."**
>
> **--John 15**

This says that we are to bear much fruit. This is not talking about harvesting of souls; that is "gathering of fruit" (see John 4:35-38). The "bearing of fruit" is talking about the fruit of the Holy Spirit:

> **22 But the fruit of the Spirit is love, joy, peace, patience, kindness, goodness, faithfulness,**

23 gentleness, self-control; against such things there is no law.

--Galatians 5

The gifts of the Holy Spirit are given in an instant. However, **fruit grows** and it takes time to develop. According to John 15:8, we are going to prove that we are Christ's disciples if the fruit of the Holy Spirit is really growing in our lives.

In an earlier chapter, I called your attention to the last fruit of the Spirit listed, the neglected one, that of "self-control." Many Christians may have love, joy and peace, but when it comes to eating, other fleshly appetites and lust for material things, they have very little self-control, and they often even laugh about it. They no longer call lack of self-control "sin." Rather, they will say, "I have a 'tendency' to over-eat" or "I have an 'inclination' to buy too many clothes." We should not call sin "a tendency" or "an inclination." We should call sin "sin" and realize that we are not "proving to be Christ's disciples" as we exhibit a lack of self-control or a lack of the other aspects of the fruit of the Spirit.

DISCIPLES CAN WITHDRAW

66 As a result of this many of His disciples withdrew, and were not walking with Him anymore.

--John 6

Many disciples may start walking with Christ, but as the teaching gets stronger and the requirements become greater, a number of them withdraw and no longer walk with Christ as disciples. What a sad state that must be for an individual. As disciples, Jesus demands much of us: to be holy, pure and perfect, to abide in His word and to spend long hours with Him in prayer and fasting.

As we count the cost of the life to which He is calling us, we need not withdraw from walking as His disciples. Rather, we can do all these things rejoicing, knowing that He will supply all of the strength we need to obey Him in all He asks us to do, and in Him we will find fullness of joy.

THINGS THAT WILL BE TRUE OF HIS DISCIPLES

There are a number of things that Jesus says will naturally be true of us, if we are disciples. We need to check these over to be sure that these things are true of us, if we consider ourselves to be His disciples. I believe the Lord wants me to simply list them without comment.

1. Disciples believe in Him:

> **11 This beginning of His signs Jesus did in Cana of Galilee, and manifested His glory, and His disciples believed in Him.**
>
> --John 2

2. Disciples spend time with Jesus:

> **22 After these things Jesus and His disciples came into the land of Judea, and there He was spending time with them and baptizing.**
>
> --John 3

3. Disciples come to Jesus:

> **36 Then He left the multitudes, and went into the house. And His disciples came to Him, saying, "Explain to us the parable of the tares of the field."**
>
> --Matthew 13

4. Disciples follow Jesus:

> **21 And another of the disciples said to Him, "Lord, permit me first to go and bury my father."**
> **22 But Jesus said to him, "Follow Me; and allow the dead to bury their own dead."**
> **23 And when He got into the boat, His**

disciples followed Him.

--Matthew 8

5. Disciples obey Jesus:

22 And immediately He made the disciples get into the boat, and go ahead of Him to the other side, while He sent the multitudes away.

--Matthew 14

6. Jesus expects disciples to do miracles:

15 And when it was evening, the disciples came to Him, saying, "The place is desolate, and the time is aleady past; so send the multitudes away, that they may go into the villages and buy food for themselves."
16 But Jesus said to them, "They do not need to go away; you give them something to eat!"

--Matthew 14

7. Disciples are taught by Jesus:

23 And turning to the disciples, He said privately, "Blessed are the eyes which see the things you see,
24 for I say to you, that many prophets and kings wished to see the things which you see, and did not see them, and to hear the things which you hear and did not hear them."

--Luke 10

8. Disciples fast:

33 And they said to Him, "The disciples of John often fast and offer prayers; the disciples of the Pharisees also do the same; but Yours eat and drink."
34 And Jesus said to them, "You cannot make the attendants of the bridegroom fast while the bridegroom is with them, can you?
35 "But the days will come; and when the

bridegroom is taken away from them, then they will fast in those days."

--Luke 5

REWARDS OF DISCIPLES

There are many rewards that Jesus gives to His disciples. We will just look briefly at a few of these. Some of these are probably available to all Christians, but they are explicitly promised to His disciples. One of the things that He gives to His disciples is authority over demons and disease:

1 And having summoned His twelve disciples, He gave them authority over unclean spirits, to cast them out, and to heal every kind of disease and every kind of sickness.

--Matthew 10

In addition to authority, Christ also gives His disciples liberty from religious traditions. This is pointed out beautifully in the following example:

1 At that time Jesus went on the Sabbath through the grainfields, and His disciples became hungry and began to pick the heads of grain and eat.

2 But when the Pharisees saw it, they said to Him, "Behold, Your disciples do what is not lawful to do on a Sabbath."

3 But He said to them, "Have you not read what David did, when he became hungry, he and his companions;

4 how he entered the house of God, and they ate the consecrated bread, which was not lawful for him to eat, nor for those with him, but for the priests alone?

5 "Or have you not read in the Law, that on the Sabbath the priests in the temple break the Sabbath, and are innocent?

6 "But I say to you, that something greater than the temple is here.

> 7 "But if you had known what this means, 'I DESIRE COMPASSION, AND NOT A SACRIFICE,' you would not have condemned the innocent.
> 8 "For the Son of Man is Lord of the Sabbath."
>
> --Matthew 12

Jesus certainly did not give His disciples the liberty to sin, but He did give them freedom from many of the religious traditions of the day. (Of course, we do not have any religious traditions here in twentieth century America!) One very beautiful thing about being a disciple of Jesus is that He considers you part of His very own family:

> 49 And stretching out His hand toward His disciples, He said, "Behold, My mother and My brothers!
> 50 "For whoever does the will of My Father who is in heaven, he is My brother and sister and mother."
>
> --Matthew 12

Jesus said that His disciples were "His family" and He had family love for them. He did not say that the multitudes who followed Him--many of whom were believers--were His family. He only called the disciples His family. One thing about family members is that you are willing to share with them secrets that you are not willing to tell anyone else. This is exactly what Jesus did with the disciples:

> 5 While he was still speaking, behold, a bright cloud overshadowed them; and behold, a voice out of the cloud, saying, "This is My beloved Son, with whom I am well-pleased; listen to Him!"
> 6 And when the disciples heard this, they fell on their faces and were much afraid.
> 7 And Jesus came to them and touched them and said, "Arise, and do not be afraid."
> 8 And lifting up their eyes, they saw no one,

except Jesus Himself alone.
9 And as they were coming down from the mountain, Jesus commanded them, saying, "Tell the vision to no one until the Son of Man has risen from the dead."

--Matthew 17

Things were revealed to Peter, James and John there on the Mount of Transfiguration that were a secret between them and Jesus. Many times He explained to His disciples the secret meaning of a parable, which others did not get to hear. As we come into and abide in the disciple relationship with Jesus, He will teach us such secrets. Would you like to know more of the secret things of God? Then here is the path.

Another reward of a disciple is that he can be continually filled with joy and the Holy Spirit:

52 And the disciples were continually filled with joy and with the Holy Spirit.

--Acts 13

THE SUPREME REWARD OF A DISCIPLE

The privileges and rewards of being a disciple are many, but the supreme reward of a disciple is that he becomes like his Master. How exciting, to follow Jesus, to sit at His feet, to learn from Him and to eventually become like Him--that makes it all worthwhile.

Jesus tells us plainly that the expected thing for a disciple is not to become greater than his teacher, but to become like his teacher:

24 "A disciple is not above his teacher, nor a slave above his master.
25 "It is enough for the disciple that he become as his teacher, and the slave as his master. . . ."

--Matthew 10

Hopefully, you and I are disciples of Jesus and we yearn to become like our Teacher. As His bondslaves, we yearn to become like our Master.

This is pointed out even more beautifully in Luke. It tells us what will happen when a pupil (which is the same as a disciple) is fully trained:

> **40 "A pupil is not above his teacher; but everyone, after he has been fully trained, will be like his teacher. . . ."**
>
> **--Luke 6**

Isn't that fantastic! After you and I, as disciples, have been fully trained, Jesus promised that we "will be like our Teacher"--Jesus! Hallelujah! What a glorious time that will be when we come into the fullness of the image of Jesus Christ.

MAKING DISCIPLES FOR JESUS

As we pointed out earlier, men can have disciples, just as Jesus can. For example, when the Pharisees were talking to the disciples of Jesus, they had this to say:

> **28 And they reviled him, and said, "You are His disciple, but we are disciples of Moses. . . ."**
>
> **--John 9**

The Pharisees plainly said that they were disciples of Moses. So we know that Moses had disciples.

The Scriptures are also clear on the fact that John the Baptist had disciples:

> **35 Again the next day John was standing with two of his disciples,**
>
> **36 and he looked upon Jesus as He walked, and said, "Behold, the Lamb of God!"**
>
> **37 And the two disciples heard him speak, and they followed Jesus.**
>
> **--John 1**

In these verses we see that John had disciples and that, praise God, his disciples left him and became the disciples of Jesus! There may be human beings around today who are Christians, or even Christian leaders, who have disciples. They would do well to follow the example of John the Baptist and turn the focus of their disciples upon Jesus, so they could become disciples of Jesus Christ.

One problem with being a disciple of another human being is that the disciple will take on the characteristics of the person doing the teaching or the discipling, both good and bad. The Scriptures tell us that this had happened with the disciples of the Pharisees. When the Pharisees sent some of their disciples to Jesus, these disciples were just as much hypocrites as the Pharisees were, for they had taken on the characteristics of the Pharisees:

> **15 Then the Pharisees went and counseled together how they might trap Him in what He said.**
> **16 And they sent their disciples to Him, along with the Herodians, saying, "Teacher, we know that You are truthful and teach the way of God in truth, and defer to no one; for You are not partial to any.**
> **17 "Tell us therefore, what do You think? Is it lawful to give a poll-tax to Caesar, or not?"**
> **18 But Jesus perceived their malice, and said, "Why are you testing Me, you hypocrites? . . ."**
> --Matthew 22

There are some precious people around today who are trying to make other Christians into their disciples. I'm not sure that that is the best thing to do. It is good for a Christian to help another Christian to grow in Christ, to be his "big brother" and even his teacher, but disciples should all be directly of Jesus Christ. In fact, Jesus commanded us to do this very thing:

> **19 "Go therefore and make disciples of all the nations, baptizing them in the name of the Father**

and the Son and the Holy Spirit,
20 teaching them to observe all that I commanded you; and lo, I am with you always, even to the end of the age."

--Matthew 28

It is interesting that Jesus didn't say, "Go out and win converts of all the nations." He wanted us to go out and **make disciples** of all the nations, disciples of Christ. He wants us to help the people whom we win to Christ to become all that we have talked about in this chapter, plus more that the Scriptures have to say about being a disciple of Jesus.

Verse 20 of Matthew 28 tells us that we are to teach these new disciples to observe **all** that Jesus commanded. This certainly states that everything in the four Gospels is for us to observe and to teach. It does not belong to a "former dispensation." It is for **us**, and Christ Himself commanded us both to observe it and to teach His disciples to observe it.

Many precious men and women of God are involved in what is commonly known as the "discipleship movement." As long as they preach Jesus Christ as the Son of God and the only way to heaven, they are my brothers and sisters and I will love them, fellowship with them and rejoice in their ministries. However, if they try to rule every area of other people's lives (which is really trying to "play God" in the lives of others), as I have seen some do, they are wrong. If they try to get other Christians to become "their disciples," which means to become like them, then I think they need to reevaluate.

If someone asks me if I am for discipleship, my answer is a definite "Yes"; however, I am for discipleship "Jesus style." With all my heart, I want to see men and women become disciples, but I want these to be disciples of **Jesus Christ**. The end result of their discipleship of Christ will be that they will become like Jesus Christ.

SUMMARY AND CONCLUSION

We have looked at the fact that there are requirements for being a disciple of Christ, which are very high. One has to be willing to deny oneself, to give up one's possessions, and to love Jesus more than one's own family and even one's own life. A disciple must love other Christians and other disciples. He must abide in the word of Jesus and in His truth. A disciple must be willing even to be tortured to death rather than deny Jesus Christ.

As we become a disciple of Christ, we will spend time with Him, we will get to know Him, He will teach us and we will gladly follow and obey Him, as we become conformed to His image.

The rewards of disciples are incredible. Jesus gives them an authority that He does not give to other believers. They have liberty from religious traditions and the joy of the Holy Spirit is evident in their lives. The disciples really become part of the intimate family of Jesus, sharing His secrets and His special "family love." However, the supreme reward is that the disciple, when fully taught, will become like his Master.

The great commission really is that we go out and make **disciples of Jesus** of all the nations and teach them and help them to observe all that Jesus commanded. Isn't it wonderful that we have the privilege of being His disciples and becoming like Him? All of this must begin some place. Let's now see where it should begin.

17
LET IT BEGIN IN ME

Schubert wrote THE UNFINISHED SYMPHONY. Perhaps the name of this book should have been THE UNFINISHED BOOK, because in many senses this book will never be, nor ever could be finished.

I say that because there are a vast number of chapters that legitimately could be added to this book.

There could be a chapter about how Christ taught, delving into the way He used parables with the multitudes and clear explanations for those who were really hungry to learn.

There could be a chapter on Christ's evangelism and how He won believers. He did not answer any questions of the woman at the well, for example, and yet He brought her to a state of believing in Him. He dealt very harshly with those who thought they were righteous and very gently with the obvious sinners. He witnessed both to the masses and to individuals. Evidently, reaching men and women with the message of the Kingdom of God was very high on His priority list.

There could be a chapter on Jesus' selection and training of His close followers. He poured His life into those who were willing to go all the way with Him, concentrating much of His time and efforts on them, rather than on the weaker ones of His flock. (This was quite opposite to what most pastors do today.)

There could be a chapter on Jesus' relationship to the civil authority, the law, the taxes, as well as to the religious authority. We could examine His attitude toward these authorities and how He dealt with them.

It is obvious that He strongly and bluntly came against the religious leadership of that day, without attempting to have any unity with them.

We could discuss Jesus' use of the gifts of the Holy Spirit in more depth. He demonstrated the gift of knowledge on occasion (the coin in the fish's mouth, for example--Matthew 17:27). He had the gift of wisdom in dealing with questions from the leaders. Almost every one of the gifts of the Holy Spirit were exhibited by Christ at one time or another during His time here on earth.

There could be a chapter on how Christ overcame the world and another on how He met temptation and overcame Satan.

As you can see, this list could go on and on before we could even begin to plumb the depths of what Jesus was really like. For this reason alone, this book could never truly be finished.

EACH INDIVIDUAL WILL BE DIFFERENT

Another reason this book could never be finished is that we could write a separate chapter on every believer who really decides to "go for it" and to try, with all of his being, to become like Jesus Christ. I could share with you the tremendous changes that the Lord has already made in my life as I have been writing this book, and I know that there are going to be more changes as I press on toward that mark of becoming like Jesus.

Fortunately, we are not all cast in the same mold. God knows how many hairs are on each of our heads. He knows every fault, every thought, and every need that we have.

We are each an absolutely unique individual to Him, even more so than each snowflake, which is a customized creation. A young, healthy athlete and, say, an elderly lady, who is a very serious librarian type, both trying to become like Jesus Christ, may look very different on the outside, but on the inside they will become much alike. The holiness, righteousness, purity and other qualities that God is going to work in their lives are going to show out through their natural personalities. So every true disciple of Jesus is going to be uniquely different. In fact, I hope that many of you will write to me and tell me about the things that happen in your lives as you seriously seek to become like Jesus. Perhaps I could do another book of just those stories!

With all my heart, I hope that no one tries to use this book as a "formula" or a legalistic method of becoming like Jesus Christ. That is certainly not the intent of the book. All I have been able to do here is to give you a direction, a goal. I have tried to lay down some principles and ideas.

God may lead someone to read the Bible through ten times in a year, while He leads another person to read it perhaps even less than we have suggested. God may have one person spending many hours a day in prayer and another, just an hour, or possibly even less. I am interested in you doing what God tells you to do. If you ask Him, He will tell you what you need to do in order to become like Jesus Christ.

As you ask Him, God will show you any changes you need to make in order to become like Jesus. I know that as I have prayed thousands of times, "O God, help me to become like Jesus Christ," He has made big changes in my life and is continuing to make changes in answer to that prayer. I know that He will do the same for you. I don't claim to be there yet, but I am pressing toward that goal.

I believe it is those people who become pure, holy and righteous like Christ--who really **become like Him**--that God is going to use as His overcomer army at the end of this age. These are what I call the "stage three Christians." Those who have made a bondslave commitment, who have made becoming like Jesus Christ the goal of their lives, and who are moving on into victory and power will be overcomers in Christ's glorious end-time army.

Lest you misunderstand, I am **not** talking about an elite group. This is a group of bondslaves. There is no such thing as a proud slave. These Christians are ones who have given up everything to try to become like Jesus, realizing their own unworthiness and that only Jesus is worthy. Their Example is Jesus, Who Himself was a humble bondslave.

If the last two paragraphs did not make much sense to you, please get a copy of my book YOU CAN OVERCOME. It explains this in much more detail and I truly believe it can be a tremendous help to you. (See last page of this book for an order form.)

BRING OTHERS INTO A RIGHT RELATIONSHIP WITH FATHER GOD

The mission of our life, as we become like Christ, will be the same mission that Jesus had. His mission was to get people into a right relationship with Father God. There are those who, in their evangelism, want to get people into a good relationship with Jesus Christ. That is commendable, because coming to God through Jesus Christ is essential. There are others who go further than that and help Christians come into a good relationship with the Holy Spirit, as well as with Jesus. However, very few are going all the way, as Jesus did, in getting people into a right relationship with Father God.

Jesus stated this mission repeatedly during His ministry:

> **6 Jesus said to him, "I am the way, and the truth, and the life; no one comes to the Father, but through Me. . . ."**
>
> --John 14

> **44 "But I say to you, love your enemies, and pray for those who persecute you**
> **45 in order that you may be sons of your Father who is in heaven; . . ."**
>
> --Matthew 5

We know that the only way to the Father is through Jesus Christ. Thus, as we bring people into a right relationship to Father God, we must first bring them to Christ. However, having a relationship with Christ is not the ultimate end. Bringing people into a right relationship with the Father is the "ultimate end" or goal that Jesus had, and it should be ours as well.

Jesus wanted men to be righteous and to do good works, so that the Father would get the glory:

> **16 "Let your light shine before men in such a way that they may see your good works, and glorify your Father who is in heaven. . . ."**
>
> --Matthew 5

As we encourage people to move in the direction of goodness, righteousness and holiness, we--like Jesus--want to keep emphasizing that it is the Father Who gets the glory. Jesus not only wants us to glorify the Father, but to be like the Father:

> **48 "Therefore you are to be perfect, as your heavenly Father is perfect. . . ."**
>
> --Matthew 5

Jesus taught that it was the Father Who was going to do the rewarding:

> **1 "Beware of practicing your righteousness before men to be noticed by them; otherwise you have no reward with your Father who is in heaven. . . .**
>
> **6 "But you, when you pray, go into your inner room, and when you have shut your door, pray to your Father who is in secret, and your Father who sees in secret will repay you. . .**
>
> **14 "For if you forgive men for their transgressions, your heavenly Father will also forgive you.**
> **15 "But if you do not forgive men, then your Father will not forgive your transgressions. . . .**
>
> **18 so that you may not be seen fasting by men, but by your Father who is in secret; and**

> your Father who sees in secret will repay you. . . ."
>
> --Matthew 6

Also, in a beautiful way, Jesus taught that not only would the Father reward us, but the Father would care for us:

> 26 "Look at the birds of the air, that they do not sow, neither do they reap, nor gather into barns, and yet your heavenly Father feeds them. Are you not worth much more than they? . . .
>
> 31 "Do not be anxious then, saying, 'What shall we eat?' or 'What shall we drink?' or 'With what shall we clothe ourselves?'
> 32 "For all these things the Gentiles eagerly seek; for your heavenly Father knows that you need all these things.
> 33 "But seek first His kingdom and His righteousness; and all these things shall be added to you. . . ."
>
> --Matthew 6

Again and again, throughout His ministry, the Father was the One to Whom Jesus directed people's attention. Jesus also pointed out that it is the Father Who gives us gifts:

> 11 "If you then, being evil, know how to give good gifts to your children, how much more shall your Father who is in heaven give what is good to those who ask Him! . . ."
>
> --Matthew 7

Jesus taught that it was by obeying the Father that we enter into the kingdom of heaven:

> 21 "Not everyone who says to Me, 'Lord, Lord,' will enter the kingdom of heaven; but he who does the will of My Father who is in heaven."
>
> --Matthew 7

We have just taken a few verses from three chapters in Matthew and already you can see that Jesus' heart was to bring people into a right relationship with their loving, heavenly Father. As we become like Jesus Christ, we too will yearn to see people come into that right relationship with Father God.

As God remolds our hearts and our lives, developing the characteristics of Jesus within us, we will long to help non-Christians receive salvation. We will yearn for Christians who have received Christ to receive the baptism of the Holy Spirit and the supernatural power that Father God wants to give to them. We will long to see those who have already received the baptism of the Holy Spirit move on to come into a deep, loving relationship with Father God, as His bondslaves. Just like Jesus did, let's help people move ever closer to our precious heavenly Father.

LOVE IS THE BOTTOM LINE

If I had to pick one word that characterized the life of Christ, I believe it would be the word "love." He loved Father God so much that He wanted to do His will, even if that required dying a death of torture on the cross. He loved people so much that He was willing to sacrifice much, and even lay down His life, in order to meet their needs. He loved them so much that He was willing to pray all night in intercession for them and fast, so that He could cast out demons. He was willing to pay the price to bring the good news to the poor, to heal the blind and to bring anyone to the Father who was willing to come. What a beautiful heart of love and compassion Jesus had. Oh, that we too might have a love like Jesus had for the Father and our fellow human beings!

> 36 "Teacher, which is the great commandment in the Law?"
> 37 And He said to him, " 'YOU SHALL LOVE THE LORD YOUR GOD WITH ALL YOUR HEART, AND WITH ALL YOUR SOUL, AND WITH ALL YOUR MIND.'

38 "This is the great and foremost commandment.
39 "The second is like it, 'YOU SHALL LOVE YOUR NEIGHBOR AS YOURSELF.'
40 "On these two commandments depend the whole Law and the Prophets."

--Matthew 22

Jesus said that the whole Law, that is the first five books of the Bible, and all of the Prophets, which is most of the rest of the Old Testament, depend upon the two greatest commandments, which He outlined in the preceding verses. Essentially, He said that if we really were to do those two things, we would be obeying the whole Old Testament.

Jesus had that kind of love outlined in Matthew 22--He loved the Father with all His heart, soul and mind, and He loved His neighbor even more than His own life. How I yearn to have that kind of love too, both for God the Father and for my fellow human beings. As Christians, we should have love for all people in general, but especially for our fellow Christians:

35 "By this all men will know that you are My disciples, if you have love for one another."

--John 13

12 "This is My commandment, that you love one another, just as I have loved you.
13 "Greater love has no one than this, that one lay down his life for his friends. . . ."

--John 15

Just as Jesus loved us enough that He was willing to give up His very life for us, He is commanding us to love each other in the same way. There is a day coming, during times of persecution, when we may indeed have to lay down our lives for one another. Now is the time to develop this Christlike love for each other.

Sometimes this love that we are talking about--for the Father, for other Christians and for non-Christians--does not come naturally. The Bible tells us that we are not to passively sit and wait for it to happen; rather, we are to pursue it:

> **1 Pursue love, yet desire earnestly spiritual gifts, but especially that you may prophesy.**
>
> **--1 Corinthians 14**

This verse says that we are to desire spiritual gifts, but we are to pursue love. We are to actively, aggressively pursue love for God, for our neighbors and for our fellow believers.

In reading through the Gospels, one characteristic of Jesus that stands out is His tremendous compassion for people, which is really an expression of love. Again and again we read phrases such as this:

> **36 And seeing the multitudes, He felt compassion for them . . .**
>
> **--Matthew 9**

> **34 Moved with compassion, Jesus touched their eyes; and immediately they regained their sight . . .**
>
> **--Matthew 20**

> **41 Moved with compassion, He stretched out His hand, and touched him and said to him, "I am willing; be cleansed."**
>
> **--Mark 1**

One way to pursue love might be to ask the Father to give you the kind of compassion that Jesus had for people, and then to actively look for God to reveal opportunities for you to express His love to people in need.

Oh, that we could love God and our neighbor as Jesus did. He had compassion for the multitudes, He wept over His friend Lazarus who died, and He lamented over Jerusalem. He yearned to "gather the people under His wings" and to protect them from harm and the consequences of their sin (Matthew 23:37-39). What a tremendous love Jesus had. Love is so very important. Remember 1 Corinthians 13. We could do all of the things outlined in this book, even to the point of martyrdom, and it would all be worthless without love.

Love is the ultimate key. May it permeate your being. Love everyone you meet. Love your enemies. Love those who do not like you, those who disagree with you, and those who give you a hard time. Love your children, love your spouse, love everyone in your church, and love your pastor, even when he does not preach well. Love yourself and, most of all, love Jesus and Father God with all your heart, soul, mind and strength. Seek to love like Jesus loved.

Remember, God is love (1 John 4:8). It is certainly true that Christ displayed this love and, if we become like Him, our epitaph could read: "(Our name) was a child of God through Jesus Christ, whose major characteristic was love."

A HELPFUL CHECKLIST

As I said near the beginning of this chapter, God will lead various individuals in different ways. His will for one person is not necessarily His will for another. Thus, the chapters in this book and even this following checklist are in no way meant to be a legalistic list, or even a complete one, but rather a guide. The concept of becoming like Jesus is so vast that it is helpful to break it up into smaller pieces in order to comprehend it. Yet becoming like Him involves letting Jesus live out His life through us, not doing a list of things.

The responsibility for us to become like Jesus is not His alone. He expects us to do some things. Allow the Holy Spirit to use this checklist to prompt you into action. You may want to go through this list from time to time to check the things that you are actively working on or the things that you have done:

1. I RESOLVE DAILY TO WALK HUMBLY BEFORE MY GOD AND TO GIVE HIM AND JESUS CHRIST THE GLORY AND CREDIT FOR EVERYTHING GOOD THAT I DO AND FOR EVERY BLESSING. I HAVE MADE A COMMITMENT TO BE A BONDSLAVE OF GOD.

2. I HAVE DECIDED TO MAKE BECOMING LIKE JESUS CHRIST THE GOAL OF MY LIFE. (I believe that preceding this one should be a commitment to be a bondslave of Father God. Becoming like Jesus Christ is part of the working out of the stage three of the Christian life.)

3. I AM COMMITED TO PERIODIC FASTING, AS GOD LEADS ME. (A suggested goal might be to have a seven- to ten-day fast several times a year. God could lead you to go on some shorter fasts and possibly even a longer one. Remember, fasting has incredible benefits, such as putting dynamite behind prayer and increasing the power to cast out demons.)

4. I COMMIT TO HAVE A TIME OF PRAYER ALONE WITH GOD EACH DAY AND I AM AIMING AT AN HOUR OR MORE. (We know that prayer changes things and no true revival in a nation, a community or an individual occurs without intensive, fervent prayer.)

5. I AM COMMITED TO READING THE SCRIPTURES, MEDITATING ON THEM AND KNOWING THEM MUCH BETTER. (For about twenty minutes a day you can use the Omega Reading Plan, which takes you through Psalms and Proverbs and the four Gospels twice during the year, as well as once through the rest of the Bible. This reading plan has been mightily used of God in many people's lives. Allow Him to show you particular passages from the Scriptures for you to meditate on and to absorb, as He works them into your life.)

6. I HAVE ASKED GOD TO SHOW ME ANY IMPURITIES IN MY LIFE AND I AM REMOVING THESE.

7. I HAVE CLEANSED MYSELF, ANOINTED MYSELF AND DEDICATED MYSELF TO BE HOLY, SEPARATED FROM UNCLEAN THINGS, AND RESERVED EXCLUSIVELY FOR GOD'S USE. (This does not mean that you will never sin again, but if you do, the sin will be doubly bad, since in addition to the sin you are desecrating a holy individual of God.)

8. I AM SEEKING FIRST TO BE PART OF GOD'S KINGDOM, TO ALLOW HIM TO RULE MY LIFE, AND TO BE RIGHTEOUS LIKE JESUS.

9. I AM YEARNING TO BE PERFECT, LIKE JESUS COMMANDED, AND TO HAVE A HEART LIKE DAVID HAD, ALWAYS INQUIRING OF THE LORD.

10. I AM WILLING TO BE OBEDIENT TO GOD AND I AM ASKING HIM TO GIVE ME A HEART OF COMPASSION AND A REAL DESIRE TO DO GOOD WORKS. I desire to visit the sick and the imprisoned, to feed the hungry, to clothe the naked and to help meet physical needs.

11. I HAVE BEEN BAPTIZED WITH THE HOLY SPIRIT AND HAVE RECEIVED HIS SUPERNATURAL POWER. I desire to be an instrument through which the Holy Spirit can manifest His gifts, for the edification of the Body of Christ.

12. I AM WILLING TO BE USED BY GOD TO HEAL PEOPLE, WHENEVER HE COMMANDS. When I do this at His command, I know healing will occur.

13. THROUGH CHRIST, I HAVE AUTHORITY OVER DEMONS AND I AM WILLING TO FAST IN ORDER TO EXERCISE THAT AUTHORITY IN ITS FULLNESS, TO THE GLORY OF GOD.

14. I AM WILLING TO SEEK OUT AND ATTACK EVIL, THE WORLD AND SATAN, KNOWING THAT I WILL OVERCOME THEM IN THE POWER OF CHRIST, IN HIS NAME, AND TO HIS GLORY. I WILL BE AN OVERCOMER FOR JESUS.

15. I AM WILLING TO PAY WHATEVER PRICE IS NECESSARY TO BECOME LIKE JESUS CHRIST. I am willing to suffer rejection, rebuke and other mental and emotional abuse. I am willing to suffer physically. I will gladly be persecuted for the truth, and I am willing to lay down my life for Jesus Christ.

16. I AM WILLING TO MEET ALL OF THE REQUIREMENTS OF A DISCIPLE OF JESUS, AND I HAVE MADE THE COMMITMENT TO BE HIS DISCIPLE. I know that the end result of being His disciple is that I will become like Him.

17. I AM NOT GOING TO WAIT; I AM STARTING NOW TO BECOME LIKE JESUS CHRIST, FOR HIS GLORY.

ABIDE IN CHRIST

There are two extremes in approaches to becoming like Jesus Christ. One extreme is to try to do it in one's own energy. Trying to become like Jesus in one's own power tends to leave one very frustrated.

The other extreme is Christians who sit back and wait for Christ to live out His life through them, making no effort themselves. This is just like a man sitting on his front porch thinking that if God wanted him to witness to someone, God could bring an unsaved person by his front porch. God is certainly able to do that, but He does expect us to get off our "front porches" and to put some effort into becoming like Jesus Christ. Yet He does not expect us to do it in our own strength or power, but in the power of the Holy Spirit and under His direction.

Jesus very beautifully taught about this subject toward the end of His ministry:

> **1 "I am the true vine, and My Father is the vinedresser.**
> **2 "Every branch in Me that does not bear fruit, He takes away; and every branch that bears**

fruit, He prunes it, that it may bear more fruit.
3 "You are already clean because of the word which I have spoken to you.
4 "Abide in Me, and I in you. As the branch cannot bear fruit of itself, unless it abides in the vine, so neither can you, unless you abide in Me.
5 "I am the vine, you are the branches; he who abides in Me, and I in him, he bears much fruit; for apart from Me you can do nothing.
6 "If anyone does not abide in Me, he is thrown away as a branch, and dries up; and they gather them, and cast them into the fire, and they are burned.
7 "If you abide in Me, and My words abide in you, ask whatever you wish, and it shall be done for you.
8 "By this is My Father glorified, that you bear much fruit, and so prove to be My disciples. . . ."

--John 15

As you can see in this passage, the emphasis is on abiding in Christ. It is only as we abide in Christ that the fruit is produced in our lives. We cannot put our emphasis on the fruit bearing. The emphasis needs to be on abiding in Christ. However, just like in this analogy, the branch that grows forth from the trunk of the vine--the vine being Christ--is not inactive. It must put forth a bud, which then develops into fruit. The Lord wants us to abide in Him totally and to let Him provide the "sap" or the energy and the power. But He then expects us to do our part with that which He has provided and to move toward becoming like Jesus Christ. As the two work in concert, the end result will be fruit in our lives that will make us more and more like Jesus Christ!

A FINAL WORD

As I have tried to emphasize, we do not become like Jesus by conforming to a list of rules or legalistic procedures. The chapters in this book are guidelines to help point you in the right direction, but becoming like Jesus is a transformation that must come from within. As the Lord changes us on the inside and truly becomes King over every area of our lives, the changes will become evident externally. Think of it like the metamorphosis that takes place as a caterpillar is transformed into a beautiful butterfly.

When Moses came down from the mountain after beholding God's glory, his face shone (Exodus 34:28-29). As we focus our eyes and our attention on the Lord, His glory is similarly reflected in us. The Bible tells us that we are being transformed into the same image that we are beholding:

> **18 But we all, with unveiled face beholding as in a mirror the glory of the Lord, are being transformed into the same image from glory to glory, just as from the Lord, the Spirit.**
>
> --2 Corinthians 3

Romans 8:29 says that we are "predestined to become conformed to the image of His Son." Romans 12:2 commands us to "be transformed" by the renewing of our minds. Ephesians 4:23,24 encourages us to be renewed in the spirit of our minds and to put on the "new self, which is in the likeness of God." Again and again the Scriptures exhort us to actually pursue becoming like our Lord and Savior, Jesus Christ, and to allow the power of the Holy Spirit to manifest His glory in us, until we are a reflection of His very nature.

As I said earlier, this book could never truly be complete. In some ways, I really do not know how to end it. I do know that Jesus wants you to abide in His presence and in the presence of His Father. He wants you not only to be baptized by the Holy Spirit, but to walk in the Spirit. "Walking in the Spirit" means to be walking continuously filled and controlled by the Holy Spirit.

As we seek His face, He will reveal Himself to us, and the more we fellowship with Jesus, the more we will become like Him. The more we love Him, the more we will want to be like Him. The more we love the Father, the more we will want to be a good and a perfect son (or daughter).

Satan would like to convince you that you can never come close to becoming like Christ. He will tell you not even to bother trying. God says that you can. You have the power through the Holy Spirit (the same power Jesus used), you have the Way, and you have Jesus Christ as your Example. God wants you to begin to move in that direction. He will help you, He will give you the power and the strength, and the end result will glorify Father God and Jesus Christ.

I pray that becoming like Jesus Christ will be the burning goal of your life. If anybody asks you what your life's goal is, I hope that your instant response will be, "To be like Jesus." I also hope you will pray many times every day, asking God to make you like Christ. He will answer those prayers and you will become conformed to His image and will follow in His steps. Go for it! Praise God, you can make it!

APPENDIX A

HOW TO BECOME A CHRISTIAN

If you are reading this I am assuming that you are not sure that you have received Jesus Christ as your personal Savior. Not only is it possible to know this for sure, but God wants you to know. The following is what 1 John 5:11-13 has to say:

> 11 And the witness is this, that God has given us eternal life, and this life is in His Son.
> 12 He who has the Son has the life; he who does not have the Son does not have the life.
> 13 These things I have written to you who believe in the name of the Son of God, in order that you may know that you have eternal life.

These things are written to us who believe in the name of the Son of God, so that we can know that we have eternal life. It is not a "guess so," or "hope so" or "maybe so" situation. It is so that we can know for certain that we have eternal life. If you do not have this confidence, please read on.

In order to get to the point of knowing that we have eternal life, we need to first go back and review some basic principles. First, it is important to note that all things that God created (the stars, trees, animals, and so on) are doing exactly what they were created to do, except man. Isaiah 43 indicates why God created us:

> 7 ". . . Everyone who is called by My name,
> And whom I have created for My glory,

> **Whom I have formed even whom I have made."**

Here it says that humans were created to glorify God. I am sure that neither you nor I have glorified God all of our lives in everything that we have done. This gives us our first clue as to what "sin" is. We find more about it in Romans 3:

> **23 for all have sinned and fall short of the glory of God . . .**

This says that we have all sinned and that we all fall short of the purpose for which we were created--that of glorifying God. I have an even simpler definition of sin. I believe that sin is "living independent of God." A young person out of high school can choose which college to attend. If he makes this decision apart from God, it is "sin." This was the basic problem in the garden of Eden. Satan tempted Eve to eat the fruit of the tree of "the knowledge of good and evil." He said that if she would do this, she would know good from evil and would be wise like God. This would mean that she could make her own decisions and would not have to rely on God's wisdom and guidance. Since you and I fit in the category of living independent of God and not glorifying Him in everything we do, we need to look at what the results of this sin are.

First let me ask you what "wages" are. After thinking about it, because you probably receive wages from your job, you will probably come up with a definition something like "wages are what you get paid for what you do." That is a good answer. Now let's see what the Bible has to say concerning this, in Romans 6:

> **23 For the wages of sin is death, but the free gift of God is eternal life in Christ Jesus our Lord.**

Here we see that the wages of sin is death--spiritual, eternal death. Death is what we get paid for the sin that we do. Yet this passage also gives us the other side of the coin: that is, that through Jesus Christ we can freely have eternal life, instead of eternal death. Isn't that wonderful?!

But let's return for a moment to this death penalty that the people without Christ have hanging over their heads, because of the sin that they live in. In the Old Testament God made a rule: "The soul who sins will die" (Ezekiel 18:4). If we were able to live a perfect, sinless life, we could make it to heaven on our own. If we live anything less than a perfect life, according to God's rule, we will not make it to heaven, but instead will be sentenced to death. All through the Bible we find no one living a good enough life to make it to heaven.

This brings us to the place where Jesus Christ fits into this whole picture. His place was beautifully illustrated to me when I was considering receiving Christ as my Savior, by a story about a judge in a small town.

In this small town, the newspapermen were against the judge and wanted to get him out of office. A case was coming up before the judge concerning a vagrant--a drunken bum--who happened to have been a fraternity brother of the judge when they were at college. The newspapermen thought that this was their chance. If the judge let the vagrant off easy, the headlines would read, "Judge Shows Favoritism to Old Fraternity Brother." If the judge gave the vagrant the maximum penalty, the headlines would read, "Hardhearted Judge Shows No Mercy to Old Fraternity Brother." Either way they had him. The judge heard the case and gave the vagrant the maximum penalty of thirty days or $300 fine.

The judge then stood up, took off his robe, laid it down on his chair, walked down in front of the bench and put his arm around the shoulders of his old fraternity brother. He told him that as judge, in order to uphold the law, he had to give him the maximum penalty, because he was guilty. But because he cared about him, he wanted to pay the fine for him. So the judge took out his wallet and handed his old fraternity brother $300.

For God to be "just," He has to uphold the law that says "the soul who sins will die." On the other hand, because He loves us He wants to pay that death penalty for us. I cannot pay the death penalty for you because I have a death penalty of my own that I have to worry about, since I, too, have sinned. If I were sinless, I could die in your place. I guess God could have sent down millions of sinless beings to die for us. But what God chose to do was to send down **one** Person, who was equal in value, in God's eyes, to all of the people who will ever live, and yet who would remain sinless. Jesus Christ died physically and spiritually in order to pay the death penalty for you and me. The blood of Christ washes away all of our sins, and with it the death penalty that resulted from our sin.

The judge's old fraternity brother could have taken the $300 and said thank you, or he could have told the judge to keep his money and that he would do it on his own. Similarly, each person can thank God for allowing Christ to die in his place and receive Christ as his own Savior, or he can tell God to keep His payment and that he will make it on his own. What you do with that question determines where you will spend eternity.

Referring to Christ, John 1:12 says:

> **12 But as many as received Him, to them He gave the right to become children of God, even to those who believe in His name . . .**

John 3:16 says:

> **16 "For God so loved the world, that He gave His only begotten Son, that whoever believes in Him should not perish but have eternal life. . . ."**

Here we see that if we believe in Christ we won't perish, but we will have everlasting life and the right to become children of God. Right now you can tell God that you believe in Christ as the Son of God, that you are sorry for your sins and that you want to turn from them. You can tell Him that you want to accept Christ's payment for your sins, and yield your life to be controlled by Christ and the Holy Spirit. (You must accept Christ as your Savior **and your MASTER.)**

If you pray such a prayer, Christ will come and dwell within your heart and you will know for sure that you have eternal life.

If you have any questions about what you have just read, I would encourage you to go to someone that you know, who really knows Jesus Christ as his Savior, and ask him for help and guidance. After you receive Christ, I would encourage you to become a part of a group of believers in Christ who study the Scriptures together, worship God together and have a real love relationship with each other. This group (body of believers) can help nurture you and build you up in your new faith in Jesus Christ.

If you have received Christ as a result of reading these pages, I would love to hear from you. My address is at the end of this book.

Welcome to the family of God.

James McKeever

APPENDIX B

MEET THE AUTHOR

James McKeever

James McKeever has been a frequent guest on Pat Robertson's "700 Club" and on other Christian television programs. He is in demand as a speaker at major Full Gospel Businessmen's (FGBMFI) meetings. In speaking at Christian rallies, fairs and conventions, he has shared the program with the following: Josh McDowell, Dr. Bill Bright, Terry Bradshaw, Dr. Walter Martin, Phil Keaggy, Leon Patillo, Paul Little, Dr. Ted Engstrom, Dr. Carlton Booth, Bob Turnbull, Andre Kole, Dr. Raphy Byron, and many other outstanding men of God.

Mr. McKeever is president of Omega Ministries, a nonprofit organization established under the leading of the Holy Spirit to minister to the body of Christ by the traveling ministry of many anointed men of God, through books, cassettes, seminars, conferences, and the newsletter, END-TIMES NEWS DIGEST. The various ministries of Omega Ministries are supported by the gifts of those who are interested.

Mr. McKeever is rapidly becoming one of America's well-known Christian authors. Among his books and booklets are: CHRISTIANS WILL GO THROUGH THE TRIBULATION--AND HOW TO PREPARE FOR IT, REVELATION FOR LAYMEN, FINANCIAL GUIDANCE FOR CHRISTIANS, THE COMING CLIMAX OF HISTORY, YOU CAN OVERCOME, ONLY ONE WORD, HOW TO KNOW THE WILL OF GOD, WHY WERE YOU CREATED?, and KNOWLEDGE OF GOOD AND EVIL.

Mr. McKeever makes his living as an international consulting economist, lecturer, author, and world traveler. His financial consultations are utilized by scores of individuals from all over the world who seek his advice on investment strategy and international affairs. He has spoken at monetary, gold and tax haven conferences in London, Zurich, Bermuda, Sydney, Amsterdam, and Hong Kong, as well as all over the North American continent and Latin America.

As an economist and futurist, he has shared the platform with such men as Ronald Reagan, Gerald Ford, William Simon, William Buckley, Harry Browne, Harry Schultz, Philip Crane, Alan Greenspan, heads of foreign governments and many other outstanding thinkers.

Mr. McKeever is the editor and major contributing writer of THE MCKEEVER STRATEGY LETTER (MSL) and Omega's FINANCIAL GUIDANCE, a financial newsletter for Christians. He was formerly editor of INFLATION SURVIVAL LETTER. For five years after completing his academic work, Mr. McKeever was with a consulting firm which specialized in financial investments in petroleum. Those who were following his counsel back in 1954 invested heavily in oil.

For more than ten years he was with IBM, where he held several key management positions. During those years, when IBM was just moving into transistorized computers, he helped that company become what it is today. With IBM, he consulted with top executives of many major corporations in America, helping them solve financial, control and information problems. He has received many awards from IBM, including the "Key Man Award" and the "Outstanding Contribution Award." He is widely known in the computer field for his books and articles on management, management control and information sciences.

After leaving IBM, Mr. McKeever founded and was president of his own consulting firm. In addition to directing the activites of more than 100 employees, he personally gave consultation to the chief executives of client organizations. Some of the men who sought his counsel were Dr. Bill Bright, Nicky Cruz, Dr. Ted Engstrom, Dr. Lloyd Hubbard, Josh McDowell, and Dr. Stanley Mooneyham.

In 1972, Mr. McKeever sold his interest in this consulting firm and resigned as president in order to devote his "business" time to writing, speaking and consulting.

In addition to this outstanding business background, Mr. McKeever is an ordained minister. He has been a Baptist evangelist, pastor of Catalina Bible Church for three and a half years (while still with IBM) and is a frequent guest at Christian conferences. He has the gifts of teaching and prophecy and an in-depth knowledge of the Bible.

DETAILED OUTLINE

YOU CAN OVERCOME

by Jim McKeever

By far the most important preparation for Christians to make for the difficult days ahead is spiritual preparation. This third book by Jim McKeever entitled YOU CAN OVERCOME deals with the spiritual preparation for the end times.

The author feels that this is likely the most important book that he will ever write. In each of Christ's letters to the seven churches in the book of Revelation, special rewards are promised to the "overcomers." Christians in general have read this and would like to become overcomers, but they don't understand what it really means to be an overcomer, nor how to go about it according to the Bible.

A term in the New Testament that is equivalent to overcomer is "bondslave" of Jesus Christ. This book explains what a bondslave is and how one becomes a bondslave of Christ.

Many Christians are concerned about the "mark of the beast." The Bible says that God is going to seal his bondslaves in their foreheads. Neither Satan nor the beast, nor anyone else, could remove God's seal from the bondslaves' forehead and replace it with the mark of the beast.

Thus, if you become a bondslave, an overcomer, and are sealed of God in your forehead, it will be impossible for you to take on the mark of the beast! Also, those who are sealed in their forehead by God are protected from much that's coming upon the earth.

Not all Christians are bondslaves of God. In the end times of this age, becoming a bondslave, an overcomer, is absolutely essential. This book tells you how. Please don't miss this incredible book.

(You may use the convenient order form on pages 407-408 to order this book.)

THE COMING CLIMAX OF HISTORY

by Jim McKeever

Most major works that deal with an analysis of prophecy and the end times take one small slice out of the broad prophetic spectrum. Until this book, THE COMING CLIMAX OF HISTORY, there has never been a work that beautifully integrates the prophetic works of the Old Testament and the New Testament. Other works have left many questions unresolved such as exactly where did the dry bones of Ezekiel fit in and at what point is the sun darkened and the moon turned to blood? In this book Jim McKeever pulls together many of those loose ends with startling insights into the way that all these prophecies fit together. Yet the concepts that he outlines are backed up one hundred percent by the Scriptures.

He lays out the timetable that God has for the remainder of this age and for the periods of time yet to come. This book will force Christian teachers and thinkers to re-examine many of their concepts placed against his outline of future events. One of the beautiful things about the extraordinary book is that it is written in such a way that the average reader cannot only read it but actually understand it. The logic of this book is very clear so that anyone can follow the author easily. You can see why he arrives at these conclusions from the Bible passages.

As the return of Jesus Christ grows nigh, it is incredibly important for every Christian to understand how this age will end. This book will be most helpful to Christians in this capacity.

FINANCIAL GUIDANCE FOR CHRISTIANS

by Jim McKeever

This book is a must for anyone interested in being a good steward over the assets that God has entrusted to him. Being written from a biblical perspective by a noted free-market economist and investment counselor, this book is one of a kind and is filled with valuable information.

The forms in this book will help you analyze your present financial status, factoring in inflation, so as to enable you to intelligently plan and invest.

The chapter titles are as follows:

1. The Foundation is First
2. Three Critical Trends
3. Hurricane Inflation
4. How to Get Money to Invest
5. Developing Your Plan of Action
6. Savings versus Investing
7. Real Estate
8. Gold and Silver
9. Collectibles
10. Stocks and Bonds
11. Commodities
12. Tax Considerations
13. Insurance, Wills and Your Estate
14. The Multinational Individual
15. Prayer, Planning, Prayer, Action
16. Tyranny of the Urgent

This book has recently been updated for the mid-1980's, and includes all the latest information, taking into consideration the changes from the Reagan administration.

(You may use the convenient order form on pages 407-408 to order this book.)

(You may use the convenient order form on pages 407-408 to order this book.)

(You may use the convenient order form on pages 407-408 to order this book.)

CASSETTES BY JIM McKEEVER

CASSETTE ALBUMS

Qty Contribution

__ $________ Becoming an Overcomer (6 tapes) $30

__ ________ Omega World Convention 1983
St. Louis (6 tapes) $40

__ ________ Annual End-Times Conference 1982
St. Louis (6 tapes) $30

__ ________ Annual End-Times Conference 1981
Medford (6 tapes) $30

__ ________ The Book of Revelation is Understandable
(16 tapes) $60

__ ________ How to Avoid the Mark of the Beast*
(4 tapes) $20

__ ________ Highlights of Revelation*
(4 tapes) $20

__ ________ Rapture and the Tribulation*
(4 tapes) $20

*From radio program END TIMES PERSPECTIVE

__ ________ TOTAL ENCLOSED FOR CASSETTE ALBUMS

__ ________ Additional Gift for Omega Ministries

- -

Omega Ministries
P.O. Box 1788
Medford, OR 97501

BC-001

Please ship me the cassettes indicated above.

Name ________________________________

Address ________________________________

City, State ______________________ Zip ________

DEEPER LIFE BOOKLETS
by Jim McKeever

HOW YOU CAN KNOW THE WILL OF GOD

One of the most frequent questions asked of Christian leaders by believers is some form of "How can I know the will of God?"

In this excellent booklet, of the Deeper Life series, Jim McKeever gives a clear and Biblical answer to that.

He first discusses the reasons why God may not be guiding an individual. He then discusses the five ways that God guides a Christian: 1) multitude of counselors, 2) circumstances, 3) the Scriptures, 4) direct revelation, and 5) peace in your heart.

This booklet shows how a Christian can recognize and be tuned into these different ways that God can guide him.

ONLY ONE WORD

In this booklet the author gives a profound insight into how to establish a deep and exciting relationship with Christ. One pastor said of this booklet, "Everybody in the church should review this booklet constantly. It should be reread until it is memorized and becomes a part of each believer." Hundreds of Christians have written saying that this booklet provided the key for greater fulfillment and happiness in their Christian life.

KNOWLEDGE OF GOOD AND EVIL

In the garden of Eden, God gave His first commandment to man by instructing Adam and Eve not to eat of the Tree of the Knowledge of Good and Evil. Does that commandment have any implications for us today? The teaching of this biblically-based booklet is that God still does not want man to have the knowledge of good and evil. The author explains how we can have God guide our decision making rather than to "lean" on our own understanding or logic.

WHY WERE YOU CREATED?

The message of this outstanding devotional booklet is that everything in nature does what it was created to do except man. People, even Christians, do not know what the Bible says they were created to do. This produces conflict and purposelessness in the lives of multitudes of Christians. The booklet explains why we were created and tells what we must do to be in tune with God's creative purposes.

(You may use the convenient order form on pages 407-408 to order these booklets.)

COMMITMENT TO BE A BONDSLAVE AND AN OVERCOMER TO THE GLORY OF GOD THE FATHER, AND HIS SON, JESUS CHRIST

TO THE GOD OF ETERNITY,

I am voluntarily becoming a bondslave of Yours. I have no property nor possessions of my own. I have no time nor rights of my own. I am willing to permanently be Your slave.

I am willing to put on Your armor and to fight against Your enemies. I am willing to do absolutely anything You tell me to do, even if it goes against my knowledge of what is good. I am willing to die for You. Nothing is more important than doing Your will–not my family, my (former) possessions, my job, nor even my own life.

Through Your power I will be an overcomer, not to my glory, but only to Your glory and the glory of Your Son and my Savior, Jesus Christ.

I make this lifetime commitment, not because I have to, nor because of rewards. I make it because of my love for You, because I desire to please You, and because I want to be as close to You as possible throughout eternity.

Signed ______________________ Date __________

Witness ______________________ Date __________

JOIN WITH US

If you would like to join with other committed bondslaves to keep in touch and to possibly help each other, send us a copy of this page. We feel that the Lord is raising up an army and we want to be part of His special troops. Perhaps this part of God's army will become known as "The Omega Force." At some point, we may have a conference just for bondslaves that will not be announced to anyone else.

We are going to need each other when persecution starts. Let's help one another to be good soldiers for Jesus Christ.

To: James McKeever, P.O. Box 1788, Medford, Oregon 97501

☐ Yes, I would like to keep in touch with others who have also made a commitment to be a bondslave and an overcomer.

Name ______________________________

Address ______________________________

City, State ______________________ Zip __________

Home phone (   ) ____________ Business phone (   ) ____________

Occupation ______________________________

COMMITMENT TO BE A BONDSLAVE AND AN OVERCOMER TO THE GLORY OF GOD THE FATHER, AND HIS SON, JESUS CHRIST

TO THE GOD OF ETERNITY,

I am voluntarily becoming a bondslave of Yours. I have no property nor possessions of my own. I have no time nor rights of my own. I am willing to permanently be Your slave.

I am willing to put on Your armor and to fight against Your enemies. I am willing to do absolutely anything You tell me to do, even if it goes against my knowledge of what is good. I am willing to die for You. Nothing is more important than doing Your will—not my family, my (former) possessions, my job, nor even my own life.

Through Your power I will be an overcomer, not to my glory, but only to Your glory and the glory of Your Son and my Savior, Jesus Christ.

I make this lifetime commitment, not because I have to, nor because of rewards. I make it because of my love for You, because I desire to please You, and because I want to be as close to You as possible throughout eternity.

Signed ______________________________ Date ____________

Witness _____________________________ Date ____________

JOIN WITH US

If you would like to join with other committed bondslaves to keep in touch and to possibly help each other, send us a copy of this page. We feel that the Lord is raising up an army and we want to be part of His special troops. Perhaps this part of God's army will become known as "The Omega Force." At some point, we may have a conference just for bondslaves that will not be announced to anyone else.

We are going to need each other when persecution starts. Let's help one another to be good soldiers for Jesus Christ.

To: James McKeever, P.O. Box 1788, Medford, Oregon 97501

☐ Yes, I would like to keep in touch with others who have also made a commitment to be a bondslave and an overcomer.

Name ____

Address ____

City, State ______________________________ Zip __________

Home phone (   ) ______________ Business phone (   ) __________

Occupation ____

TO THE AUTHOR

The various services and materials available from Mr. McKeever are shown in summary on the reverse side. Please indicate your area of interest, remove this page and mail it to him.

Mr. McKeever would appreciate hearing any personal thoughts from you. If you wish to comment, write your remarks below on this reply form.

Comments:

ORDER FORM BC-001

Omega Publications
P. O. Box 4130
Medford, OR 97501

Please rush the materials I have indicated below to:

Name ______________________________

Address ______________________________

City, State ____________________ Zip __________

I am enclosing a check for:

$ _____ for ___ additional copies of BECOME LIKE JESUS at $6.95 each
$ _____ for ___ copies of YOU CAN OVERCOME at $6.95 each
$ _____ for ___ copies of FINANCIAL GUIDANCE FOR CHRISTIANS at $5.95 each
$ _____ for ___ copies of REVELATION FOR LAYMEN at $5.95 each
$ _____ for ___ copies of CHRISTIANS WILL GO THROUGH THE TRIBULATION, $5.95
$ _____ for ___ copies of THE COMING CLIMAX OF HISTORY at $6.95 each
$ _____ for ___ copies of the booklet ONLY ONE WORD at $1.00 each
$ _____ for ___ copies of the booklet WHY WERE YOU CREATED? at $1.00 each
$ _____ for ___ copies of the booklet KNOWLEDGE OF GOOD AND EVIL at $1.00 each
$ _____ for ___ copies of the booklet HOW YOU CAN KNOW THE WILL OF GOD, $1.00 ea.

TOTAL AMOUNT ENCLOSED $ ______________

Please send me more information about:

- [ ] Your financial newsletter for Christians, FINANCIAL GUIDANCE
- [ ] Your Christian newsletter, END-TIMES NEWS DIGEST
- [ ] Your newsletter for sophisticated investors, MCKEEVER STRATEGY LETTER
- [ ] Your speaking at our church or Christian conference